Philosophy and the Emotions

ROYAL INSTITUTE OF PHILOSOPHY SUPPLEMENT: 52

EDITED BY

Anthony Hatzimoysis

CAMBRIDGE
UNIVERSITY PRESS

PUBLISHED BY THE PRESS SYNDICATE OF THE UNIVERSITY OF CAMBRIDGE
The Pitt Building, Trumpington Street, Cambridge, CB2 1RP,
United Kingdom

CAMBRIDGE UNIVERSITY PRESS
The Edinburgh Building, Cambridge CB2 2RU, United Kingdom
40 West 20th Street, New York, NY 10011–4211, USA
477 Williamstown Road, Port Melbourne, VIC 3207, Australia

Printed in the United Kingdom at the University Press, Cambridge
Typeset by Michael Heath Ltd, Reigate, Surrey

*A catalogue record for this book is available
from the British Library*

Library of Congress Cataloguing-in-Publication Data

Philosophy and the emotions/edited by Anthony Hatzimoysis.
    p. cm.—(Royal Institute of Philosophy supplement; 52)
    Includes bibliographical references and index.
    ISBN 0-521-53734-7 (pb.)
    1. Emotions (Philosophy) I. Hatzimoysis, Anthony. II. Series.

B815.P45 2003
128'.37—dc21

2003043576

ISBN 0 521 53734 7 paperback
ISSN 1358-2461

B
815
.P45
2003

Contents

Preface   v

Notes on Contributors   vi

I. Emotions, Thoughts and Feelings: What is a 'Cognitive
Theory' of the Emotions and Does it Neglect Affectivity?   1
ROBERT C. SOLOMON

II. The Emotions and their Philosophy of Mind   19
RICHARD WOLLHEIM

III. Basic Emotions, Complex Emotions, Machiavellian
Emotions   39
PAUL E. GRIFFITHS

IV. Emotion, Psychosemantics, and Embodied Appraisals   69
JESSE PRINZ

V. Emotions and the Problem of Other Minds   87
HANNA PICKARD

VI. Emotional Feelings and Intentionalism   105
ANTHONY HATZIMOYSIS

VII. Emotions, Rationality, and Mind/Body   113
PATRICIA GREENSPAN

VIII. The significance of recalcitrant emotion
(or, anti-quasijudgmentalism)   127
JUSTIN D'ARMS AND DANIEL JACOBSON

IX. The Logic of Emotions   147
AARON BEN-ZE'EV

X. Emotion and Desire in Self-Deception   163
ALFRED R. MELE

XI. Emotion, Weakness of Will, and the Normative
Conception of Agency   181
KAREN JONES

Contents

XII. Narrative and Perspective; Values and Appropriate
   Emotions   201
   PETER GOLDIE

XIII. Passion and Politics   221
   SUSAN JAMES

IX. Don't Worry, Feel Guilty   235
   J. DAVID VELLEMAN

Index   249

Preface

'Philosophy' is the name of a calm passion: the love of wisdom. Looking inside oneself for the springs of such passion might make a nice case of soul-searching, but is not necessarily the best means for advancing philosophical inquiry. The papers in this volume arise from an international symposium on emotions, and provide material for a continuing dialogue among researchers with different philosophical itineraries.

Each essay addresses, in varying detail, the nature of emotions, their rationality, and their relation to value. Chapters I to VIII map the place of emotion in human nature, through a discussion of the intricate relation between consciousness and the body. Chapters IX to XI analyse the importance of emotion for human agency by pointing to the ways in which practical rationality may be enhanced, as well as hindered, by powerful or persistent emotions. Chapters XII to XIV explore questions of normativity and value in making sense of emotions at a personal, ethical, and political level.

I am very pleased to acknowledge the generous support of the Royal Institute of Philosophy, British Academy, Mind Association, and the Research and Graduate Support Unit of the University of Manchester. Finally, I would like to thank all the philosophers who contributed to the conference of the 'Philosophy and the Emotions' —their paper abstracts are available at:

http://fssl.man.ac.uk/philosophy/emotions/papers.htm.

Anthony Hatzimoysis

Notes on Contributors

Aaron Ben-Ze'ev is Professor of Philosophy, Rector of the University of Haifa, and co-director of the Centre for the interdisciplinary research on Emotions. He has published in philosophy of mind and the emotions, including the books *The Perceptual System* (1993), *Straight From the Heart: Emotions in Everyday Life* (1998), *The Geography of Emotions* (2000), and *The Subtlety of Emotions* (MIT Press, 2000).

Justin D'Arms is an Associate Professor of Philosophy at The Ohio State University. He is currently working on a collaborative book project with Daniel Jacobson, which develops a novel version of sentimentalist metaethics. He has published articles on metaethics, moral psychology, and evolutionary explanations of morality and behaviour. He also has research interests in normative ethics and practical reason.

Peter Goldie is a Lecturer in Philosophy at King's College London. He is the author of *The Emotions: A Philosophical Exploration*, Oxford: Clarendon Press, 2000, and the editor of *Understanding Emotions: Mind and Morals*, Aldershot: Ashgate Publishing, 2002. His current philosophical interests include character and narrative.

Patricia Greenspan is Professor of Philosophy at the University of Maryland, having previously taught at the Universities of Indiana, Ohio, Chicago, and Harvard. She has published extensively in the areas of moral psychology and philosophy of mind, including the books *Emotions and Reasons: An Inquiry into Emotional Justification* (1988), and *Practical Guilt: Moral Dilemmas, Emotions, and Social Norms* (1995).

Paul Griffiths is Professor at the History and Philosophy of Science Department at the University of Pittsburgh, having previously held positions at Otago University in New Zealand and at the University of Sydney. He has worked on many topics in the philosophy of biology and philosophy of psychology, as well as on the nature of scientific categories and 'natural kinds'. He is Associate Editor of the journal *Biology and Philosophy*, author of *What Emotions Really Are: The Problem of Psychological Categories* (1997) and author (with Kim Sterelny) of *Sex and Death: An Introduction to the Philosophy of Biology* (1999).

Notes on Contributors

Anthony Hatzimoysis is a Lecturer in Philosophy at the University of Manchester. His work focuses on the relation between values and the self, with particular emphasis on the metaphysical and epistemological aspects of normative thought.

Daniel Jacobson is associate professor of philosophy at Bowling Green State University. He is currently working on a collaborative book project with Justin D'Arms, which develops a novel version of sentimentalist metaethics. In addition to his work in ethical theory and moral psychology, Jacobson has published on J. S. Mill, political philosophy, and aesthetics.

Susan James is Professor of Philosophy at Birkbeck College of the University of London. Her areas of research are early-modern philosophy, political philosophy and feminist philosophy. She is the author of *The Content of Social Explanation* (1984), *Passion and Action: The Emotions in Seventeenth-century Philosophy* (1997), and *Beyond Equality and Difference*, (ed. with Gisela Bock, 1992).

Karen Jones is Assistant Professor at the Sage School of Philosophy at Cornell University, and Visiting Professor at the Philosophy Program of the Research School of Social Sciences at the Australian National University. She has written extensively on ethics (especially moral psychology), philosophy of the emotions, social and political philosophy, and feminism.

Alfred R. Mele, the William H. and Lucyle T. Werkmeister Professor of Philosophy at Florida State University, is the author of *Irrationality* (Oxford, 1987), *Springs of Action* (Oxford, 1992), *Autonomous Agents* (Oxford, 1995), *Self-Deception Unmasked* (Princeton, 2001), and *Motivation and Agency* (Oxford, forthcoming). He is the editor of *The Philosophy of Action* (Oxford, 1997) and co-editor of *Mental Causation* (Oxford, 1993) and *Handbook of Rationality* (Oxford, forthcoming). His primary research interests are in philosophy of action, philosophy of mind, and metaphysics.

Hanna Pickard is a Prize Fellow in Philosophy at All Souls College, Oxford. Her research interests are predominantly in the philosophy of mind and psychology, and include our awareness and knowledge of our own bodies and actions, personal identity and the self, other minds, emotion and cognition, and mental disorder.

Notes on Contributors

Jesse Prinz is associate professor of philosophy at the University of North Carolina, Chapel Hill. He is author of *Furnishing the Mind; Concepts and their Perceptual Basis and Emotional Perception*. He has held positions at the University of Maryland, Washington University in St. Louis, the California Institute of Technology, and the University of London.

Robert C. Solomon is Quincy Lee Centennial Professor of Business and Philosophy and Distinguished Teaching Professor at the University Texas at Austin. He is the author of *The Passions, In the Spirit of Hegel, About Love, A Passion for Justice, It's Good Business, Ethics and Excellence, Up the University, The Joy of Philosophy* and (with Kathleen M. Higgins) *A Short History of Philosophy* and *What Nietzsche Really Said*, and many other books.

Richard Wollheim taught at University College London from 1949 to 1981, and was Grote Professor of the Philosophy of Mind and Logic from 1963 onwards. He now teaches at the University of California Berkeley. He is the author of books in the philosophy of mind and the philosophy of art, including *Art and its Objects, Freud, The Thread of Life, Painting as an Art*, and *On the Emotions*. He is a Fellow of the British Academy and a Member of the American Academy of Arts and Sciences, and has been honoured by the International Psychoanalytical Association.

J. David Velleman is James B. and Grace J. Professor of Philosophy at the University of Michigan, Ann Arbor. His publications include *Practical Reflection* (Princeton University Press, 1989) and *The Possibility of Practical Reason* (Oxford University Press, 2000).

I. Emotions, Thoughts and Feelings: What is a 'Cognitive Theory' of the Emotions and Does it Neglect Affectivity?

ROBERT C. SOLOMON

I have been arguing, for almost thirty years now, that emotions have been unduly neglected in philosophy. Back in the seventies, it was an argument that attracted little sympathy. I have also been arguing that emotions are a ripe for philosophical analysis, a view that, as evidenced by the Manchester 2001 conference and a large number of excellent publications, has now become mainstream. My own analysis of emotion, first published in 1973, challenged the sharp divide between emotions and rationality, insisted that we reject the established notion that the emotions are involuntary, and argued, in a brief slogan, that 'emotions are judgments.' Since then, although the specific term 'judgment' has come under considerable fire and my voluntarist thesis continues to attract incredulousness the general approach I took to emotions has been widely accepted in both philosophy and the social sciences. When Paul Griffiths took on what he misleadingly characterized as 'propositional attitude' theories of emotion as the enemy of all that was true and scientifically worthy, I knew that we had made it.[1] Such ferocious abuse is surely a sign that we had shifted, in Kuhnian terms, from being revolutionary to becoming the 'normal' paradigm. The current counter-revolution of affect programmes and neuro-reductionism says a lot about who we are and how far we have come. (Progress in philosophy is moved more by this drama of one outrageous thesis after another—once called 'dialectic'—than by cautious, careful argument.)

The view that I represent is now generally referred to as the 'cognitive theory of emotions,' a borrowing from psychology and 'cognitive science.' The cognitive theory has become the touchstone of all philosophical theorizing about emotion, for or against. But what exactly is a 'cognitive' theory of emotions? The label 'cognitive theory' is not mine, and I fought it for years, not because

[1] P. Griffiths, *What Emotions Really Are* (Chicago, 1998).

it was wrong but because 'cognition' is so variously or ill-defined. In this talk, I would like to take on 'cognition' directly and try to say what I think it is and what it isn't, with particular reference to emotion. But to begin with, I want to reject, or at any rate call into question, the very *dimensions* of the emotional phenomena that are now under investigation. In recent work by Le Doux, Panksepp, and Damasio, for example, an emotion is sometimes presented as if it is more or less over and done with in 120 milliseconds, the rest being mere aftermath and cerebral embellishment. An emotion, so understood, is a preconscious, pre-cognitive, more or less automatic excitation of an affect programme. Now, I do not deny for a moment the fascinating work that these researchers have done and are doing, but I am interested, to put it polemically, in processes that last more than five minutes and have the potential to last five hours, five days, or five weeks, months, or even years. I am interested, in other words, not in those brief 'irruptive' disturbances but in the long-term narratives of Othello, Iago, Lily Bart and those of my less drama-ridden but nevertheless very emotional friends. I am interested in the meanings of life, not short-term neurological arousal.

Those bold and intriguing discoveries in the neurobiology of emotion have stimulated a mantra of sorts, 'emotion *before* cognition,' which rather leaves the cognitive theory, so to speak, with its pants down. (A fair turn around, one might argue, from my old slogan, 'emotions are judgments,' i.e., not Jamesian feelings or neurological events.) But the very statement of the new mantra provokes a cognitivist rejoinder: Surely the very fact of a *response* indicates some form of recognition, and (just to say the obvious) recognition is a form of cognition. What gets thrown into question, therefore, is not the intimate connection between emotion and cognition but the nature of cognition itself. Cognition is not to be understood only as conscious and articulate. There are primitive pre-conceptual forms of cognition, 'a cognitive neuroscience of emotion.'[2] These are not the forms of cognition or emotion that primarily interest me, perhaps, but they are extremely important in understanding not only the very brief phenomena studied by the neuroscientists but also the long-term emotional psycho-dramas that do interest me. Whatever else I may have meant or implied by my slogan 'emotions are judgments,' I was not thinking of necessarily conscious—and self-conscious—reflective, articulate judgments.

[2] R. Lane and L. Nadel, *The Cognitive Neuroscience of Emotion* (Oxford, 1999).

What is a 'Cognitive Theory' of the Emotions

Emotions as 'Thoughts' and Other Things

'Cognition' is a not very informative technical term. It demands a translation into the vernacular. (If the charge against me is that I am stuck in what is now called, 'folk psychology,' I can live with that. Jerry Fodor may overstate the case when he insists that, 'folk psychology is the only game in town,' but it is certainly the Mother of All Games in Town.) The number of candidates that have been put forward to front the cognitive theory is impressive. Many authors, Jeffrey Murphy and Kendall Walton, for example, suggest *beliefs*. Jerome Neu, one of the prominent voices in the philosophy of emotions for more than twenty years, suggests that the cognitive elements that matter most are *thoughts*, a view that (at least nominally) goes back to Descartes and Spinoza.[3] Several philosophers (including myself) defend the theory that emotions are *evaluative judgments*, a view that can be traced back to the Stoics. Cheshire Calhoun has suggested 'seeing as' and Robert Roberts has offered us 'construal' as alternative, more perceptual ways of understanding cognition in emotion.[4] Other theorists, especially in psychology and cognitive science, play it safe with 'cognitive elements' or 'cognitive structures'.[5] Some psychologists split on the question of whether 'appraisals' are 'cognitions,' sometimes leading to a narrowed and critically vulnerable conception of both.[6] Many philosophers play it safe with the technical term 'intentionality,' although interpretations of this technical concept are often even less helpful than 'cognition.'[7] Pat Greenspan has played it coy with 'belief warrant' while rejecting the 'cognitive' theory in its more committal forms.[8] Michael Stocker is more directly combative when he rejects all of this in the defence of 'affect' and 'affective states,' although I have always suspected and will again here that Stocker's 'affect'

[3] Jerome Neu, *Emotion, Thought & Therapy* (Routledge, 1978).

[4] C. Calhoun, 'Cognitive Emotions?' in C. Calhoun and R. Solomon, *What is an Emotion?* (Oxford University Press, 1984); Robert Roberts, 'Propositions and Animal Emotion' *Philosophy* **71**, 147–56.

[5] E.g. A. Ortony, G. L. Clore and A. Collins, *The Cognitive Structure of Emotions* (Cambridge University Press, 1988); Robert Gordon, *The Structure of Emotions: Investigations in Cognitive Philosophy* (Cambridge University Press, 1987).

[6] R. Lazarus, J. Averill and E. Opton 'Towards a Cognitive Theory of Emotion', in *Feelings and Emotions*, Magda B. Arnold (Academic Press, 1970).

[7] A. Kenny, *Action, Emotion and Will* (London: Routledge, 1963).

[8] P. Greenspan, *Emotions and Reasons: An Inquiry into Emotional Justification* (New York: Routledge, 1988).

3

sneaks in a lot of what others portray as cognition.[9] Ronald De Sousa suggests 'paradigm scenarios,' an intriguing and more contextual and behavioural conception that is intended (among other things) to undermine the cognitive theory. (De Sousa, 1987)

Sometimes, the interpretation is absurdly more than the concept will bear, for example, in the overly committed conceptions of 'cognition' as *knowledge* (and therefore in some sense veridical). But it should be obvious that the cognition constituents of emotion can be wrong or mistaken. As my favourite philosophical author Nietzsche writes, 'The falseness of a judgment is not necessarily an objection to [it]. The question is to what extent it is life-promoting, life-preserving ...'[10] Whether or not the falseness of a cognition is an objection to an emotion (sometimes it is, sometimes it ain't), it is amply clear that whether or not it is an emotion or not is independent of its truth.

So, too, 'cognition' is interpreted in an overly narrow typically passionless cognitive science framework as 'information.' But while every emotion may presume information (for instance, in the recognition of its object) no amount of information (including information about one's own physiological and mental states) is sufficient to constitute an emotion. By the same reasoning I think the common linkage between emotion and belief is misleading. Beliefs and emotions are related in many important ways, belief as precondition or presupposition of emotion, and belief as brought about by emotion (say, by way of wishful thinking or rationalization).

Belief isn't the right sort of psychological entity to *constitute* emotion. Beliefs are necessarily dispositions, but an emotion is, at least in part, an *experience*. A belief as such is not ever experienced. Beliefs are propositional attitudes while many emotions are not (which is what's wrong with Griffiths's characterization). If Fred loves Mary and hates spinach, the objects of his emotions are Mary and spinach, respectively, not propositions. If Fred believes that spinach is good for you (and that, perhaps, is *why* he loves it) the object of his belief (but not his emotion) is the proposition that spinach is good for you.

Appraisal and evaluation or what Ortony *et al.* call 'valenced reactions' are necessary in emotion, even on the most basic neurological level, and belief too readily slides into the exclusively factual and epistemic if not into mere information. But an emotion is always

---

[9] M. Stocker, with E. Hegeman, *Valuing Emotions* (Cambridge University Press, 1996).

[10] F. Nietzsche, *Beyond Good and Evil* (New York: Random House, 1967).

value- or valence-laden.[11] Emotion as cognition does not point merely to information processing, and it cannot be captured in any list of beliefs or in terms of passionless states of knowledge.

Furthermore, there is considerable confusion concerning the 'level of awareness' of cognition, with neurological ('hard-wired') response at one end of the spectrum and then consciousness as re-cognition, as self-consciousness, as reflection, as articulation, and as deliberation at the other. The ambiguity of the word 'conscious-ness,' referring as it does both to unreflective awareness (the emo-tional experience) and to reflective self-consciousness (our recogni-tion that we have such-and-such emotion), is the source of many problems, though I would argue that it is also the simple-minded dualism, based on the metaphor of 'reflection' (that is, mental activ-ity versus the *observation* of that activity) that is at fault here. In the sense of consciousness as awareness, every emotion is (necessarily) conscious. In the sense of consciousness as articulate and self-con-scious reflection, an emotion can become conscious only if one has (at the minimum) a language with which to 'label' it and articulate its constituent judgments. Thus I would challenge Jerome Neu's Blake-inspired title, 'A Tear is an Intellectual Thing,' on the grounds that it is not the *intellect* that is typically engaged in emotion. Thus I will also reject the view that cognitive theory— once distinguished from the intellect—*excludes affect*. The fact that many if not most emotions are non-reflective has no bearing on the question whether affect (so-called) might be an essential part of the cognitive aspect of emotional experience.

In his early work, and I see little evidence of radical change since, Jerome Neu took the defining element of emotion to be the very Spinozistic notion of a 'thought.' He makes it quite clear that one cannot have an emotion (or a particular kind of emotion) without certain types of thoughts. Emotions, simply stated, *are* thoughts, or dispositions to have thoughts, or defined by thoughts. (I am not considering here the very general Cartesian sense of '*cogitationes*' that would include virtually any mental process, state, or event, making the claim that emotions are thoughts utterly uninformative.) At the very least, Neu is correct when he says that thoughts are indicative of emotions and are produced during emotions.

I think that the notion of a 'thought' is too specific and involves too much intellect to provide a general account of the emotions. To be sure, a person with an emotion will have thoughts appropriate to the emotion and the context shaped and constrained by his or her

[11] A. Damasio, *Descartes' Error* (London: Macmillan, 1994).

5

language and culture. In the case of adult human emotions, I think that this may necessarily be so. But if belief is too dispositional to capture the essence of emotion, thoughts are too episodic for emotions, which often turn out to be enduring processes rather than mere episodes. Thus a thought may punctuate and manifest an emotion, but it is in itself not a process. *Thinking*, of course, is a process, but thinking is clearly too cerebral, too explicit, to characterize most emotions. A thought is a momentary appearance. It is a more or less articulate formation, and it is more or less independent of perception. Most thoughts involve words and the use of language, whether or not the thought is explicitly couched in words. Thus my thought of Paris (a postcard view of the Seine, looking towards Notre Dame) is a visual image but it's being a thought *of Paris* requires a complex act of recognition on my part. Thus I would say that dogs and babies may have emotions, perceptions and make judgments, but they do not have thoughts.

Philosophers since Frege confuse the matter by taking 'the thought' to be the proposition expressed by the thought, but the proposition alone (a logical construction) is never tantamount to a thought in the psychological sense, as an episodic phenomenon. Much less is a proposition (or a set of propositions) ever tantamount to an emotion. Thus the absurdity of Donald Davidson's much heralded analysis of emotion (following Hume's example of pride) in terms of a syllogism of propositions in logical sequence.[12] Philosophers also confuse the matter by conflating thoughts and thinking (Davidson, again), but although both might be involved in emotion (some emotions certainly 'get us thinking') it is *having* thoughts and having them without necessarily thinking that is most pronounced both as symptom and as constituent of emotion. When I have recurrent thoughts of violence or recurrent sexual fantasies a plausible hypothesis is that I have the appropriate (or rather, *in*appropriate) emotion. But insofar as thought is an aspect of emotion (rather than just a symptom or sign), it cannot merely be a proposition (or a set of propositions), and it must not be tied too tightly to the activity of thinking. (I would argue that it is also important not

---

[12] Donald Davidson (1977) 'Hume's Cognitive Theory of Pride' reprinted in Davidson (1980) *Essays on Actions an Events* (Oxford University Press), 277–90. Davidson's view was taken very seriously by many philosophers who never showed any interest in emotion, much less in any cognitive theory of emotion. But what gets left out of Davidson's reconstruction—as Hume himself clearly recognized—was pride, that is, the emotion. See Annette Baier, 'Hume's Analysis of Pride', *Journal of Philosophy*, **75** (1978), pp. 27–40.

to insist that thinking *cannot* be an aspect of emotion but rather only an antecedent or consequence of emotion.)

One feature of thoughts of particular interest to me which more or less follows from the distinction between thought and thinking is the fact that thoughts do not always appear by way of organized activity (like thinking) but rather appear in at least three ways, which I would summarize as 'conjured up' (when, for example, I think my way through a problem or try to remember the answer to a query), 'invited' (as when I work on a problem, give up on it for the evening, and the answer 'comes to me' in the middle of the night), and 'uninvited' (as when a thought 'pops' into my head, unwanted and unanticipated). This triple feature of thought is particularly relevant to the question whether and in what sense one can choose one's emotions for it is true both that one can (through thinking) choose one's thoughts and that thoughts can come unbidden. Insofar as thoughts are essential aspects of emotion one might note that thoughts are sometimes straightforwardly voluntary and even 'willed' (as in thinking), but thoughts also display considerable degrees of involuntariness, as when they 'pop' into my head (or, as Nietzsche wrote, 'A thought comes when *it* will, not when I will.')

Peter Goldie makes the interesting argument that while thoughts are voluntary, our imagination often 'runs away with us.' This depends on the nature of the distinction between thought and imagination. If a 'thought' is something abstract and merely conceptual (such as the *idea* that some one could possibly run off with my wife) while an image is by its very nature something fully fleshed and robust (such as an exquisitely detailed scenario in which my wife is having sex with another man) Goldie's claim is surely correct. But why should we restrict ourselves to such an emaciated sense of 'thought' or such an overly provocative sense of imagination? I think that Goldie is thinking primarily of thoughts 'conjured up' as opposed to thoughts merely invited or uninvited. I would say that both our thoughts and our imaginations are sometimes wilful, sometimes obsessive and beyond our control. Either way, wilful or obsessive, it is evidence that we have a strong emotion (whether or not we acknowledge it or know what it is) and it is suggestive of a sense in which our emotions are not in our control.

Beyond Belief

'Belief' has now become a catch-all term in cognitive science that specifies very little while it suggests something very specific. (Thus emotion theorists in the late eighties, for instance Ronnie De Sousa and Robert Gordon, spent considerable time arguing that emotion cannot be captured by any combination of belief and desire but inevitably found that they were trying to get hold of a jellyfish.) Belief is too loosely tied to perception to account for those cases where one has an emotion immediately upon coming upon a situation, and it is too tightly tied to the logic of propositions to explain, for example, how it is that we can often hold conflicting (but not literally contradictory) emotions at the same time (what Patricia Greenspan raises as 'the problem of mixed emotions.')

Belief is typically described as a state, and though emotions may be states (that is, if they are of considerable duration and one ignores the dynamic engagement that goes on in emotion), it is surely inadequate to suggest that thus all emotions are states. That is why beliefs are often taken to be only 'cognitive preconditions' of emotion, not constitutive of emotion, since emotions are dynamic and often in flux while belief, as a holding onto a proposition, is a steady state. One either believes a proposition or not (although one might misleadingly express doubt or scepticism by saying that he or she 'sort of' believes that *p*.) Furthermore, beliefs are not experiences, though to be sure they shape and explain experiences. In Neu's vocabulary, they are always explanatory (they must always be postulated to explain behaviour and utterance in the third-person case) and not phenomenological. Belief may be perfectly appropriate in *explaining* emotion but it is inappropriate in the *analysis* of emotion.

These doubts about 'belief' explain the appeal of 'perception' as the 'cognitive element' most appropriate to the analysis of emotion. Ronnie De Sousa makes this case, as did John Dewey years ago, and I think that perception does indeed capture the heart of one kind of emotional experience, that which I would call 'immediate' (though without bringing in the heavy philosophical baggage that term conjures up in the history of epistemology). That is, in those examples where I have an emotional reaction to a situation unfolding right in front of my eyes, i.e. the sorts of examples employed (for obvious reasons) by William James in his classic analysis of emotion. Pointing out the close link between emotion and perception seems to me a plausible way of proceeding. Indeed one of its virtues is that it blocks the insidious distinction (still favoured by some positivistic psychologists) that perception is one thing, appraisal, evaluation, interpretation, and emotional response are all something else. Again, I prefer the concept of judgment precisely because it maintains these close ties to perception but at the same time, is fully conceivable apart from perception.

But when the trigger of an emotional response is a thought or a memory, the perception model looses its appeal. In general, when the object of emotion is something not immediately present, it makes little sense to say that the emotion is essentially a kind of perception. Take the appeal of such notions as 'construal' or 'seeing as.' Cheshire Calhoun defended 'seeing as' in criticizing my theory many years ago (in a book we co-edited).[13] As I have been revising my own 'judgment' theory over the years I have come more and more to construe 'judgment' as 'construal,' though I still think that 'judgment' has a number of advantages, not least of which is that it smacks less of reflection and is more pointedly less concerned with perception and other 'immediate' circumstances. 'Seeing as,' to be sure, is too tied to vision and thus perception, although (of course) it can be treated as a metonym (as Husserl, for instance, used the term) and extended to not only all of the senses but to all cognitive processing as well. But many of our emotions concern merely imaginary, distant, or abstract (but not therefore impersonal) concerns, and the 'seeing as' metonym is seriously stretched. Perhaps the point is better conceived in terms of 'construal,' a more consciously complex (as well as arguably voluntaristic) notion, but then I think the bias towards reflection cancels out these advantages.

Which brings me to Ronnie De Sousa's very fruitful idea of a 'paradigm scenario.' In his book, *The Rationality of Emotion*, De Sousa does not take this as a specification of cognition so much as an alternative to cognition. I have openly expressed my intrigue and admiration regarding this notion. Part of what is so exciting about it is that (unlike virtually all of the cognitive theories I have mentioned so far) it has an explicitly developmental and evolutionary bent. It takes a bold step in the direction of speculating how it is that we come to have the cognitions (or whatever) that constitute emotions, namely, by being taught to respond in certain ways (or taught what responses are appropriate) in specific situations. It thus has the virtue of being quite particularist, as opposed to those overly ambitious cognitive theories that try to draft broad generalizations that govern or constitute emotions. I would note that De Sousa as always been deeply involved in the theatre (and is pretty theatrical himself) and his theatrical shifting from emotion content to emotion context and behavioural training has always seemed to me a huge step forward in emotion research. It goes much further than superficially similar theories of 'action readiness' in that it postulates not only an ingredient in emotion and emotional experience but the

[13] C. Calhoun and R. Solomon, *What is an Emotion?* (Oxford University Press 1984).

Robert C. Solomon

dynamic of emotion as well. In what follows, I will also find two more virtues in De Sousa's theory, its explicit bringing in the body in a behavioural (not physiological) mode and its explicitly social nature, where other people are not just objects of our emotions or those who (in some sense) share our emotions but, in a critical sense, co-conspirators in the cultivation of our emotions.

Emotions as Judgments

Back there in ancient history, in 'Emotions and Choice' (1973) and *The Passions* (1976), I suggested 'judgment' to capture many of these insights. If Neu had the camaraderie of the neo-Stoical Spinoza, I could claim a linkage with the original Stoics, although I obviously rejected their conclusion that emotions as judgments are as such irrational. Briefly put, I take judgment in a way that is not episodic (although, to be sure, one can make a judgment at a particular moment). It is not necessarily articulate or for that matter conscious. (Neu clearly follows Freud in maintaining that thoughts, too, can be unconscious.) I take it as uncontroversial that animals make all sorts of judgments (e.g. whether something is worth eating, or worth chasing, or worth courting) but none of these are articulated or 'spelled out,' nor are they subject to reflection. We make non-reflective, non-deliberative, inarticulate judgments, for instance, kinaesthetic judgments, all the time. Kinaesthetic judgments are rarely deliberative and rarely merit conscious attention. Michael Stocker has a poignant story about his falling on the ice, thus making both his fear and his bodily awareness painfully conscious. But the example only illuminates the fact that such judgments are not usually conscious at all.

Judgments, unlike thoughts, are geared to perception and may apply directly to the situation we are in, but we can also make all sorts of judgments in the utter absence of any object of perception. Thus while I find the language of 'thought' just too intellectual, too sophisticated, and too demanding in terms of linguistic ability, articulation, and reflection, to apply to all emotions, judgment seems to me to have the range and flexibility to apply to everything from animal and infant emotions to the most sophisticated and complex adult human emotions such as jealousy, resentment, and moral indignation. In other words, I find the following to be essential features of emotion and judgment: they are episodic but possibly long-term as well. They must span the bridge between conscious and non-conscious awareness. They must accept as their

10

What is a 'Cognitive Theory' of the Emotions

'objects' both propositions and perceptions. They must be appropriate both in the presence of their objects and in their absence. They must involve appraisals and evaluations without necessarily involving (or excluding) reflective appraisals and evaluations. They must stimulate thoughts and encourage beliefs (as well as being founded on beliefs) without themselves being nothing more than a thought or a belief. And (of considerable importance to me), they must artfully bridge the categories of the voluntary and the involuntary.

Thus emotions are like judgments. And emotions necessarily involve judgments. Does this entitle me to say that emotions *are* judgments? Well, not by logic alone, needless to say. But as a heuristic analysis and a way of understanding the peculiarities of emotion, I think so. But, of course, an emotion is not a single judgment. (In many traditional philosophical analyses, in Hobbes, Descartes, and Spinoza, the complex character of an emotion is reduced to a single one-liner.) An emotion is rather a complex of judgments and, sometimes, quite sophisticated judgments, such as judgments of responsibility (in shame, anger, and embarrassment) or judgments of comparative status (as in contempt and resentment). Emotions as judgments are not necessarily (or usually) conscious or deliberative or even articulate but we certainly *can* articulate, attend to, and deliberate regarding our emotions and emotion-judgments, and we do so whenever we think our way into an emotion, 'work ourselves up' to anger, or jealousy, or love. The judgments of love, for instance, are very much geared to the perceptions we have of our beloved, but they are also tied to all sorts of random thoughts, day-dreaming, hints and associations with the beloved, with all sorts of memories and intentions and imaginings. A judgment may be made at a certain time, in a certain place ('I loved you the first time I ever saw you') but one continues to make, sustain, reinforce, and augment such judgments over an open-ended amount of time.

I am willing to admit that different cognitive candidates may work better or worse for different emotions, and here I see further reason to heed and embellish the warning that Amelie Rorty and Paul Griffiths (for very different reasons) have issued, that 'emotion' is not an adequate category for cross-the-board analysis. Different emotions employ different kinds of cognition. This is the virtue, perhaps, of such non-committal notions as 'cognitive elements' or 'cognitive structures.' They are elastic enough to cover just about anything vaguely conceptual, evaluative, or perceptual. But while these seem to me to be useful conceptual tools for

Robert C. Solomon

working out the general framework of cognitive theory,[14] they clearly lack the phenomenological specificity that I am calling for here. Judgment seems to me to be, all in all, the most versatile candidate in the cognitive analysis of emotion. But by embracing (without distinction) the whole host of cognitive candidates, it is left open whether some emotions might be better analysed in terms of perception, others in terms of thoughts or judgments, others in terms of construals. The real work will have to be with regard to particular emotions, and often with specific regard for the particular instance of a particular sort of emotion.

What is Affect? Emotions, Feelings, and the Body

Michael Stocker and, more recently, Peter Goldie, have accused the cognitive theory of neglecting feelings, or 'affect.' I admit that in *The Passions* I was dismissive of the 'feeling theory' that then seemed to rule what passing interest there was in the emotions (particularly in the work of William James and his successors). I argued that whatever else it might be, an emotion was no mere feeling (interpreting this, as James did, as a bodily set of sensations). But what has increasingly concerned me ever since is the role of the body in emotion, and not only the brain. In my original theory, it was by no means clear that the body had *any* essential role in emotion. I presumed, of course, that all emotional experience had as its causal substratum various processes in the brain, but this had little to do with the nature of emotion as such, as experienced. But as for the various physiological disturbances and disruptions that serve such a central purpose in William James' analysis that the '*sensation IS the emotion*' (with all of the oomph that italics and caps can capture) and in later accounts of emotion as 'arousal,' I was as dismissive as could be, relegating all such phenomena to the causal margins of emotion, as merely accompaniments or secondary effects.

What has led me to this increasing concern about both the role of the body and the nature and role of feelings in emotion is in fact just the suspicion that my own cognitive theory had been cut too 'thin,' that in the pursuit of an alternative to the feeling theory I had veered too far in the other direction. I am now coming to appreciate that accounting for the feelings (not just sensations) in emotion is not a secondary concern and not independent of appreciating the essential role of the body in emotional experience. By this I do not

[14] Ortony *et. al.* (1988).

mean anything having to do with neurology or the tricky mind-body relationship linked with Descartes and Cartesianism but rather the concern about the kinds of *bodily experience* that typify emotion and the bodily manifestations of emotion in immediate expression. In retrospect, I am astounded that facial expression is hardly mentioned in *The Passions* (although, to be sure, my interest increased enormously when I met Paul Ekman some years later.) These are not mere incidentals. But understanding them will provide a concrete and phenomenologically rich account of emotional feelings in place of the fuzzy and ultimately content-less notion of affect.

The role of physiology in feeling is not straightforward. On the one hand, many physiological changes (including autonomic nervous system responses) have clearly experiential consequences, for instance flushing and the quickening of the heart beat. Many others (including most neurological activities) do not. James was rather indiscriminate in his specification of bodily and 'visceral' disturbances, but when he clearly referred to just those bodily processes (not necessarily disturbances) that had clear experiential or phenomenological effects, he did indeed capture something of what goes on in the *feeling* of emotion, although he short-changed the nature of the emotion itself. I now agree that feelings have been 'left out' of the cognitive account, but I also believe that 'cognition' or 'judgment' properly construed captures that missing ingredient. The analogy with kinaesthetic judgments suggests the possibility of bringing feelings of the body into the analysis of emotion in a straightforward way.

What are the feelings in emotion (though, to be sure, an emotion may last much longer than any given feelings, and feelings may outlast an emotion by several minutes or more)? The workings of the autonomic nervous system (quickened pulse, galvanic skin response, the release of hormones, sweating) have obvious phenomenological manifestations (feeling excited, 'tingly,' feeling flushed). Moreover, the whole range of bodily preparations and postures, many of them but not all of them within the realm of the voluntary, have phenomenological manifestations. Here too the well-catalogued realm of facial expression in emotion plays an important role. So do other forms of emotional expression. The category of 'action readiness' defended by Nico Frijda and others seems to me to be particularly significant here, not in terms of dispositional analysis of emotional behaviour but rather as an account of emotion feelings. Anger involves taking up a defensive posture. Some of the distinctive sensations of getting angry are the often subtle and

13

Robert C. Solomon

usually not noticed tensing of the various muscles of the body, particularly those involved in physical aggression. All of these are obviously akin to kinaesthetic feelings, the feelings through which we navigate and 'keep in touch with' our bodies. But these are not just feelings, not just sensations or perceptions of goings-on in the body. They are also *activities*, the activities of preparation and expression. The feelings of our 'making a face' in anger or disgust constitute an important element in our experiences of those emotions.

The voluntary status of these various emotion preparations and expressions is intriguing. Many gestures are obviously voluntary and the feelings that go along with them are the feelings of activity and not passivity. Many bodily preparations, even those that are not autonomic nervous system responses, are not voluntary and our feelings are more of the 'what's happening' sort than of 'I'm doing this.' Facial expressions are an especially intriguing category in this regard. Paul Ekman and others have analysed what most of us have recognized and that is the difference between (for example) smiles that are genuine (that is, to a certain extent involuntary) and smiles that are 'forced' (that is, voluntary but to some extent incompetent). Action readiness includes both autonomic (involuntary) as well as quite conscious and reflective posturing, for example, adopting a face and stance fit for the occasion, a darkened frown and threatening gesture in anger, a 'shame-faced' expression and a gesture of withdrawal or hiding in shame, a sentimental even teary-eyed smile and a tender gesture in love. And each of these has its phenomenological manifestations, its characteristic sensations or feelings that are part and parcel of emotional experience (whether noticed or recognized as such or not).

To put my current thinking in a nutshell, I think that a great deal of what is unhelpfully called 'affect' and 'affectivity' and is supposedly missing from cognitive accounts can be identified with the body, or what I will call (no doubt to howls of indignation) *the judgments of the body*. George Downing has put the matter quite beautifully in some of his recent work.[15] He writes of 'bodily micropractices' and suggests that emotions are to a large extent constituted by these. This could, of course, be taken as just another attempt at behavioural reductionism, but Downing also insists that an emotion is essentially an experience. He also is quite happy to insist that cognitions (judgments) are also an essential part of any emotional experience. But he adds, and I have come to agree, that a good deal

[15] George Downing, 'Emotion Theory Revisited', in *Heidegger, Coping, and Cognitive Science: a Festschhrift for Hubert Dreyfus*, Vol. 2 (M.I.T. Press, 2001), pp. 245–70.

of cognition is of a radically pre-linguistic (very misleadingly called 'pre-cognitive') nature. Building on the work of Hubert Dreyfus and suggestions in Heidegger and Bourdieu, Downing insists that a good deal of emotional experience and even emotional knowledge can be identified in the development of these bodily micro-practices.

Does it make sense to call these judgments? I am sure the answer is yes, and I would defend this in two steps. First, I have already insisted that judgments are not necessarily articulate or conscious and so the sorts of discriminations we make and the construals that we perform are sometimes (often) made without our awareness of, much less reflection on, our doing so. Second, a relatively small store of human knowledge is of the form 'knowing that.' Philosophers, of course, are naturally concerned with such knowledge and that leads them not unnaturally to the prejudice that only such knowledge, propositional knowledge, is important. Not that they deny the need for all sorts of non-verbal skills of the 'knowing how' variety, but these are hardly the stuff of philosophical analysis, first, perhaps, because there may be nothing distinctively human about them (animals display such non-verbal skills at least as impressively as humans) and second, it is well-known that 'knowing how' cannot be reduced to any number of 'knowing that'-type propositions. But it is a distortion of cognition and consciousness to suggest that 'knowing that'-type propositional knowledge is in any way primary or independent of 'knowing how.' The thesis here obviously takes us back to Heidegger and Merleau-Ponty (and to a lesser extent, to Heidegger's one-time disciple Gilbert Ryle). But since I have already insisted that emotional judgments are not necessarily propositional the way is open to make the further claim that they are not necessarily 'knowing that' type cognitions either.

It goes without saying that many of our most 'knowing' responses to the world and the ways in which we bring meaning to our world have much more to do with the habits and practices we perform than the ways in which we think about and describe the world. Feelings of comfort (and discomfort) have a great deal to do with doing the familiar and finding ourselves acting in familiar ways with familiar responses. These feelings of comfort and discomfort range from felt-satisfaction, frustration and low-level anxiety to exuberant joy, full-blown anxiety, rage, and panic. Anger often involves feelings of discomfort, but to be anger (and not just frustration or irritation) the emotion must be further directed by way of some sort of blame, which in turn involves feelings of aggression and hostility, which may themselves be readily traced (as James did) to specific modes of arousal in the body (tensing of muscles, etc.). Shame is at least in part a feeling of discomfort with other people, a feeling of rejection, as love is (in part) a feeling of unusual comfort with another. One might object that there is nothing *distinctively* bodily about any of this, and I would agree. But this is only to say that the Cartesian distinction of mind and body serves us ill in such cases, that it is only as embodied and mobile social beings that we have even the most primitive cognitions about the world to begin with. And more to the point it is in light of such pre-verbal and also active and engaged judgments that we have any emotions at all. We then embellish and enrich these through language, both by increasing (exponentially) the range of descriptions and behaviours and situations in which we become engaged (adding morality, aesthetics, and politics) and by increasing (logarithmically) the kinds of reactions we can have.

Thus the judgments that I claim are constitutive of emotion may be non-propositional and bodily as well as propositional and articulate, and they may further become reflective and self-conscious. What is cognition? I would still insist that it is basically judgment, both reflective and pre-reflective, both knowing how (as skills and practices) and knowing that (as propositional knowledge). A cognitive theory of emotion thus embodies what is often referred to as 'affect' and 'feeling' without dismissing these as unanalysable. But they are not analysable in the mode of conceptual analysis. That is what is right about Griffiths' otherwise wild charges. But neither are the feelings in question simply manifestations of the biological substratum, as James and Griffiths at least sometimes suggest. There are feelings, 'affects' if you like, critical to emotion. But they are not distinct from cognition or judgment and they are not mere 'read-outs' of processes going on in the body. They are judgments *of* the body, and this is the 'missing' element in the cognitive theory of emotions.

On Emotions and Choice

It was John Rawls who made me a radical. It was more than twenty-five years ago, when I was just starting to think my way through *The Passions*, that Rawls and I were having lunch while we were both visiting the University of Michigan. I explained my blooming thesis to him, and he asked, rather matter of factly, 'But surely when you say we choose our emotions you are saying something more than the fact that we choose what to do to bring about a certain emotion?' This was John Rawls, whose Great Book had just been published, and I was not about to say, 'Oh, well, yes, only that.'

Thus began a twenty-year stint of dramatic over-statement, to the effect of *'we choose our emotions.'*

There are two immediate obstacles to any such claim that emotions are matters of choice. The first is the obvious fact that emotions *seem* to happen to us, quite apart from our preferences or intentions. This phenomenological point is reinforced by a semantic-syntactic observation, that the language of the passions (starting with the word 'passion') is riddled with passivity, 'being struck by' and so on. (Though this set of observations should be balanced with another, that we sometimes feel guilty or glad about feeling what we feel, and that we often assess our emotions as warranted or not, wise or foolish, appropriate or inappropriate).

The second is the enormous range of emotions and emotional experiences, from being startled to carefully plotting one's revenge, from inexplicable panic upon seeing a little spider to a well-warranted fear of being audited by Internal Revenue, from falling 'desperately' in love to carefully cultivating a life-long loving relationship, from 'finding oneself' in a rage to righteous and well-considered indignation and a hatred of injustice. And it is not merely the difference between different emotions that is at stake here but (as several of the listed examples indicate) a difference in kinds of emotional experience in the same sort of emotion (fear, anger, love). The enormous range of emotions suggests that no single claim about choice will suit all emotions.

The voluntariness of emotions is obviously a contentious thesis that will require far more careful explication and defence than I can give it here. Let me limit myself to a few well-chosen arguments.

First of all, I certainly did not mean that emotions were *deliberate* actions, the results of overt plans or strategies. We do not think our way into most emotions. Nor do emotions fit the philosophical paradigm of intentional action, that is, actions that are preceded by intentions—combinations of explicit beliefs and desires and 'knowing what one is going to do.' Insofar as the emotions can be defended in terms of a kind of activity or action, it is not fully conscious intentional action that should be our paradigm. But between intentional and full-blown deliberate action and straightforward passivity—getting hit with a brick, suffering a heart attack or a seizure, for example, there is an enormous range of behaviours and 'undergoings' that might nevertheless be considered within the realm of the voluntary and as matters of responsibility.

Second, I was not claiming that having an emotion is or can be what Arthur Danto once called a 'basic action' (namely an action one performs *without performing any other action*, such as wiggling one's little finger). One cannot 'simply' decide to have an emotion. One can, however, decide to do any number of things—enter into a situation, not take one's medication, think about a situation in a different way, 'set oneself up' for a fall—that will bring about the emotion. Or one might *act as if* one has an emotion, act angrily, for instance, from which genuine anger may follow. There is William James' always helpful advice: 'Smooth the brow, brighten the eye, contract the dorsal rather than the ventral aspect of the frame, and speak in a major key, pass the genial compliment, and your heart must be frigid indeed if it does not gradually thaw.' But this does not mean that we simply 'manipulate' or 'engineer' our emotions, as if *we* perform actions which affect or bring about *them*. Following Danto, one might say that virtually all human action—writing a letter, shooting a rifle, signalling a left-hand turn, working one's way through law school—involves doing something by doing something else, and this does not mean that the latter action *causes* the former. The one act (or course of action) *constitutes* the other.

Third, although it is certainly true that most of our emotions are not pre-meditated or deliberate, it is not as if *all* emotions are devoid of premeditation and deliberation. We often pursue love— the having of the emotion and not just the beloved—and we 'work ourselves into a rage,' at least sometimes with obvious objectives in mind (e.g. intimidating the other person). Whether an emotion is pre-meditated or deliberate, however, we may not experience the emotion as a choice among options. We may not think to ourselves, 'I could get angry now, or I could just resign myself to the fact that I'm a loser, or I could just forget it.' Given the situation, I simply choose to get angry. Nevertheless, I think that the notion 'choice,' like the notion of 'action,' is instructive here. It suggests a very different kind of framework for the study of emotion, one in which choice, intention, purpose, and responsibility play important if not central roles at least some if not most of the time. If we think of ourselves as authors of our emotions, we will reflect in such a way as to affect and possibly alter them. It would be nonsense to insist that, regarding our emotional lives, we are 'the captains of our fate,'[16] but nevertheless we are the oarsman and that is enough to hold that we are responsible for our emotions.

[16] The line is from William Henley's 'Invictus,' which has been forever tarnished by mass-murderer Timothy McVeigh, who quoted it immediately before his execution (June 2001).

II. The Emotions and their Philosophy of Mind

RICHARD WOLLHEIM

1. When I was invited by Yale University to deliver the Cassirer lectures,[1] I hesitated for a topic. I wanted something new. I proposed the emotions, and at that time my knowledge of the topic was so slight that I didn't know whether it was something that I had already written on or not.

I mention this fact because one thing that I have since learnt about the emotions is that such ignorance is in order. For it is one of those topics where grasping the extension of the term is inseparable from having some theory of the matter, however primitive. One way to explain this fact is to invoke the novelty of the term, for, in the sense in which it is used in this lecture, it is only about 300 years old. Another way, probably related, is to point to the fact that, not only are there belief *and* particular beliefs, desire *and* particular desires, but, when we refer to particular beliefs and to particular desires, we call them 'the belief that this' or 'the desire that that'. However there is no locution 'the emotion that this', or 'the emotion that that', which would indicate the presence of an emotion. It seems that ordinary language is an intermittent guide to the circumscription of the emotions.

However the uncertainty that I felt when I came to constructing a theory of the emotions went beyond anything I felt in demarcating the field of the emotions. For much of the time, I had the sense that I was engaged in work of pure improvisation. I tried to avoid first one rock, then another, and all the while I was aiming to keep as large a view as possible of the open sea: for without that, what is philosophy worth?

Now, somewhat more used to my own views, I see it less like that. There are, I now discern, certain basic ideas that, at one and the same time, organize my account of the emotions and correspond either to general features of the mind or to particular features of the emotions as I at any rate conceive of them. You can have a theory of the emotions—possibly even a true one—which disagrees with me

[1] Richard Wollheim, *On the Emotions: the Ernst Cassirer Lectures, 1991* (New Haven and London: Yale University Press, 1999).

19

on the details of the mind, but you will not have a theory of the emotions at all unless it takes you deeper into the substantive nature of the mind than does, say, a theory of belief.

In other words, a theory of the emotions needs a theory of the mind to go with it, and in this talk, I plan to set out those features of the mind which I have found cannot be ignored when we try to articulate an account of the emotions. If these features can seemingly be ignored elsewhere in the philosophy of mind, this is a mere coincidence, and not to be made much of.

2. When all else was uncertain, the one thing that I knew about my task ahead was that, before I could intelligibly find anything of detail to say about the emotions, I had first to locate them on a certain broad map of the mind: a map that I had been carrying with me from my first days in philosophy, and which I saw, and see, no need to revise.[2]

On this map the most salient feature is a broad fissure, effecting a division that is exclusive, though not exhaustive of the territory. On one side of the divide lie mental states, on the other side mental dispositions. By mental state, I mean those transient events, possessed of subjectivity and intentionality, which make up what William James called 'the stream of consciousness'.[3] Examples of a mental state would be perceptions, sensations, pangs of hunger and lust, daydreams and hallucinations, and passing thoughts, whether these are truly thought by the person or whether they enter the mind unbidden. One thing that James's great phrase should not deceive us into thinking is that mental events are necessarily conscious in the narrow, or determinate, sense of that term: what they are endowed with is some grade of consciousness in the broad, or determinable, sense, but they can as readily be preconscious, or unconscious, as narrowly conscious. By mental disposition, I mean those underlying modifications of the mind which are possessed of intentionality but not of subjectivity. They have histories of some richness, and they endure for some period of time up to the lifespan of the person to whom they belong. Examples of a mental disposition would be desires, beliefs, skills, virtues and vices, and habits.

It is a crucial fact in the life of the mind, as well vital to our understanding of the distinction between mental dispositions and

[2] See Richard Wollheim, *The Thread of Life: the William James Lectures for 1982* (Cambridge, Ma: Harvard University Press, 1984).

[3] William James, *The Principles of Psychology* (New York: Holt, 1890), Chapter IX.

mental states, that mental dispositions and mental states interact. In *On the Emotions* I list five such ways.

(One) a mental state can initiate a mental disposition. So, waking up and seeing a frog standing on his chest could establish in a small boy's mind a lasting fear of frogs.

(Two) a mental state can terminate a disposition. So, a moment's dizziness high up in the big tent could destroy for ever a woman's ability to walk the tight-rope.

(Three) a mental state could attenuate, or reinforce, a disposition. So, years later, seeing another frog half-buried in sedge, the boy, now an adolescent, finds his fear of frogs intensified, alternatively subsiding into a mild fascination.

(Four, and most important), the disposition, aroused by some stimulus of the moment or, to all appearances, spontaneously, manifests itself in something that the person does or endures, inwardly or outwardly, voluntarily or involuntarily. So, a woman's desire for revenge might manifest itself in the way her head swims, or in a daydream in which her rival cringes before her, or in a scowl that passes across her face, or in her engaging a hitman.

And (five) a disposition can filter, or deflect, either an outward going or an inward coming causal chain: a chain that goes, in one case, from the mind to the world, or, in the other case, from the world to the mind. So, a man's declaration of, even as it issues from his lips, starts to sound unconvincing as sudden fear intervenes and robs his words of authority. Or a woman, who revisits her childhood home after many years, finds that the pleasure she thought this would give her is soured by the incursion of memories she thought she had overcome.

Where are emotions to be located on this map?

My answer is that emotions are to be placed amongst the mental dispositions. The reasons for this are twofold: positive and negative.

The positive reason is that, if we think of emotions as dispositions, this appears to do justice to two intuitions that we have about the emotions. In the first place, emotions have histories of just the sort that dispositions have: emotions often extend over a substantial period of time, they wax and wane, and, though they can last until the death of the person who houses them, they can also come to an end through changing circumstances, through the superior strength of an opposing force, or through boredom or long absence of the object. Secondly, emotions are invariably related to mental states, actual or possible, in some cases bearing the same name, in some cases not, in all the ways enumerated above.

The negative reason is that, if we do not follow this line of thinking, if instead we make emotions out of those mental states which we otherwise think of as either initiating or manifesting the emotions, they, the mental states, show their inadequacy in that, in two respects, they are fatally dependent upon the very dispositions that they are now displacing.

In the first place, it is only through the association with dispositions that the mental states can come to acquire the importance in our lives that we naturally ascribe to the emotions. A man, let us say, has a deep fear of disagreement with anyone whom he loves. He knows that, whenever disagreement breaks out, or perhaps as soon as it is imminent, he will feel a tightening of the throat, an urge to be elsewhere. Phenomenologically such an experience is disagreeable enough, but surely, if the man, as he well might, arranges the whole of his life around this fear, it cannot be simply so as to avoid this experience: it is only by invoking the disposition that we can account for the evasiveness of his life. The avoidance of a visceral feeling is not explanatorily adequate, so the feeling cannot take over the place of the emotion. The second respect in which mental states seem inadequate takes off from the first. For, though mental states possess their phenomenology independently of the dispositions with which they are associated, it is often, not invariably but often, only through this association that their phenomenology becomes fully recognisable to us who have them. Our man with the fear of disagreement might have to depend upon the disposition to recognize what he experiences at the end of a long and painful conversation, or a difficult dinner, as the mental state that it is.

3. The map of the mind that provided my starting-point derives from Gilbert Ryle's *The Concept of Mind*,[4] and, though I have found little else in the book to agree with, the division into mental dispositions and mental states has always struck me as compelling. So much so indeed that theories of the mind that have no place for this two-tier organization seem to me, for just that reason, not to fit on to the facts of the case, on to mental reality, in any very clear way. I here have in mind Functionalism, which, with its insistence upon the 'total state' of the person, homogenizes mental dispositions and mental states, and, in most of its variants, Constructivism, which, by equating persons with well-constructed strings of mental states, finds nowhere to house mental dispositions.

However it is one thing to accept Ryle's map, and quite another

[4] Gilbert Ryle, *The Concept of Mind* (London: Hutchinson's University Library, 1949).

thing to accept the way he understands the map, or the sense he makes of the labels stamped across it. According to Ryle, to attribute a mental state to a person—once exception is made for certain recalcitrant states of which Ryle instances 'thrills, shocks, glows and ticklings', or 'hankerings, itches, gnawings, and yearnings'—is to say one or other of several things, all connected with behaviour: it is to say how the person is doing what he is doing outwardly, or it is to say what is happening to the person as the result of not doing something outwardly. To attribute a mental disposition to a person is also, it turns out, to say something about behaviour. It is to say that the person has a tendency to behave in a certain fashion: hence it is to predict, with varying degrees of assurance that, in certain circumstances, this is just what he will do. When we say that a man is angry, we are saying that he is behaving in a certain way: when we say that he is an angry man, we are saying he is likely to behave in that same way, should the opportunity arise.

If what Ryle is led to say about mental states is the more egregious error in that it goes more directly in the face of commonsense, it is arguably his characterization of mental dispositions that has the more insidious results. For there are two consequences of this characterisation that completely distort the nature of mental dispositions. If I am right about what dispositions are, we should be able to see this by taking the emotions as a test-case.

The first consequence is that no plausible account can be given of conflict of emotion within the breast of a single person. On the contrary, if Ryle is right, when a speaker is tempted to ascribe such conflict to someone, he is doing no more than confessing to an uncertainty on his part about which of two emotions he should attribute to the other. Should he predict that he will behave in this way, or in that way? Despite Ryle's references to what he calls 'commotion conditions' presumably located in the conflicted individual, his actual argument transplants the conflict from the person to whom the speaker nominally ascribes it, and positions it inside the speaker.

The second consequence of the Rylean view of mental dispositions is that the emotions lose whatever explanatory value they can ordinarily claim as far as what the person feels, or the way in which the person views the world, or how the person acts. The most that the attribution of an emotion can achieve for our understanding is that, by subsuming what the person does on one occasion under the larger pattern of what he ordinarily does, it takes away some of what might otherwise strike us as the unfamiliarity of the behaviour: as Ryle himself puts it, when a speaker tries to account for a person's outburst of anger by citing his irascible nature, he succeeds to the extent that we do when we say of what someone does 'He *would* do that'.[5]

Reductionism, I need hardly say, patterns itself all over Ryle's discussion of the mind, but it is worth observing that his account of the mind is at the point of convergence of two reductionist programmes. If one of these programmes, the reduction of mental phenomena to behavioural phenomena, is nowadays less in evidence, the other, the reduction of our understanding of phenomena to our understanding of what we characteristically say about them, is endemic to current philosophy of mind. Of course, a programme may be ill-conceived, and yet some of its individual results be eminently valuable.

4. In the course of attempting to construct a theory of the emotions, I found myself increasingly drawn to a programme for the treatment of the mind, which I have called the 'psychologization', or, more accurately, since what is at issue is a return to a pre-philosophical state of understanding, the 'repsychologization', of mental concepts.[6] I used this term to refer to, at once, the undoing of psychological reductionism, and the recognition of the reality of such psychological phenomena as mental states and mental dispositions. Though we have a general need for such a programme, this need becomes acute in the study of the emotions. We need it, I concluded, not only for the correction of some things ordinarily said about the emotions, but for the ability to say intelligibly certain further things, which, as things stand, do not, cannot, get said.

However to talk of the repsychologization of mental concepts, or realism about mental phenomena, is not itself to articulate a theory of the mind: for at least two reasons.

In the first place, there is the question, left open, which concepts should be repsychologized, which mental phenomena are we to be realists about. For instance, one could be—and, I personally think, one would be well-advised to be—a realist and an anti-reductionist about mental dispositions, and a reductionist and anti-realist about so-called character traits, such as generosity, or strictness. Secondly, repsychologization, realism, are terms for attitudes, approaches, perhaps even prejudices, and exactly what they involve is not all that clear until we start thinking locally.

Let me start then with a set of constraints that I am inclined to think we should impose upon mental dispositions if they are to be

[5] Op. cit., p. 93.
[6] *On the Emotions*, p. 6, and *passim*.

repsychologized, if we are to be realists about them. If, in a general way, they serve to flesh out the demand that mental dispositions are real, what they do in a more particular way is to prepare dispositions for the inclusion of emotions.

In the first place, mental dispositions must be held to have genuine causal powers, and not simply be redescriptions of the phenomena. Secondly, the effects brought about by these causal powers cannot be ascertained simply through analysis of the terms that designate the dispositions themselves. This is in part due to the fact that dispositions never act in isolation to produce a certain effect, and this is something that we can see very clearly when we descend to the particular case of the emotions Thirdly, the disposition itself must be allowed a real history over and above its manifestations. Specifically: we must be able to identify its beginning and its end in some way over and above the first and the last occurrence of the effects we ascribe to it. As we look deeper into not so much the nature as the history of the emotions, we shall find this constraint very important. We shall find it important in its application to another kind of disposition, desires, out of which, or such will be my claim, emotions issue.

5. 'Kind of disposition': I hope that phrase will have held you up.

The belief that the cat is on the mat and the belief that the king of France is bald are mental dispositions: the desire that the sun will shine tomorrow and the desire that peace will prevail in the Middle East are also mental dispositions. But they are mental dispositions in that they are particular mental dispositions. By contrast, when we say that emotions are mental dispositions, or when we say that beliefs are mental dispositions, or when we say that desires are mental dispositions, we are talking about kinds of mental disposition. Even if beliefs, desires, emotions, do not exhaust the kinds of disposition to which they belong—and this is not a question I shall pursue—they are salient examples of their kind. So two questions: How are mental dispositions divided into kinds? And, What is distinctive of the kind of mental disposition to which emotions belong?

My proposal is that the fundamental way in which mental dispositions are divided into kinds is according to the role or function that they carry out for the creature that houses them. Role or function is a differentiating mark of a kind of disposition. Examples: Beliefs belong to a kind of disposition the role of which is to provide the creature with a picture that claims to be true of reality. And desires belong to another kind of disposition the role of which is to provide the creature with targets at which to aim. The role of the kind of disposition to which emotion belongs is that it provides the creature with an attitude, or orientation, towards reality, or, more ordinarily, some part of reality.

If we now ask, How do our mental dispositions carry out these functions? one answer allows us to see how my proposal about dispositions and the kinds into which they fall already calls for some repsychologization of the mind. The truth is that there are several routes along which dispositions achieve their roles for those who house them, but that which is most distinctive of our psychology runs through the mental states in which they, the dispositions, manifest themselves: more precisely, the route runs through—runs through, in that it makes use of—the phenomenology of these mental states. Broadly put, mental dispositions manifest themselves in mental states that are apt, or well-adjusted, to advance the role or function of the disposition, and their aptness lies in the way in which what it is like for the person to be in that kind of state propels the person to do what, in the circumstances, will fulfil that role. So, for instance, beliefs are called upon to impress upon those who subscribe to them the particular picture of the world that they provide. And beliefs do this through manifesting themselves in states in which the content of the belief is confidently asserted. Desires are called upon to keep before the minds of those who are moved by them the targets at which they should aim. And desires do this through manifesting themselves in states in which these targets are imagined as attained.

If this suggestion about how mental dispositions characteristically fulfil their functions requires some measure of repsychologization, it is a limited measure. All that is required is the repsychologization of mental states, or the concession that mental states characteristically have phenomenology, by which I mean the conjunction, the conjunction and interpenetration, of thought-content and experience, of intentionality and subjectivity. This is minimal repsychologization of the mind.

6. And now back to the substantive claim about the role or function of that kind of disposition which is exemplified by emotion: namely, the formation of an attitude.

It is regrettable that philosophers, preoccupied, though not always gainfully, with the nature of belief and of desire, have given insufficient attention to the phenomenon of an attitude. In so far as they have, they have regularly reduced attitudes, hence emotions, to beliefs, or to desires, or to some combination of the two, and without remainder. It is to these reductions that we owe the proliferation of cognitive theories, evaluative theories, and conative theories of emotion: often enough, and interestingly enough, in the writings of one and the same philosopher.[7]

One not uncommon source of error in trying to ascertain how emotion relates to desire and to belief is to proceed by means of a certain kind of imaginary example, or so-called 'thought-experiment', in which insufficient information is initially postulated for any relevant finding to be elicited. 'Imagine' a philosopher says to his audience, 'someone who is frightened...,' Or the philosopher says, 'Imagine someone who is in love....' Then he goes on, and asks, 'Would not such a person believe this, or value that, or desire such-and-such?' And his audience, who have, in order to answer these questions, already imagined into existence characters with these emotions, will then, in interviewing them about what they are likeliest to believe, or value, or desire, be compelled to endow them with further psychology over and above the philosopher's instructions: so much so indeed that there is no telling what the answers they give draw upon over and above fear and love, hence there is no telling what their answers have to say about fear and love themselves.

At the cost of a digression, I want to elaborate on the employment of imaginary examples, and to contrast the two very different uses to which they are widely put, and which, in the bluster of argument, are often insufficiently distinguished. The first way is when we try, or ask our readers to try, to imagine a situation described a certain way, and we do so in order to establish whether the description in question makes sense. 'Imagine a three-sided figure with more than three angles', we say: or we say 'Imagine a person who strongly desires something but would never, in any circumstances, do anything to attain the object of his desires'. In this usage the experimenter looks for one or other of two responses: 'Yes, I can', 'No, I can't'. The second way is when we set ourselves, or try to get others, to imagine a situation described in a certain way, but this time, not for its own sake, but so as then to be able to go on and anticipate what we would naturally say about some eventuality that transpired in that situation. So, for instance, we might be asked, 'Imagine a situation in which someone else's memories replaced yours, and your body was then tortured, would it be you who was tortured?' Now the experimenter requires of the subject a justification for what he says: a mere 'yes' or 'no' will not

[7] Examples of reductionist treatments of attitudes or more precisely emotions are to be found in John Searle, *Intentionality* (Cambridge University Press, 1983).

do. In this second kind of case, we assume the very thing the possibility of which we are dubious about in the first kind of case: that is, whether the description of a certain situation is meaningful, and what it means.

If then it is wrong to identify emotions with either beliefs or desires, there are undoubted similarities, imperfect similarities, between, on the one hand, emotions (or attitudes) and, on the other hand, beliefs, and between attitudes and desires, on the other hand.

In the first place, attitudes are similar to beliefs in that they too influence the way the person reacts to the world. But attitudes do this, not only through what the person holds true of the world, but also through how the person imagines, or cannot but imagine, the world. And, if it is now said that much the same holds for belief, there is a further difference. An attitude does not simply depend upon what we hold true of the world, or how we imagine it. The attitude also influences what he holds true of the world, or how we imagine it. And there is no parallel to this in the case of belief. What are the constituents of a belief are more like the reasons for an attitude, and the relation between an emotion and its reasons is often a symbiotic relation. It is to be observed that, when the emotion is ready to dissipate, the reasons that we had for it, which seemed so strong while the emotion lasted, may no longer have any hold over us: there is no presumption that the reasons a person has for an attitude are reasons that, independently of that attitude, the person would, or does, endorse. This is one sense in which attitudes are irreducibly subjective: they are irreducibly subjective in that they, and their hold over the person, cannot be freed from how the feels about the world.

Secondly, attitudes are similar to desires in that attitudes too are likely to leave the person pleased or displeased with the world as he now finds it. But there is nothing in the attitude, as there is something in desire, to make these feelings directive. I have emphasized this point by saying that, at times, an emotion can be a compromise with reality: a compromise with which in turn we are amply prepared to live. Someone angry with the world is not necessarily inclined to change it, and might well get even angrier with someone who was so inclined. When living well is found the best revenge, who would necessarily want the world rectified?

Sometimes the relationship of emotion to action is obscured when an emotion has grafted on to its core meaning some kind of imperative component. Because the Ancients thought it natural to connect anger with revenge, anger became directional for them, and specifically so when they latched on to the composite concept a complicated code of when an honourable man should seek revenge and when he should tolerate harm.

And, further to obfuscate the situation, just when these imperfect similarities between emotion and belief, or between emotion and desire, give out, there are strong causal connections that can influence us. Emotions, though they are not themselves beliefs, can be caused by beliefs, and, when they are, they can take on some of belief's sensitivity to the truth: *but this is not necessary*. (We shall see more of this in a minute.) Equally emotions, though they are not themselves desires, can cause desires, and, when they do, they can take on some of the motivational force of desire: *but this is not necessary*. Now the conjunction of the similarities *and* the causal connections can lead to a confused belief in the identity of emotion and belief, alternatively in the identity of emotion and desire.

But what we should never lose sight of are the two following facts, which are basic: that there is no parallel in the life of the emotions either to the tendency of beliefs to evaporate when they are shown to conflict with the evidence, or to the tendency of desires to terminate when they are satisfied. More fundamentally, beliefs can be falsified, emotions cannot be: desires can be satisfied, emotions cannot be. And this is not just a matter of what we say, it is a matter of how things are. It is a matter of how we are.

7. Some of these unsystematic remarks about attitude, belief, and desire, about emotion, falsification, and satisfaction, can be deepened as we enlarge our perspective on to emotion.

For if—and it is a genuine 'if', for I see it as an open question—reference to role or function can suffice to identify the kinds of disposition that belief and desire exemplify, more must be said in the case of the emotions. The kind of disposition to which emotions belong is differentiated by a further mark, over and above role or function. For it is essential to emotions, and to their kind of disposition, not only that they generate attitudes, but that they standardly arise in a certain way, or that they have, within the life-history of the person, a characteristic history of their own. And it is to be noted that the two marks of an emotion—specific function and particular history—are closely bound up. For what partly accounts for the fact that an attitude is irreducibly subjective in the sense already considered—that is, that it cannot be divorced from the person's feelings in relation to the world—is that it is subjective in some further sense: that is, that it is a residue from the particular life that that person has led. The first kind of subjectivity is bound up with the specific function of an emotion, the second kind with its particular history.

Richard Wollheim

Briefly told, the history of an emotion goes thus: One, the person has a desire; two, the desire may be satisfied or frustrated; three, when either happens, the person, at one and the same time, has an experience of satisfaction or frustration, and is led to trace the fact of satisfaction or frustration to what I call a precipitating factor, which may be a person, or a thing, or an event; four, though this precipitating factor is often settled upon only after much thought and much weighing-up of factors one against another, the whole process may be clouded by the imagination, and therefore the selection of the precipitating factor need not be on rational grounds; five, the next thing to happen is that the experience of satisfaction or frustration (as the case may be) is projected on to the precipitating factor, and this gives rise to an attitude on the part of the person; six, the attitude persists, an emotion forms; and, seven, the newly formed emotion will in the course of time give rise to a variety of mental dispositions, and will manifest itself in a number of mental states. Prominent amongst the mental states that arise will be feelings, and prominent amongst the dispositions that form will be desires. It is only when desires form that the emotion has motivational force.

There are within this story two alternates, differing in the starting-point from which they set out. One sets out from the satisfaction of desire, and standardly terminates on what is called a positive emotion, or an emotion associated with pleasure, such as gratitude, joy, hope, love: the other sets out from the frustration of desire, and standardly terminates on what is called a negative emotion, or an emotion associated with unpleasure, such as grief, hatred, anger. However, since it is far from clear that satisfaction and frustration are natural correlatives—for surely frustration is a far more complex notion—from now on, I shall confine myself to the first variant. I shall ignore the consequences, the emotional consequences, of frustration.

It goes without saying that I cannot, here and now, defend this story as giving the true history of how an emotion forms. But my present charge is only to show how the story is dependent, at different points of the telling, upon a repsychologization of the mind, and showing that will, I hope, in turn bring out the wealth and complexity of that programme.

8. There are at least three distinct points at which the characteristic history of an emotion, as I have articulated it, appears to come into conflict with the nature of the mind as it is standardly conceived, and this conflict can be resolved only though repsychologization.

However, in each case, the prevailing conception is differently grounded, and the return to a pre-philosophical way of looking at the topic has a somewhat different burden placed upon it. I shall start by identifying the points of conflict

In the first place, then there is the claim that, in searching for the precipitating factor, the mind operates outside the constraints of rationality, and this appears to bring the history I have articulated into conflict with a conception of the mind that holds it to be inherently constrained by the norms of rationality. The repsychologization called for at this point is modest.

The second point at which the history of an emotion as I see it calls for repsychologization is that crucial moment in the aftermath of which emotion forms, and from which the emotion never fully escapes: the satisfaction (or frustration) of desire. For the history I recount in effect requires the equation of the satisfaction of desire with a psychological event: indeed with an experience. That this is required by the story told follows from the fact that it is only an experience that we can, in the appropriate sense, project. The details of the claim I shall consider in a moment, but the repsychologization of the mind that is called for at this second point is somewhat more than modest, and may best be described as an unfamiliar interpretation of a familiar mental phenomenon.

Finally there is the invocation of projection, and now repsychologization takes on substantive form. It no longer reinterprets a phenomenon whose existence we all accept: it asks us to accept a mental phenomenon the very existence of which does not receive widespread recognition either within or outside philosophy.

9. I now intend to look more closely at the three points at which the need for repsychologization arises, and what that need is.

The first point at which my account of the formation of the emotions comes into conflict with a depsychologized view of the mind is where, desire having been satisfied or frustrated, the mind searches for the precipitating factor, which will ultimately be the object of the emotion. For, at this point, the mind is said to be influenced by the imagination, and not to respect the constraints of rationality. And this appears to bring my account into conflict with a prevailing view of the mind as essentially rational.

Now such a view of the mind is indeed a depsychologized view, for experience teaches us that, deep down, the mind is prey to irrational forces. However so depsychologized is this view of the mind, and, on the admission of its adherents so abstracted from actuality, that it is not altogether clear whether the conflict between

Richard Wollheim

it and my account of the emotions is real or merely apparent, and this for two, and possibly three, reasons. First, because the prevailing view does not, at any rate in the first instance, aim to say anything about how the mind actually operates. What it addresses itself to is the question of the commitments that the mind makes, and its claim is that, even when the mind behaves irrationally, it of necessity accepts the very norms of rationality that it flouts. For some, but not for others, this has the consequence that limits are set to the irrational behaviour of the mind, or that the mind must, *by and large*, work rationally. Secondly, because the view of the mind at issue is driven, not so much by a consideration of how the mind actually is, as by reflection on how we have to think the mind to be. Rationality is not directly attributed to agents themselves: directly it is a constraint upon any speaker who wishes to attribute in a coherent manner thought or action to an agent. And, thirdly, because it is conceded at the outset that rationality is a constraint upon the mind only when the mind functions in a unified way, and this is not how it universally functions: the mind functions in a non-unified way when it is played upon by factors that act as causes without also acting as reasons.

It seems therefore, without going into this complex matter deeper than I want to, that what my history of an emotion requires to be true need not involve more than a redrawing of the boundary between the *a priori* and the empirical aspects of the mind in the interests of a more complex overall view of the mind. If it is now objected that this move puts at risk the intelligibility of what we can say about the mind, a retort might be that the intelligibility of what we can say about the mind is not necessarily a more perspicuous constraint than how the mind actually is.

I turn now to the second of the three points where the history of the emotions that I propose calls for the abandonment of a depsychologized view of the mind: that is, in so far as it asks for the identification of the satisfaction of desire with an experience.

A view such as that which I hold can be justified only by a complex argument, and a good starting-point would be a prevailing understanding of what it is for a desire to be satisfied, which stems from a totally depsychologized account of the mind.

This view gives a layered account, the top layer of which is provided by what I call *the linguistic thesis,* according to which the nature of a desire is fully exposed by the logical form of how we canonically attribute desires to persons. The second layer I call the *oratio obliqua thesis,* and it goes on to identify the canonical ascription of a desire with a sentence having the form 'A desires that *p*'. It is, of course, this thesis that justifies the classification of a desire as a propositional attitude.

For those who accept these two theses, the sentential complement in this analysis is now credited with doing two things in one: it gives *the object* of A's desire, and, by extension, it reveals *what it is for the desire to be satisfied*. The object of a desire and the conditions of its satisfaction are the greater part of its nature. Accordingly, when A desires that p, the object of A's desire is p, and what it is for A's desire to be satisfied is for p to be, or, as it is sometimes put, to come, true, with perhaps additionally the requirement that A knows this to be so. Artificial as the idea of something's coming true may seem, it is not clear how, without this notion, we can do justice to the temporality of desire, or to the idea that at one moment a desire is not satisfied and at another moment it is.

Central to this analysis are two ideas. The first is that a proposition (or a sentence) provides the core of any mental phenomenon. The second is that the interactions between any mental phenomenon and either the world or some other mental phenomenon is to be understood in terms of how this propositional (or sentential) core relates to the second term. In thinking of it as a depsychologized view, I have in mind the fact that any contribution that any other aspect of the mental phenomenon might make to, say, what it is for a desire to be satisfied is disregarded.

If we have reservations about this way of looking at the matter, do we have any clues about an alternative perception of the matter?

I believe that we do, and I suggest that we go back to what I found to say about the broad, or structural, constraints on how we should conceive of mental dispositions if they are to be credited with what I have called 'psychological reality'. Let us look specifically at the second and the third constraint, the more specific motivation of which was to secure for dispositions a genuine history. The second constraint was that the event in which the disposition manifests itself cannot be fully predicted from an analysis of the description of the disposition: this is to ensure that the history of a disposition, which includes how it manifests itself, has a truly empirical character, or is subject to independent external influences. The third constraint was that, when a disposition terminates, it does so upon an event that is over and above the termination of its effects: this is to meet the charge that the introduction of the disposition tells us nothing more than we would know from a mere catalogue of the effects attributed to it. If we now put these two constraints together, and, in doing so, recognize that whatever is true of the manifestations of a disposition, must *a fortiori* be true of the event that brings the disposition to an end, then we should be ready to accept the equation of the satisfaction of a desire with (one) an event, and (two) an event the description of which cannot necessarily be inferred from the description of the disposition itself. This would have the consequence that, though the coming-true of the object might cause whatever causes the termination of the desire, it could not itself be the termination of the desire.

However as yet nothing further follows about the nature of this event. It could, for instance, be a purely neuro-physiological happening: it could, on the other hand, be an event that was external, not only to the desire, but also to the person. However that the event should be an experience finds some general support in the idea that, since a desire will begin in an experience, symmetry is restored to the history of a desire by insisting that it end in an experience. But, in order to arrive at something specific enough to deserve inclusion in the history of an emotion, repsychologization must go below the purely structural level, and it must engage more significantly with what I call 'the place of desire in our lives'.

We might start on such an inquiry by contrasting desire and its satisfaction with the vicissitudes of other psychological phenomena to which desire bears an initial similarity.

Let us begin with the case where we take out a bet on the coming about of a certain state of affairs, which we do not otherwise desire. Once we have placed the bet, we acquire an interest in the event, but this interest is purely instrumental: it will bring us in money. Next let us adjust the situation somewhat, and consider two variations upon it. One would be where the state of affairs upon which we bet is something that we independently desire. Another would be where the state of affairs that we independently desire is, because of external factors, so highly unlikely to be realized that we take out a bet against its occurrence, on the grounds that, if it does not come about, we shall at least have the solace of winning our bet. Now, in all three cases, what is preserved is a stark contrast between, on the one hand, the direct interest that nature has implanted in us in our desires and their satisfaction and, on the other hand, the various more oblique forms of interest that we can come to acquire in the winning of a bet. A way of putting the matter would be to point out that the interest we have in a bet is always mediated by our attitude to money, which is invariably complex. Nothing in the same way mediates our interest in the satisfaction of our desires: though this does not have the consequence that we are always prompted to act on all our desires. Some of our desires we would rather die than act on, even if we shall always regret, to some degree, their failure to be satisfied.

I have elsewhere sought to express the asymmetry between the interest that desire gives us in certain states of affairs and the somewhat different interest that a bet gives us in possibly the same state of affairs us by saying that what desire does is that it 'sensitises' us to something in, or perhaps even out of, the world. It is as though desire creates a niche within us, which is waiting to be occupied by its object. If that is truly so, then it is implausible that this carving out of our sensibility should not enter into the psychological picture at the moment when desire meets its object, or when the niche comes to be filled: that is, in the moment of satisfied desire.

As to the readily anticipated objection to calling something of which it has been conceded that it is (one) an event, and (two) psychological, an 'experience', this, I believe, comes from thinking that an experience is something more specific in its nature than it is. It comes, like many other errors about the mind, from taking sensation as the prototype of experience. As with certain other psychological terms, it is in part experience that teaches us the extension of 'experience'.

If at this point someone were to claim that I have confused the satisfaction of a desire with the satisfaction of the person who has the desire, I would plead not guilty. The only shadow of plausibility that attaches to such a charge comes from taking for granted the very point that is at stake: namely, whether it is right to treat the satisfaction of desire as an experience. For otherwise it might very well be the case that both the satisfaction of the person and the satisfaction of a desire are experiential, and the two experiences can come apart. To insist that, if one is an experience, the other isn't, or (the same thing) that anyone who thinks both are has confused the two, is to beg the question against me.

10. The formation of the attitude that is the core of the emotion has, as I have set it out, two components to it: (one), the experience of satisfaction, and then (two), the projection of this experience on to what is taken as the precipitating factor.

I turn now to the second component, and, in doing so, move the discussion into an area where the repsychologization of the mind calls upon us, not just to tolerate philosophically unfamiliar interpretations of psychological phenomena, but to tolerate philosophically unfamiliar phenomena.

So what is projection?

A warning is in place: through two historical contingencies—one is that projection belongs to a group of mental activities, such as introjection, denial, splitting, which Freud was the first to study systematically, and the other is that, when he did so, he studied them under the technical appellation 'defence-mechanisms'—it is widely held that projection is an artefact of psychoanalytic theory. In other words, projection—and, on this view, the same would go for the correlative terms, like introjection, denial, splitting—is used as a mere place-holder, seemingly to designate an event, but the event is one for which there is in principle no evidence. The event is postulated solely so as to isolate, and then to explain some arbitrarily selected stretch of mental life, which is identified as pathological.

But this, it strikes me, is to rush to a conclusion

In point of fact, as Freud himself came to recognize, defence is only one of several ends to which the defence-mechanisms may be directed, and some of these ends, hence some of the occasions on which these mechanisms are deployed, have nothing whatsoever to do with pathology: with either its avoidance or its formation.

But, that issue apart, there is no reason to suspect that the events to which terms like projection are supposed to refer simply dissolve, under analysis, into the effects they are supposed to explain. One way of showing them to be more robust than that is to credit them with some structure, or inner mechanism, for the moving parts of which evidence might be forthcoming.

I shall try to build up a case along these lines for the psychological reality of projection. It will take the form of three observations of increasing specificity.

In the first place, projection is a mental activity. In this respect, projection resembles thinking, inferring, or focusing the gaze, and, along with them, is to be located in a third area that needs to show up on our original map of the mind, distinct from those occupied by mental states and by mental dispositions. Our mind would have a singularly static character if there were no place on the map for mental activity. A distinctive mark of a mental activity is that, though a desire may play a part in its initiation, there is no place for a related instrumental belief. We are, for example, likely to want to get rid of that which we project, but we do not have a belief to the effect that projection is an opportune way of bringing this end about.

Secondly, mental activities fall roughly into two kinds: one kind consists of activities that can be reconstructed as one-stage processes, and the other kind of activities that need to be reconstructed as two-stage processes. Likely examples of one-stage mental activities would be negating, querying, and the carrying out of an immediate inference. But the kind of mental activity to which the defence-mechanisms belong is one that falls into two stages, of which characteristically the first stage consists in some sequence of mental states, and the second stage consists in the coming-to-be, alternatively, in the going-out-of-existence, of a mental disposition, and the two stages are connected in the following way: the first stage has the function of bringing about the second stage, on which it terminates. In an early stage of thinking about mental activities of this second kind, I hit upon the following example: Irritated that I can no longer recall a line from a favourite poem, I start from the beginning, and recite to myself, one by one, the preceding lines until, as I arrive at the forgotten line, it will, with luck, suddenly spring to mind, and thus reenter my accessible cognitive stock. A line, once known, since forgotten, is now remembered. Reciting the lines (stage one) involves a series of mental states, and this then induces (stage two) the revival of an old disposition: this time, knowledge.

The third observation concerns projection specifically. Projection is certainly a two-stage, not a one-stage, mental activity, and, as a start, it is plausible to analyse it along lines similar to those which I have used in the account given of recalling a line of poetry.

So a first approximation goes thus: I am in a certain condition in which I am not happy: let us say, a state of melancholy. Accordingly (stage one) I start to imagine that I am, at one and the same time, expelling this condition from myself, and investing another with it. This stage takes the form of entertaining a number of mental states, which have a process of expulsion as their content. Then (stage two) I find myself believing that the other person is now in this condition instead of me: 'instead of me', for my condition now lightens. Stage two is that for which stage one was entertained, and stage one delivers stage two.

In point of fact, this story, if correct, gives the mechanism, not of projection as such, but of what I have come to call 'simple projection'.

In simple projection, the person comes, at stage two, to think that the other is in the very same condition that he, the person, was initially in and is in no longer. In complex projection, by contrast, the person comes to think, not that the other is in the very condition that he was in, but that the other is in a condition that *matches*, or *corresponds to*, the condition that he has shaken off. It should be clear that complex projection occurs whenever a psychological property is projected on to something inanimate, which of necessity has no psychology. Escaping from our melancholy, we come to find the estuary, as it oozes its way to the sea, melancholy: but, since the estuary is without a psychology, what is ascribed to the estuary is not our melancholy, but something that matches it. 'Match' is a difficult idea.

Richard Wollheim

However it might now be pointed out that there is such a substantial difference between projection as I have been spelling it out and the original case of a two-stage mental activity, when a line of poetry is recalled through an inner mechanism, that doubt is cast on whether the latter can serve as anything approximating to a model for the former. The difference between the two cases is on the level of phenomenology, and it centres on the transition from stage one to stage two of the mental activity.

For, it might be said, we can all see how reciting lines 1, 2, and 3 of a poem might bring it about that line 4, if once known, would erupt into consciousness. There is enough of what has been called *thematic affinity* to underwrite a causal connection between the two stages of the process. But how could imagining that I am getting rid of some unwanted condition of mine bring it about that that condition would vanish, or abate. The thematic affinity here is so broken-backed that it looks as though it could only underwrite a magical link.

I believe that the answer that is required at this stage involves invoking the phenomenon of phantasy. For the links between different phantasies are often of this kind: that, in certain cases where, if one phenomenon brought about another, we would be forced to say that it was magic, the phantasy of one will bring about the phantasy of the other. So phantasizing that I have cast some bad part of myself out of myself can leave me with the phantasy that I am much improved. And this can in turn leave me with a further phantasy about the efficacy of my mental processes.

11. I conclude abruptly because I wish to preserve the impression that I have still done no more than let you sample the detail involved in what I have been calling the psychologization, the repsychologization, of mental concepts. This programme, at one moment, leads us to a certain overall picture of the mind, at another moment it leads us to a certain particular view of familiar mental phenomena, and at yet other moments it leads us to recognize the existence of mental phenomena we thought that the philosophy of mind could do without. I hope to have said enough to suggest the difficulties that there are in constructing a plausible account of the emotions if we do not invoke such a programme.

III. Basic Emotions, Complex Emotions, Machiavellian Emotions[1]

PAUL E. GRIFFITHS

1. Emotion Episodes

According to the distinguished philosopher Richard Wollheim, an emotion is an extended mental episode that originates when events in the world frustrate or satisfy a pre-existing desire (Wollheim, 1999). This leads the subject to form an attitude to the world which colours their future experience, leading them to attend to one aspect of things rather than another, and to view the things they attend to in one light rather than another. The idea that emotions arise from the satisfaction or frustration of desires—the 'match-mismatch' view of emotion aetiology—has had several earlier incarnations in the psychology of emotion[2]. Early versions of this proposal were associated with the attempt to replace the typology of emotion found in ordinary language with a simpler theory of drives and to define new emotion types in terms of general properties such as the frustration of a drive. The match-mismatch view survived the demise of that revisionist project and is found today in theories that accept a folk-psychological-style taxonomy of emotion types based on the meaning ascribed by the subject to the stimulus situation. For example, the match-mismatch view forms part of the subtle and complex model of emotion episodes developed over many years by Nico Frijda (Frijda, 1986). According to Frijda, information about the 'situational antecedents' of an emotion—the stimulus in its context, including the ongoing goals of the organism—is evaluated for its relevance to the multiple concerns of the organism. Evaluation of match-mismatch—the degree of compatibility between the situation and the subject's goals—forms part of this process. The result of the evaluation process is an understanding of the situation in

---

[1] In preparing this paper I am indebted to comments on the draft delivered to Royal Institute of Philosophy 2001 at the University of Manchester and later that summer to a seminar in the Department of Philosophy, Kings College London.

[2] See, for example, (Mandler, 1984).

Paul E. Griffiths

terms of the possible actions it affords and the urgency of adopting a course of action. This understanding may in turn initiate physiological changes readying the organism for action and the formation of dispositions to act on various anticipated contingencies. Each stage of the emotion process is regulated by cognitive activity outside the emotion process itself, and the whole emotion process operates in a 'continual updating' mode leading to a varied emotion episode, rather than 'running its course' to result in a single emotion. Many other 'cognitive appraisal' theories of emotion share Frijda's conception of an ongoing process of evaluation with feedback and hence are theories of emotion episodes rather than theories of the elicitation of a single emotion. But at the heart of all these models are claims about the features of the emotion-eliciting situation that lead to the production of one emotion or another at some point in the episode. These claims are usually expressed as a set of dimensions against which the situation is assessed, one of which often corresponds to match-mismatch. Many theorists label points in the resulting evaluation hyperspace with the names of emotion categories, which would seem to imply that the type-identity of an emotion is determined by the evaluation process[3].

Research in the 'dimensional appraisal' tradition consists mainly in documenting the association of regions in the hyperspace defined by the proposed dimensions of evaluation with particular emotional responses. Frijda's model has been criticized for its very comprehensiveness—its desire to account for every finding documented in this rich empirical literature (Scherer, 1999). This form of criticism is well known to philosophers of science from the example of Darwin's 1868 theory of pangenesis. A comprehensive theory that fits all the known data is unable to perform one of the vital functions of theory, which is to contradict the 'facts', leading to their re-examination and the progressive transformation of the empirical base. In contrast to Darwin's theory of pangenesis, Mendelian genetics contradicted not only much accepted low-level theory about heredity but also contradicted what appeared to be the simple, factual outcome of many breeding experiments. One might hope that a psychological theory of emotion would have the same effect—leading us to re-examine some of our existing beliefs.

Appraisal theorists have also become sensitive to the charge that their models are not based on the reality of emotion processes, but rather on the image of those processes recorded in folk-wisdom. This is because appraisal models have traditionally been tested by

---

[3] For a review of appraisal theories, see Scherer, 1999.

asking people who have experienced a particular emotion to report on the appraisal process, or even by asking people to report on the relevance of certain dimensions of evaluation to certain emotion concepts. This comes close to 'conceptual analysis by numbers' or, as the leading appraisal theorist Klaus Scherer has expressed it, to studies that 'do little more than explicate the implicational semantic structures of our emotion vocabulary' (Scherer, 1999: 655). This challenge to appraisal theory can be met in a number of ways, including studies that manipulate situational factors relevant to the dimensions of appraisal and predict the resultant change in emotion, and studies that rely on objective measures of emotion rather than self-report. The ongoing effort to test appraisal theories as theories of emotion, rather than as elucidations of folk theory, has led to a consensus that emotions do not walk in step with cognitive evaluation of the stimulus unless the notion of 'cognitive evaluation' is broadened to include sub-personal processes (Teasdale, 1999). Appraisal theorists have come to accept that even such apparently conceptually complex dimensions of evaluation as Richard Lazarus's 'core relational themes' (Lazarus, 1991) can be assessed: 1. Without the information evaluated being available to other cognitive processes, 2. Before perceptual processing of the stimulus has been completed, and 3. Using only simple, sensory concepts to define the property that has to be identified. Some evidence supporting such 'multi-level appraisal theories' will be considered at more length in section three, as will their philosophical implications.

2. Basic Emotions

The emotion episodes which are the main focus of Wollheim's work, and that of other well-known philosophers[4], are very different entities from the most intensively studied emotions—the so-called 'basic emotions' of the Tomkins-Izard-Ekman tradition (Griffiths, 2001). Research on the basic emotions began in the 1860s with Darwin's efforts to reveal the 'true and original' forms of human emotional behaviour. Having found painting and sculpture too dominated by convention to be of any use for this purpose, he took the innovative step of using photographs to establish which facial expressions were reliably recognized as indicating certain emotions by men and women in England. Darwin's *The Expression of the Emotions in Man and Animals* (Darwin, 1872) is illustrated

[4] E.g. Greenspan, 1988; Greenspan, 1995; Nussbaum, 2001.

Paul E. Griffiths

with many of the wonderful images he used in these experiments, some taken from life and others posed by hired actors. Then, as he so often did, Darwin used his network of correspondents across the world to extend his investigations. In search of indigenous peoples not corrupted by exposure to European facial expressions Darwin contacted colonists at the edges of European expansion. In Australia, for example, he contacted a missionary in 'a remote part of Gippsland' and another correspondent who had ventured 'several hundred miles in the interior of Queensland'. Neglected for decades, Darwin's ideas on emotion were revived by animal behaviourists like Konrad Lorenz in the 1950s and were spectacularly confirmed in the 1960s. In one famous series of experiments the American psychologist Paul Ekman, again searching for subjects not exposed to European cultural conventions, worked amongst the Fore people of the New Guinean highlands. Using an ingenious experimental design that avoided the problem of translating the names of emotions into another language Ekman showed his subjects photographs of actors posing facial expressions associated with certain emotions. Then he asked them to pick out the face of a character in a story—a man sitting at the bedside of his dead child, for example, or a man unexpectedly confronted by a wild pig. The Fore informants reliably identified the correct faces—those Westerners would label as sadness and fear. Ekman also filmed the faces of Fore people acting out some of the same incidents and students back in the United States proved equally adept at identifying the intended emotion from these films (Ekman, 1972). At around the same time, human ethologists demonstrated the early emergence of some of these expressions in human infants (Eibl-Eibesfeldt, 1973) and primatologists reasserted the homology between human facial expressions and those of non-human primates (Chevalier-Skolnikoff, 1973).

So for the past thirty years, there has been a consensus that certain 'basic emotions' are found in all human cultures. These are commonly called fear, anger, disgust, sadness, joy and surprise (not to be confused with the simpler, reflex-like startle response). Naturally enough, when used in this context all these emotion words refer to phenomena less rich and varied than those they refer to in common speech. Each basic emotion has a distinctive facial expression and for most of them there is evidence of distinctive physiological responses, distinctive changes in the voice and evidence of cognitive phenomena like focusing attention on the emotion stimulus. Psychologists have disputed whether the basic emotions are really *basic*, that is, whether the other emotions are really all based on these six. They have also disputed whether the basic emotions are emotions, suggesting instead that they are mere building blocks that form parts of more complex psychological states, and that it is these complex states that better deserve the name 'emotions'. Emotions or not, however, the basic emotions clearly form part of what is going on in emotion episodes. The characteristic facial and other behaviours associated with the basic emotions are one criterion by which people apply emotion terms. Homologous and analogous states in animals are normally called emotions and both biologists and neuroscientists take it for granted that human emotions are some kind of elaboration of these animal emotions. Finally, the basic emotions are almost the only affective phenomena about which there is a strong consensus in the scientific literature. A philosophical theory of emotion must have some way, however dismissive, of accommodating these empirical findings. My own view is that rather than dismissing them, we can build on these findings about basic emotions to obtain insights into the nature of the more complex emotions that are of primary interest to philosophers.

3. 'Affective primacy' and 'twin-pathway' models of emotion

A controversial claim associated with research into the basic emotions is the 'affective primacy thesis'. Affective primacy means that emotional responses are independent of the rational evaluations we make of things; that we can be afraid of things that we know are not dangerous and angry about things we firmly believe to be just. In contrast, the 'cognitive' tradition in the philosophy of emotion has treated the connections between emotion and beliefs and desires about as set of conceptual truths (Deigh, 1994; Griffiths, 1989). Robert Solomon states that:

> 'all emotions presuppose or have as their preconditions, certain sorts of cognitions—an awareness of danger in fear, recognition of an offence in anger, appreciation of someone or something as loveable in love. Even the most hard-headed neurological or behavioural theory must take account of the fact that no matter what the neurology or the behaviour, if a person is demonstrably ignorant of a certain state of affairs or facts, he or she cannot have certain emotions.' (Solomon, 1993: 11).

Many psychologists, however, claim to have demonstrated experimentally that emotions can occur in the absence of the

Paul E. Griffiths

relevant cognitions. The best known of these is Robert Zajonc, who showed that subjects can form preferences for stimuli to which they have been have been exposed subliminally so that their ability to identify those stimuli remains at chance levels (Zajonc, 1980). Many results have since been obtained which confirm Zajonc's discovery. Arne Öhman and his collaborators have conditioned subjects to dislike angry faces and subsequently elicited the conditioned emotional response when those angry faces were masked by neutral faces so that subjects reported no conscious experience of them (Esteves and Öhman, 1993; Öhman, 1986). In a later study, subjects were exposed to subliminal images of snakes, spiders, flowers and mushrooms. Although the subjects showed no ability to identify which stimulus they had been exposed to, subjects with previously established snake phobia showed elevated skin conductance responses to the snake images and subjects with spider phobia showed this response to the spider images (Öhman and Soares, 1994)[5].

The original controversy aroused by Zajonc's results concerned whether emotions involve a 'cognitive evaluation of the stimulus' (Lazarus, Coyne and Folkman, 1984; Zajonc, 1984a, 1984b). It has become clear that this was not a helpful formulation, and that what is really at issue is whether the information processing that leads to an emotional response is separate from that which leads to paradigmatically cognitive processes such as conscious report and recall, and whether the two kinds of information processing are different in kind. The predominant view at the present time is that emotions involve states that are, in some sense, representational and which constitute, in some sense, an evaluation of the stimulus (Charland, 1997; Izard, 1992; Lazarus, 1999). These states, however, can occur at many 'levels' (in a sense to be clarified below) and an evaluation that leads to an emotion can be separate from, and can contradict, the evaluation of the same stimulus that is verbally reportable and integrated with the organisms other reportable beliefs. Under normal conditions, of course, the beliefs a subject has about an emotion stimulus match their emotional response to that stimulus, but this is not always the case, and the affective primacy thesis was basically correct in its assertion that even under normal conditions there are two (or more) processes going on (Ekman, 1980; Griffiths, 1990; Rozin, 1976; Zajonc, 1980). In Paul Ekman's work these ideas are embodied in his concept of an 'automatic appraisal mechanism'—a cognitive subsystem dedicated to determining whether a stimulus will elicit a basic emotion and able to operate independently of the

[5] For a brief overview, see Öhman, 2002.

cognitive systems that lead to conscious, verbally reportable appraisals of the same stimulus.

This 'twin-pathway' approach to the elicitation of emotion has been solidly confirmed in the case of fear by the neuroscientist Joseph LeDoux (LeDoux, 1996; LeDoux, 1993). LeDoux distinguishes between 'cognitive computations' which yield information about stimuli and the relations between them, and 'affective computations' which yield information about the significance of stimuli for the organism and lead to physiological and behavioural responses appropriate to that significance. In fear, and probably at least some other basic emotions, key aspects of affective computation occur in the amygdala. The emotional evaluation of a stimulus can be driven by inputs at various levels of analysis. At a very early stage of perceptual processing, minimally processed data from thalamic sensory relay structures follows the 'low road' to the amygdala. This is the ultimate 'quick and dirty' route to rapid emotional response. Meanwhile, perceptual information follows a slower 'high road' to the visual, auditory, somatosensory, gustatory and olfactory cortices, projections from which to the amygdala allow responses to stimuli in a single, sensory modality. Lesions to these pathways inhibit emotional responses to stimulus features in the corresponding modalities. Finally, the amygdala receives inputs from brain regions associated with full-blown, polymodal, perceptual representations of the stimulus situation and with memory, allowing the emotional response to be triggered by complex, contextual features of the stimulus. However it is triggered, it is the final response in the amygdala that is associated with fear conditioning, and conditioned fear responses to simple sensory-perceptual stimuli have been shown to be relatively hard to modify.

Twin (or multiple) pathway models of emotion have considerable implications for the theories of emotion episodes discussed in section one. They bolster existing concerns about the extent to which self-report data accurately reflect actual emotion processes. As Öhman puts it: 'Thus, rather than being an important factor in the shaping of emotion, as assumed by most cognitively-oriented emotion theorists... from the present perspective, conscious cognitive mechanisms enter late in the sequence of events, with the primary aim of finding some order in and evaluating what is going on. Therefore, self-reports may be a misleading route to the understanding of emotion...' (Öhman, 1999: 345). Findings like those of LeDoux have also increased the attraction of multi-level appraisal theories (Teasdale, 1999), which preserve the guiding insight that emotional states are directed onto states of affairs in the world without having to force emotions onto the procrustean bed of the traditional 'cognitive theory' of emotion.

Twin pathway models also have major implications for the philosophy of emotion, as I have argued elsewhere (Griffiths, 1990, 1997). What is at stake for philosophers is our ability to discover the nature of emotional processes by exploring the semantic relations between emotion terms. This approach rests on the idea that emotions are mental representations and that emotional cognition manipulates these representations on the basis of their representational content. Hence emotional processes can be explored via the semantic 'logic' of emotions. Solomon's strictures on any future neuroscience,quoted above, depend on just this assumption. But twin-pathway models suggest that emotional representations are separate from representations of the same objects used for other purposes and perhaps also different in kind. The 'separateness' (e.g. modularity or informational encapsulation) of emotional representations means that the way in which emotional and other representations interact, if they interact at all, depends on details of cognitive architecture as well as on the content of the representations. This architecture, of course, cannot be determined by studying the logical relations between emotion words. If, in addition, emotional representations are different in kind from other representations, then further problems arise. Contemporary naturalized theories of mental representation envisage the existence of several grades of representation (Dretske, 1981, 1988; Millikan, 1984). Many of the fine-grained semantic distinctions we make in natural language may fail to get a grip on representational states with more coarse-grained semantics. Millikan has also suggested that primitive mental representations may unite the functions of beliefs and desires in a single, undifferentiated functional role. Stephen Stich has explored the possibility that 'sub-doxastic' mental representations may fail to respect the logical operations that we expect to govern full-fledged beliefs (Stich, 1983). A good, and close, analogy is that between emotional representations and states of the early stages of visual processing. The states of edge and motion detectors in the visual system, for example, are clearly 'representations' in some general sense of that term, but we do not expect to be able to characterize the representational content of these states using sentences of English while preserving all the semantic and inferential properties of those sentences! The representational content of an edge detector is only vaguely gestured at by the sentence 'This is an edge' and this is not because of a lack of work on the 'logic of edges'. If emotional representations are, as research suggests, separate, and perhaps qualitatively distinct, from conscious, verbally reportable representations of the same stimuli, then traditional philosophical analysis of the 'logic' of fear and anger must be reconceived as akin to the 'logic' of memory or the 'logic' of perception. Such analytic projects represent the elucidation of a folk theory of the mind and are potentially as important as studies of folk-physics or ethnobiology, but they bear only an indirect and problematic relationship to the psychology of emotion. Failure to distinguish between elucidating the folk theory and studying emotion processes themselves is unlikely to lead to a good account of either.

4. Beyond the basic emotions

After this brief sketch of the basic emotions literature, I want to explore how we might build on the understanding of these emotions to model the complex emotions that mediate human social interaction; the emotions that are of greatest interest to philosophers, particularly aestheticians and moral psychologists. Numerous suggestions already exist as to how to do this. Some contemporary evolutionary psychologists believe that we can understand human emotion by straightforwardly extending the basic emotions approach to the rest of our emotional lives. Even a person's capacity to 'experience existential dread by considering their own death' may be an adaptation to some specific problem in human evolution (Gaulin and McBurney, 2001: 266). Following this strategy, David Buss argues that the brain houses specialized circuits devoted to sexual jealousy (Buss, 2000). Like the fear circuits in the amygdala, these reacts to special inputs such as unusual scents or violations of rules about personal space and uses special-purpose computational algorithms to decide that a partner is committing adultery, often far in advance of any evidence that would provide rational grounds for that belief. The jealousy module in men causes them to behave violently to their partner as a deterrent to possible adultery, and Buss has speculated that it may even contain special rules for spouse-murder. Although better founded than, for example, Victor Johnston's suggestion that women experience negative emotions during menstruation to encourage them to get pregnant next time (Johnston, 1999: 135), Buss's claims still do not have the scientific credentials of Ekman's claims about the basic emotions or LeDoux's analysis of the fear circuits. Nevertheless, the basic emotions approach has been very successful, leading to one of the few areas of consensus in the science of emotion. It is only understandable if some psychologists believe that the correct approach is more of the same. Ekman himself has suggested a more extended list of sixteen basic emotions, amusement, anger, contempt, contentment, disgust, embarrassment, excitement, fear, guilt, pride in achievement, relief, sadness/distress, satisfaction, sensory pleasure and shame (Ekman, 1999). In contrast to most other advocates of an extended basic emotions approach, however, Ekman continues to insist that basic emotions are a distinctive class of psychological phenomena marked out by their automaticity, by unique behavioural and physiological signatures and by the existence of homologous states in other primates. He believes that empirical evidence of these features will probably be forthcoming for the states on his extended list. More doctrinaire evolutionary psychologists resist the demand for such evidence. Steven Gaulin and Donald McBurney argue that it is inappropriate to demand that an emotion have a distinctive facial expression, since it may be more adaptive to keep emotions secret (a view discussed at more length below). They suggest that many emotions are unique to humans, have no homologues in other primates and so cannot be studied using the comparative method. Finally, they urge that the recognition of new emotional adaptations should not be prevented by the inability of current measurement techniques to identify any distinctive physiology associated with that adaptation (Gaulin and McBurney, 2001: 264–7). While in line with the general theoretical position adopted by many contemporary evolutionary psychologists (Cosmides and Tooby, 2000), these arguments threaten to extend the meaning of 'basic emotion' to cover just about any phenomenon in the general domain of motivation and emotion for which a plausible evolutionary rationale can be suggested. Ekman's approach has the advantage that it identifies a range of broadly comparable and individually well-characterized psychological states. I have argued elsewhere that the methodological value of a list of basic emotions is to have a list of states of more or less *the same kind*, so that we can look for psychological and neurological principles about states of that kind (Griffiths, 1997).

In contrast to the evolutionary psychologists, the other currently popular attempt to build a more general theory on the foundation of the basic emotions draws a fundamental distinction between 'primary' (basic) and 'secondary' emotions. This is the revival of the early C20 James/Lange theory in the work of neuroscientist Antonio Damasio and his philosophical interpreters (Charland, 1995; Damasio, 1994; Damasio, 1999; Prinz, Forthcoming). These authors have argued that the phenomenology that accompanies basic emotions is the perception of bodily changes caused by the subcortical circuits that drive those responses. They argue further that these 'somatic appraisals' play important functional roles in cognition and action. More complex emotions involve subtly differentiated somatic appraisals and cognitive activity realized in the neo-cortex that accompanies some combination of basic emotions. Primary emotions are part of our evolutionary inheritance, shared by all normal humans and tied to specific types of stimuli. Secondary emotions are acquired during development, show cultural and individual variation and are sensitive to more complex and abstract features of the stimulus situation. This approach identifies each emotion with one type of somatic appraisal and focuses on the functions of emotions in the internal, cognitive economy of the organism.

In this paper, however, I want to introduce and explore a very different strategy for building on the basic emotions to illuminate complex emotional episodes. The strategy draws on recent work by 'transactional' psychologists of emotion (Fridlund, 1994; Fridlund, 1989; Parkinson, 1995). In contrast to somatic appraisal theorists, these theorists focus on the functions of emotion in interactions between organisms rather than their function in the organism's internal cognitive economy. From a transactional perspective, emotions are moves people make as they negotiate how they will be treated by others and how they will think of themselves and their situation in life. Sulking, for example, in which people sabotage what would normally be mutually rewarding interactions with a social or sexual partner and reject attempts at reconciliation after conflict, can be seen as a strategy for seeking a better global deal in that particular relationship. People sulk because of what sulking will achieve, as much or more than because of what has happened. Interpretations of emotional behaviour as 'strategic' or goal-directed behaviour are a familiar feature of the literature on the 'social construction' of emotions (Griffiths, 1997: 137–167). The work I discuss here is significantly different, because it takes a 'strategic' or goal-directed perspective on the basic emotions and locates the origins of these features of emotion in an evolutionary account of mind. I suggest that a socially-oriented ('Machiavellian') perspective on the basic emotions can be incorporated into a theory of extended emotion episodes containing many emotional and cognitive events as parts—what Ekman has called 'emotion plots' (Ekman, 1999: 55)—in such a way as to provide biological underpinnings for ideas that have traditionally been associated with social constructionist or more generally culture-based account of emotion.

Paul E. Griffiths

5. Emotions as Social Transactions

There is a fundamental evolutionary puzzle about the conventional view that basic emotions have obligate facial expressions. Why would evolution produce organisms that are obliged to continually inform friend and enemy alike about their motivation and likely future behaviour? As discussed above, some evolutionary psychologists have disputed Ekman's longstanding view that each evolved emotion has a distinctive facial signature. They argue that this will only be true for those emotions that it is in the interests of the organism to reveal. The best-known advocate of this view, however, is Alan Fridlund (Fridlund, 1994). Rather than arguing that there will be some emotions with facial signatures and some without, Fridlund makes a general prediction across the whole range of emotions that organisms will produce displays when it is advantageous for them to do so and not at other times. Emotional behaviours, he argues, are primarily signals to other organisms and as such their production takes account of the presence of other organisms and of their relationship to the organism producing the display.

Several psychologists have conducted experiments to test this perspective on emotion, mostly seeking to find 'audience effects'—cases in which social context influences whether a particular stimulus elicits emotional behaviour. For example, José Miguel Fernández-Dols and María-Angeles Ruiz-Belda have documented audience effects on the production of the so-called 'true smile'—the pan-cultural expression of happiness (Fernández-Dols and Ruiz-Belda, 1997). In a study of Spanish soccer fans they found that a wide range of facial, vocal and other behaviour occurred when the favoured team scored a goal. Smiles, however, occurred almost exclusively when one fan turned to another and sought to share their enthusiasm. Fernández-Dols and Ruiz-Belda found the same pattern in medal winners at the 1992 Barcelona Olympics. Gold medallists produced many signs of emotion during the medal ceremony, but smiled almost exclusively when interacting with the audience and officials. They concluded that happiness merely facilitates smiling, making it more likely to occur when the actual precipitating factor is present. That precipitating factor is a social interaction in which one person seeks to affiliate with another. Obviously, people do smile and produce other classical emotional expressions when they are alone, but several studies suggest that they do so much less often than we suppose. Even such apparently reflexive displays as faces produced in response to tastes and smells appear to be more marked in a social setting than in solitary subjects (Fridlund, 1994: 155–7). There are also different ways of being 'alone'. Fridlund has shown that solitary subjects who are mentally picturing themselves as taking part in a social interaction produce more emotional facial signals than subjects thinking only of the emotional stimulus and how it makes them feel. Fridlund has described this as 'implicit sociality' and remarked that his subjects display to the 'audience in their heads'(Fridlund, 1994; Fridlund *et al.*, 1990).

Experiments like these are open to objection that they merely reveal the operation of what Ekman has termed terms 'cultural display rules'. According to the display rule conception, the occurrence of an emotion always initiates a set of expressive movements, give or take a few caveats about stimulus intensity, but subjects sometimes prevent those movements from actually occurring by utilizing the same muscles in a voluntary movement pattern. The operation of a display rule can become as automatic as any other, habitually performed action. Fully enculturated adults can respond to social cues that require them to modulate the expression of emotions as smoothly and unconsciously as they respond to features of the traffic when driving. In a well-known experiment, Ekman and his collaborators showed American and Japanese college students neutral and stress inducing films while they were alone in a room. The repertoire of facial behaviours shown during the stress phase by the two sets of subjects was very similar. However, when an experimenter was introduced into the room and asked questions about the subject's emotions as the stress film was shown again, the facial behaviour of the Japanese diverged radically from that of the Americans (Ekman, 1971, 1972). Ekman interpreted this as the operation of a cultural display rule in Japanese subjects, a rule forbidding the expression of negative emotions in the presence of authority figures. In support of this interpretation, he was able to document the momentary onset of negative emotional expressions prior to formation of the characteristic final facial configuration of the Japanese subjects. This phenomenon of emotion 'leakage' helps make clear the difference between the display rule and transactionalist theories of the social modulation of emotion. For Ekman, the emotion process itself is distinct from the process of strategically modulating information flow. The automatic appraisal system that triggers an affect program takes no notice of display rules. Instead, the affect program response and the display rule compete for control of output systems. Leakage is a side effect of the intrinsically conflict-based architecture of this system for controlling emotional behaviour. For the transactionalist, however, the strategic modulation of information flow is an intimate part of the emotion process itself. If leakage occurs, it must have some strategic function.

There is a standard transactionalist account of the strategic function of 'leakage', an account that can be traced back to the work of the ethologist Robert A Hinde (Hinde, 1985a, 1985b). Hinde's flagship examples are threat displays in birds, which, he argued, are adaptive either as bluffs or because the display elicited in response provides information that the first bird can use to assess its options. In neither case is the probability of the threat display, or its intensity, a simple consequence of the probability that the bird will attack (or, anthropomorphically, of 'how angry it is'). Hinde used a distinction between emotional 'expression' and emotional 'negotiation' to mark the difference between his view of emotion signals and the views of earlier ethologists (Hinde, 1985a, 1985b). Emotional displays seen as expressions of emotion are unconditional predictors of future behaviour, in the sense that they reveal a motivational state. that will persist and explain the future behaviour. Emotional displays seen as negotiation are *conditional* predictors of behaviour. They predict how the first organism will behave if one or more organisms make one or other of a range of possible response. The second kind of display does not reveal an enduring motivational state, because the organism's future emotional state will depend on how other organisms respond to the display. Hinde suggested that 'emotional behaviour may lie along a continuum from behaviour that is more or less expressive to behaviour concerned primarily with a process of negotiation between individuals.' (Hinde, 1985a: 989). Fridlund compares these ethological ideas to a study on human lying which contrasted two conditions, one in which subjects lied to keep secret a surprise birthday party, and one on which they lied to avoid telling someone the painful truth. In the latter condition, but not the former, subjects equivocated (Bavelas, et al., 1990). Fridlund draws a parallel between the ambiguous speech of these human agents, who are conflicted as to whether to tell the truth or to avoid an unpleasant personal interaction, and animals unsure whether to flight or flee. Both use ambiguous signals of intention to probe the likely response of the audience to an action. From this perspective 'leakage' is not the result of the architecture of the brain, but an adaptive behaviour in which animals both convey information to others and obtain information that helps them form a more definite motivation.

Since Hinde wrote, the concept of 'Machiavellian intelligence' has moved to centre stage in discussions of the evolution of human cognition (Byrne and Whiten, 1988; Whiten and Byrne, 1997). Intelligence is 'Machiavellian' to the extent that the evolutionary forces which shaped it concern social competition within primate groups. Machiavellian intelligence is the result of an intra-species arms race in which increased intelligence at the level of the population merely raises the bar for success at the level of the individual. Hinde's seminal papers were a response to developments in behavioural ecology in the 1970s, particularly in the theory of animal signalling, which prefigure the Machiavellian intelligence concept. His concept of emotional negotiation and the general idea that emotions are social transactions are therefore very naturally regarded as applications of the Machiavellian intelligence perspective to emotion, an idea embodied in the title of this paper. Like more traditional conceptions of intelligence, emotions are Machiavellian in a general sense simply to the extent that they find their dominant evolutionary functions in social competition. It is, however, useful to distinguish some more specific ways in which emotion may be 'Machiavellian'. A fundamental distinction, and one that is particularly useful in reconstructing the debate between Ekman and Fridlund, is between the Machiavellian *expression* of emotion and the Machiavellian production of emotion. It seems to be common ground, at least amongst theorists who are prepared to interpret human emotion as a product of evolution, that the expression. of emotion is Machiavellian. The contextual factors that predict whether an emotion is expressed are of the sort that are likely to have been significant in human evolution—factors such as conformity to group standards and the status of the individual in the group. The sensitivity of emotional expression to such factors is very plausibly part of our evolved social competence. This need not imply, of course, that the specific rules to which individuals conform in one culture or another can be explained in evolutionary terms. Evolution can be equally relevant when the task is to understand how cultures generate their patterns of difference from a shared developmental system. The generic fact that there are display rules, for example, is very likely to have an evolutionary explanation. Learning to utilize evolved facial expressions appropriately in a social setting turns out to be as critical for infant monkeys as it is for infant humans (see below).

If the Machiavellian expression of emotions is common ground amongst evolutionary theorists of emotion, the Machiavellian production of emotion is a more controversial idea. A Machiavellian perspective on the production of emotion would imply something like the following:

Paul E. Griffiths

The Machiavellian Emotion Hypothesis: Emotional appraisal is sensitive to cues that predict the value to the emotional agent of responding to the situation with a particular emotion, as well as cues that indicate the significance of the stimulus situation to the agent independently of the agent's response.

Put in the language of appraisal theories, the hypothesis is that the appraisal hyperspace has 'strategic' dimensions. Current appraisal theories identify multiple dimensions that assess the organism-relative significance of what has happened. The Machiavellian emotions hypothesis predicts that there will also be dimensions that assess the payoff to the organism of having the emotion. Putting the hypothesis in more philosophical terms, the emotional appraisal ascribes to the environment the property of affording a certain strategy of social interaction. This process, like the process described by Frijda, might operate in ' continuous updating mode' leading to a continuous modulation of the organisms strategies of interaction.

A Machiavellian theory of the production of basic emotions might apply to any or all levels of appraisal. First, the triggering of basic emotions via the slower, 'high road' structures might display an evolved sensitivity to social context. Although this idea seems plausible I am going to put less emphasis on it, for two reasons. First, I suspect that the behavioural consequences of this high-level process would be very be hard to distinguish empirically from the operation of complex display rules or from the effect of broader aspects of the psychology of emotion that fall under the general rubric of 'coping processes'. Second, I will suggest below that some of the best evidence for a Machiavellian perspective on the production of emotions comes from work on non-human animals, work which probably illuminates the 'low road' to emotion. I will concentrate, therefore, on the idea that the 'low road'—Ekman's 'automatic appraisal mechanism'—may display an evolved sensitivity to social context that is Machiavellian in nature.

Most of the evidence so far produced by transactional psychologists working with human subjects can be accounted for by a Machiavellian perspective on the expression of emotion, without endorsing the more radical thesis of Machiavellian production. Research on audience effects is intrinsically unsuited to distinguishing the hypothesis that an emotion does not occur in inappropriate social contexts (Machiavellian production) from the hypothesis that it is not expressed in those contexts (Machiavellian expression). As I have sketched above, the existence of emotion 'leakage' does not straightforwardly discriminate between these two interpretations. Nor does the persistence of reduced levels of emotional behaviour in asocial settings, which can be accounted for by Fridlund's concept of 'implicit sociality' (displaying to the audience in your head), an explanation that has some empirical support. Studies of the eliciting conditions for emotions are more likely to be able to discriminate between Machiavellian expression and Machiavellian production. One intriguing study, based on retrospective self-report of actual emotion episodes, found that the occurrence of anger rather than sadness as the response to a loss was predicted, not only by traditionally recognized factors such as intentional action by a human agent or breach of a norm of behaviour, but also by the possibility of obtaining restitution or compensation, a finding that seems to fit the Machiavellian emotion hypothesis (Stein, Trabasso, and Liwag, 1993). However, the best evidence I can currently find for the existence of Machiavellian factors in emotion production comes from studies on non-human animals. These studies also suggest that Ekman's concept of a display rule needs to be amended in a way that makes even Machiavellian expression a more integral part of the actual emotion process that it at first seems.

6. Machiavellian Emotion in Animals

Audience effects are common in animals. In one well-known study, Peter Marler and Christopher Evans found sophisticated audience effects in Golden Sebright chickens. These birds give two alarm calls, one for aerial predators and another for terrestrial predators. Although solitary chickens are clearly afraid when they see an aerial predator, they do not produce the relevant alarm call. Likewise, male chickens call excitedly when they find food, but only if there are female chickens in the vicinity. The evolutionary rationale for these audience effects is obvious: there is no point warning chickens who aren't there or demonstrating foraging ability to other males. Marler and Evans say that their findings are compatible with Ekman's concept of display rules. The solitary chickens show many other signs of fear when they see an aerial predator, and they may still be excited by finding food even when they produce no calls. But the very application of the display rule concept to chickens involves a very significant revision of that concept. Display rules those were originally introduced as 'learnt, cultural display rules' (Ekman, 1972). Their function was to explain how earlier researchers had been misled about the extent of cultural variability in human emotion, as gauged by facial behaviour. The suggestion was that basic emotions and their facial displays are part of humanity's evolutionary heritage, but are modified differently in every culture as a result of social learning. The chicken 'display rules', however, are not culture-specific but species-typical, and it is most unlikely that their development in individual chickens requires learning in the sense that a human infant might be supposed to acquire a display rule by imitation or by reinforcement of initial performances. In Marler and Evans's usage, the concept of a display rule has is reduced to marking the bare distinction between Machiavellian expression and Machiavellian emotion outlined in the previous section. The chicken's appraisal of what it has found as a high value food item and its consequent emotional state have an existence independent of the chicken's Machiavellian decision to reveal this emotion to conspecifics.

I will suggest below that the distinction between having an emotion and expressing it may be distinctly problematic in non-human subject. But even if the role of Machiavellian processes in simple minds is restricted to the expression of independently existing emotional states, this carries an important message for the study of human emotions. It provides a powerful argument against the idea that Machiavellian processes imply the sort of sophisticated cognitive abilities that naturally come to mind when we hear phrases like 'negotiation' and 'sensitivity to social context'. The existence of audience effects in animals is in tension with some basic stereotypes about emotion. Emotions are the paradigm of something that happens without regard for the consequences. Emotions are also stereotypically 'biological'. Something sounds right in Konrad Lorenz's epigram that animals are highly emotional people of limited intelligence: emotions are part of our 'animal nature'. Producing or suppressing behaviours so as to take account of social relationships, however, seems like a complex, cognitive achievement. It suggests processes that involve deliberation, perhaps even conscious deliberation. So the idea that the emotion system implements strategies of social interaction naturally suggests the idea that these aspects of emotion are learnt, and perhaps culture-specific, rather than being part of our evolutionary heritage. But this inference may well be entirely spurious. The existence of sophisticated audience effects in animals suggests that the social, manipulative aspects of emotion may be as evolutionarily ancient as any others. The appraisal process that sets off a transparently Machiavellian response like sulking may very well resemble the ancient, 'low road' to fear uncovered by LeDoux.

Basic Emotions, Complex Emotions, Machiavellian Emotions

Further support for this perspective comes from the vital role of emotion in primate social cognition. The role of experience in the development of emotional responses in primates is well known. A series of deprivation experiments conducted in the 1960s by Harry F. Harlow and his collaborators demonstrated the vital role of appropriate social contact in the development of the emotional phenotype in the rhesus macaque (Harlow, 1986). Monkeys deprived of appropriate social interaction as infants are unable to interact effectively with peers, including sexual partners. An inability to respond to social contact with positive emotion, or with appropriate levels of negative emotion, seems to be an important mechanism producing these social deficits. It is also well known that lesions to the amygdala, the likely seat of much affective computation, produce severe social dysfunction in rhesus monkeys (Emery and Amaral, 2000). These results, however, involve damage to the emotional phenotype that is too devastating to allow any evaluation of the Machiavellian emotion hypothesis, as opposed to the uncontroversial general claim that the emotions play an important role in social behaviour. Other studies, however, have uncovered subtler deficits. William Mason reports that rhesus macaques deprived of social contact as infants produce a range of grossly normal facial behaviours which are generally interpreted as expressions of fear (grimace), friendliness (lipsmacking) and threat (threat faces) (Mason, 1985). What seems to be lacking in these animals is an ability to utilize these facial expressions to manage their relationships with other monkeys. Mason reports two dysfunctional patterns of behaviour that are particularly interesting in the context of the present discussion. Normal monkeys use facial affiliation signals to form alliances to defeat dominant individuals and to maintain confidence in each other's support during that project. Socially deprived monkeys are unable to accomplish this. They also fail, unlike normal monkeys, to use facial expressions to redirect aggression from dominants against third parties. Mason explains these results in terms of the role of social experience in elaborating complex eliciting conditions for emotional behaviour. Infant monkeys begin by producing these behaviours in response to relatively simple, context independent stimuli. Later on, 'As a result of functional elaborations, refinements, and transformations of the schemata [*of elicitors for expressive behaviour*] present in early infancy, experience creates new sources of social order, new possibilities for the regulation and control of social life.' (Mason 1985: 147). The monkeys, in other words, learn to produce the same behaviours in response to subtler, context dependent stimuli, and by doing so are able to manage their social interactions with other animals in a rewarding manner.

One possible interpretation of these results is that socially skilled, adult monkeys experience emotions in the same way as the socially deprived monkeys, but have learnt to suppress them when they are socially inconvenient or fake them when they are socially useful. This interpretation confines Machiavellian social cognition to the management of social expression and excludes it from emotion production. Frankly, however, it is hard to attach any operational meaning to the idea that rhesus monkeys pretend to feel friendship for one another or pretend to be angry. It is easier to make sense of the inverse claim that they pretend not to have emotions. Perhaps some emotional responses are repressed by a relatively automatic version of a display rule, but it seems equally conceivable that the production of emotional responses is inhibited by the cues that might be supposed to figure in that display rule, so that, for instance, actions that might generate anger if performed by a subordinate or equal simply do not generate anger when performed by a dominant. Contextual inhibition of this kind is consistent with the neural connectivity of the primate amygdala (Emery and Amaral, 2000: 167). The positive case, in which rhesus monkeys pretend to have emotions, is really quite implausible. When an animal produces a threat display but flees when challenged, as occurs in the examples Hinde used to introduce the idea of emotional negotiation, this can be described in functional terms as a 'bluff'. This, unfortunately, invites an anthropomorphic interpretation in which the organism is acting angry but not feeling angry. If that interpretation means anything there must be a distinction between genuine ('sincere') agonistic displays and fakes. The very idea of human anger seems to presume a fixed relationship between the production of displays and the motivation of later behaviour that runs counter to the idea of regarding an agonistic display as a behaviour in its own right. Yet, in the case of animals, that is exactly what ethologists do.

The fact that the concept of emotional sincerity seems largely otiose in the study of animal cognition explains why the transactional perspective on emotion emerged quite rapidly after the abandonment of the classical ethological theory of drives. For Konrad Lorenz, an emotion was the subjective aspect of the performance of an instinctive behaviour. The sequence of behaviour leading up to this 'consummatory act' is driven by the accumulation of 'action-specific energy' in a reservoir. If the behaviour is prevented by the presence of an inhibiting stimulus, this energy 'overflows' to produce 'displacement activities' (Lorenz, 1996). In the classic example, a cat confronting a rival but unwilling to attack begins to wash itself. In this context, unexpressed emotions serve to explain an apparently observable phenomena: 'I think it is probable that displacements do serve a function as outlets, through a safety valve, of dangerous surplus impulses' (Tinbergen, 1952: 52). However, the drive-discharge model of instinctive behaviour was rejected by most students of animal behaviour by the early 1960s e.g. (Hinde, 1956). The idea of unexpressed emotions in animals came to seem like nothing more than unwarranted anthropomorphism. The complex relationship between emotional behaviour and motivational states was conceptualized instead through a strategic understanding of the role of those behaviours in social interaction. In the seminal papers cited above, Hinde brought this perspective home to the study of emotion in humans.

7. Machiavellian Emotions in Humans

There is a straightforward evolutionary continuity argument for Machiavellian emotion production in humans. The automatic appraisal system in humans is homologous to the corresponding emotional appraisal system in other primates. If primates exhibit sensitivity to strategically significant features of social context it seems likely that the hominid line began its divergence from other primates already equipped with this ability. The Machiavellian intelligence perspective suggests that the ability to negotiate social relationships was the dominant factor driving the evolution of increased human cognitive ability. Given these background presuppositions, it seems highly unlikely that the emotion system would lose its sensitivity to social context during human evolution.

What would a Machiavellian theory of human emotion production look like? Numerous emotion theorists have suggested that emotions may be self-serving, occurring not when the situation objectively warrants the judgment embodied in the emotional appraisal, but rather when it suite the agent to interpret the situation in this light. Jean Paul Sartre famously took this view (Sartre, 1962). Emotions are a class of mental processes in which people regain psychic equilibrium by altering their perception of reality rather than altering reality itself. Affective cognition is thus like the fable of the sour grapes—unable to discharge the desire for the grapes by obtaining them, we discharge it by ascribing to the grapes the property of being undesirable. Likewise, according to Sartre, anger ascribes to a person the property of being hateful precisely because he stands between the agent and the satisfaction of her desires. That is the difference between the emotion of anger and rational coping with the conflicting needs of others. In anger, rather than give up some of our desires, we reinterpret the world to allow us to hang on to them. According to Sartre, the involvement of the body in emotion is a device for turning these psychic acts into involuntary happenings. Sartre compares a person in the grip of emotion to the florid hysterics of the Salpetrie. Emotions are psychosomatic symptoms used to make our pretences real to ourselves and to others. Emotions as Sartre describes them are intrinsically pathological—a form of bad faith in which people reject reality out of mental weakness. But the central insight of his theory is independent of this judgment: people can use emotions to view the world in a light that is psychologically more rewarding to us than other possible interpretations. Highly adaptive versions of this process are described in the literature on 'emotional intelligence', such as using an emotional reinterpretation of the situation to motivate oneself (Salovey, *et al.*, 2000). Viewed from the perspective of contemporary emotional intelligence literature, Sartre's work seems like an insightful account of human psychology marred by the French philosophers penchant for calling a spade a conspiracy against the soil.

Sartre concentrates on the intra-personal functions of emotion, in apparent contrast to the literature on strategic emotion in animals that focuses of inter-personal functions. But the difference between these two is smaller than it at first appears. Transactionalist psychologists have stressed the importance of managing self-image as well as social image in a functional way, and it is easy to see that these goals can often be accomplished simultaneously. By interpreting another's behaviour as unreasonable I can both maintain my positive self-image and make an advantageous move in the social negotiation of the eventual outcome of my interaction with that person. A person who becomes angry when their sexual partner points out that they have failed to do enough around the house, for example, might gain both these advantages by focusing on the hurtful way the remark was made.

An interesting example with which to develop the Machiavellian perspective is romantic love. Most accounts of this emotion regard it as a device to create and maintain long-term pair bonds. According to Robert Frank, love is a 'commitment mechanism' a guarantee that a person will remain committed to a relationship even when temporarily more rewarding relationships become avail-

Basic Emotions, Complex Emotions, Machiavellian Emotions

able (Frank, 1988). A special emotion is needed for this purpose, because simple means-end rationality will dictate choosing the current best option at each moment. Melvyn Konner, in contrast, has pointed out that in traditional societies few people have the option of forming a long-term pair bond on the basis of romantic attraction. Instead, he suggests that the irruptive, passionate love that western societies treat as the occasion for the formation of life-long partnerships may have as its primary evolutionary function motivating behaviours such as mate desertion and copulation out-side the pair bond (Konner, 1982: 315–316). This suggestion has become more credible since it was first made in the light of the increasing emphasis in behavioural ecology on female promiscuity. Females in a wide range of species search for the 'best genes' independent of the need in many of the same species to maintain a stable bond with a single male to provide economic support for off-spring. In humans, mate desertion and promiscuity are risky behaviours as far as immediate survival goes. They carry a high probability of agonistic interactions with other members of the group. If the advantages of these behaviours for reproductive fitness are great enough, however, love might evolve as a special motivational system designed, not to enforce commitment when impulse argues against it, but to motivate adultery when prudence argues against it. Both theories represent evolutionary just-so-stories, with all their attendant uncertainty. But if the adultery theory were correct it would dovetail interestingly with some ideas about love from the social constructionist tradition. Constructionists have emphasized the role of emotions as 'excuses'—ways to move socially sanctioned behaviour into the realm of passive, involuntary, and thus excusable behaviour. The existence of recognized 'excuses' also allows society to tolerate a certain amount of deviance without the complete breakdown of social norms. The use of love to excuse mate desertion is one instance to which this model could be applied. The obvious prob-lem with the constructionist theory is that it requires both the indi-vidual emotional agent and their society to be sincerely convinced that the behaviour is involuntary. In earlier work I suggested that the internalization of a cultural model of behaviour in childhood might do the requisite work of 'naturalizing' the behaviour and making its function invisible to those who enact it[6]. If the adultery theory of the evolution of love is correct, however, then a process of

[6] For an analysis of social constructionism about emotion, see (Griffiths, 1997, Ch 6). The idea of love as a socially accepted excuse for adultery was first suggested to me by Peter Forrest.

this kind would have ample biological material to work with. It would simply be a matter of hyper-cognizing a certain kind of emotional experience and establishing cultural narratives in which it figures and which would be cited to explain, and implicitly excuse, desertion. The same narratives might serve the intra-personal function of allowing the individual to regard themselves as swept along by impersonal forces and thus maintain a positive self-image in the face of the damage caused to other people by their behaviour.

The ideas of the last paragraph are grossly speculative. I include them merely to make a general, theoretical point about the impact of the Machiavellian emotion perspective on emotion theory. A Machiavellian perspective on the basic emotions would allow a much tighter integration of biological and cultural theories of emotion. This would be true even if Machiavellian processes are restricted to the management of emotional expression, so long as those processes occur as an intimate part of the evolved emotion system. The basic emotions represent some of the key building blocks of complex emotion episodes. These episodes are more than just the sum of their constituent parts, but they also, inevitably, reflect the nature of those parts. What we might learn from ethological work on the Machiavellian nature of emotional behaviour in animal on the one hand and social transactional account of human psychologists on the other, is to stop contrasting spontaneous emotions with strategic, perhaps even manipulative, social interaction. Basic emotion processes and complex, culturally situated emotion episodes may, as it were, speak the same language. Emotion may be Machiavellian all the way down.

8. Conclusion

I have suggested that the basic emotions may be ' Machiavellian' in their expression and possibly also in their production, meaning that they show an evolved sensitivity to strategically significant aspects of the organism's social context. The best evidence for this, I suggest, is the presence of sophisticated social cognition in animals, where it is problematic to postulate complex psychological processes such as self-deceit and pretence. What is plausible for animal emotion, I have argued, is also plausible for low-level processes in human emotion. Finally, I have suggested that some of the narratives about self-serving or manipulative emotion associated with social constructionist accounts of emotion are easier to believe if these emotion episodes have biological underpinnings that take account of the organism's strategic situation at a sub-personal level. My suggestion is analogous to Alfred Mele's recent suggestion that self-deception can be generated by a set of simple cognitive biases that produce the appearance of a person choosing to believe something they know to be false (Mele, 2001). Similarly, a strategically sensitive emotion system might give rise to emotion episodes that appear self-serving and manipulative without the agent forming a plan to pursue their social interests or engage in manipulation.

Bibliography

Bavelas, J. B., Black, A., Chovil, N. and Mullett, J. 1990. 'Truth, lies and equivocations: The effects of conflicting goals on discourse', *Journal of Language and Social Psychology*, **9**, 135–61.

Buss, D. M. 2000. *The Dangerous Passion: Why Jealousy is as Essential as Love and Sex* (New York: Simon and Schuster).

Byrne, R. W. and Whiten, A. E. 1988. *Machiavellian Intelligence* (Oxford, New York: Oxford University Press).

Charland, L. C. 1995. 'Emotion as a natural kind: towards a computational foundation for emotion theory', *Philosophical Psychology*, **8**(1), 59–84.

Charland, L. C. 1997. 'Reconciling Cognitive and Perceptual Theories of Emotion: A Representational Proposal', *Philosophy of Science*, **64**(4), 555–79.

Chevalier-Skolnikoff, S. 1973. 'Facial expression of emotion in non-human primates', In P. Ekman (ed.), *Darwin and Facial Expression: A Century of Research in Review* (pp. 11–89). (New York and London: Academic Press).

Cosmides, L. and Tooby, J. 2000. 'Evolutionary Psychology and the Emotions', In M. Lewis and J. M. Haviland-Jones (eds), *Handbook of the Emotions* (2 edn, pp. 91–115). (New York and London: Guildford Press).

Damasio, A. R. 1994. *Descartes Error: Emotion, Reason and the Human Brain* (New York: Grosset/Putnam).

Damasio, A. R. 1999. *The Feeling of What Happens: Body and Emotion in the Making of Consciousness* (New York: Harcourt Brace).

Darwin, C. 1872. *The Expressions of Emotions in Man & Animals* (1st edn). (New York: Philosophical Library).

Deigh, J. 1994. 'Cognitivism in the theory of emotions', *Ethics*, **104**, 824–54.

Dretske, F. 1981. *Knowledge and the Flow of Information* (Oxford: Blackwells).

Dretske, F. 1988. *Explaining Behaviour* (Cambridge, MA: Bradford/MIT).

Eibl-Eibesfeldt, I. 1973. 'Expressive behaviour of the deaf & blind born',

Paul E. Griffiths

In M. von Cranach and I. Vine (eds), *Social Communication & Movement* (pp. 163–194). (London & New York: Academic Press).

Ekman, P. 1971. 'Universals and Cultural Differences in Facial Expressions of Emotion', In J. K. Cole (ed.), *Nebraska Symposium on Motivation* **4**. (pp. 207–283). (Lincoln, Nebraska: University of Nebraska Press).

Ekman, P. 1972. *Emotions in the Human Face* (New York: Pergamon Press).

Ekman, P. 1980. 'Biological & cultural contributions to body & facial movement in the expression of emotions', In A. O. Rorty (ed.), *Explaining Emotions* (pp. 73–102). (Berkeley: University of California Press).

Ekman, P. 1999. 'Basic Emotions', In T. Dalgleish and M. Power (eds), *Handbook of Cognition and Emotion* (pp. 45–60). (Chichester: John Wiley and Sons Co.).

Emery, N. J. and Amaral, D. G. 2000. 'The role of the amygdala in primate social cognition', In R. Lane and L. Nadel (eds), *The Cognitive Neuroscience of Emotion* (pp. 156–91). (New York: Oxford University Press).

Esteves, F. and Öhman, A. 1993. 'Masking the face: recognition of emotional facial expression as a function of the parameters of backward masking', *Scandinavian Journal of Psychology*, **34**(1–18).

Fernández-Dols, J. M. and Ruiz-Belda, M.-A. 1997. 'Spontaneous facial behaviour during intense emotional episodes: Artistic truth and optical truth', In J. A. Russell and J. M. Fernández-Dols (eds), *The Psychology of Facial Expression* (pp. 255–294). (Cambridge: Cambridge University Press).

Frank, R. H. 1988. *Passions Within Reason: The Strategic Role of the Emotions* (New York: Norton).

Fridlund, A. 1994. *Human Facial Expression: An Evolutionary View* (San Diego: Academic Press).

Fridlund, A. J. 1989. *Evolution and facial action in reflex, social motive, and paralanguage* (Berkeley: University of California Press).

Fridlund, A. J., Schaut, J. A., Sabini, J. P., Shenker, J. I., Hedlund, L. E. and Knauer, M. J. 1990. 'Audience effects on solitary faces during imagery: displaying to the people in your head', *Journal of Nonverbal Behaviour*, **14**(2), 113–37.

Frijda, N. H. 1986. *The Emotions* (Cambridge: Cambridge University Press).

Gaulin, S. J. C. and McBurney, D. H. 2001. *Psychology: An Evolutionary Approach* (Upper Saddle River, NJ: Prentice Hall).

Greenspan, P. 1988. *Emotions and Reasons: An Inquiry into Emotional Justification* (New York: Routledge).

Greenspan, P. S. 1995. *Practical Guilt: Moral Dilemmas, Emotions, and Social Norms* (New York: Oxford University Press).

Griffiths, P. E. 1989. 'The Degeneration of the Cognitive Theory of Emotion', *Philosophical Psychology*, **2** (3), 297–313.

Griffiths, P. E. 1990. 'Modularity & the Psychoevolutionary Theory of Emotion', *Biology & Philosophy*, **5**, 175–96.

Basic Emotions, Complex Emotions, Machiavellian Emotions

Griffiths, P. E. 1997. *What Emotions Really Are: The Problem of Psychological Categories* (Chicago: University of Chicago Press).

Griffiths, P. E. 2001. 'Emotion and Expression', *International Encyclopaedia of the Social and Behavioural Sciences* (Pergamon/Elsevier Science).

Harlow, C. M. (ed.), 1986. *From Learning to Love: The Selected Papers of H. F. Harlow* (New York: Praeger).

Hinde, R. A. 1956. 'Ethological Models and the Concept of "Drive"', *British Journal for the Philosophy of Science*, 6, 321–31.

Hinde, R. A. 1985a. 'Expression and Negotiation', In G. Zivin (ed.), *The Development of Expressive Behaviour* (pp. 103–16). (New York: Academic Press).

Hinde, R. A. 1985b. 'Was "The Expression of Emotions" a misleading phrase?', *Animal Behaviour*, 33, 985–992.

Izard, C. E. 1992. 'Basic emotions, relations amongst emotions and emotion-cognition relations', *Psychological Review*, 99 (3), 561–65.

Johnston, V. S. 1999. *Why We Feel: The New Science of Human Emotions.*

Konner, M. 1982. *The Tangled Wing: Biological Constraints on the Human Spirit* (London: William Heinemann Ltd).

Lazarus, R. S. 1991. *Emotion and Adaptation* (New York: Oxford University Press).

Lazarus, R. S. 1999. The cognition-emotion debate: a bit of history. In T. Dalgleish and M. J. Power (eds), *Handbook of Emotion and Cognition* (pp. 3–19). Chichester, New York: John Wiley and sons.

Lazarus, R. S., Coyne, J. C. & Folkman, S. 1984. Cognition, emotion & motivation: doctoring Humpty Dumpty. In K. Scherer and P. Ekman (eds), *Approaches to Emotions* (pp. 221–237). Hillsdale, New Jersey: Erlbaum.

LeDoux, J. 1996. *The Emotional Brain: The Mysterious Underpinnings of Emotional Life* (New York: Simon and Schuster).

LeDoux, J. E. 1993. 'Emotional networks in the brain', In M. Lewis and J. M. Haviland (eds), *Handbook of Emotions* (pp. 109–118). (New York: Guildford Press).

Lorenz, K. (1996). *The Natural Science of the Human Species: An Introduction to Comparative Behavioural Research. The Russian Manuscript (1944–1948)* (R. D. Martin, trans.). (Cambridge, Mass: MIT Press).

Mandler, G. 1984. *Mind and Body: The Psychology of Emotion and Stress* (New York: Norton).

Mason, W. A. 1985. 'Experiential influences on the development of expressive behaviours in Rhesus monkeys', In G. Zivin (ed.), *The Development of Expressive Behaviour* (pp. 117–152). (New York: Academic Press).

Mele, A. R. 2001. *Self-Deception Unmasked* (Princeton: Princeton University Press).

Millikan, R. G. (1984). *Language, Thought & Other Biological Categories* (Cambridge, Mass.: M.I.T. Press).

Paul E. Griffiths

Nussbaum, M. C. 2001. *Upheavals of Thought: The Intelligence of Emotions* (Cambridge, New York: Cambridge University Press).

Öhman, A. 1986. 'Face the beast and fear the face: animal and social fears as prototypes for evolutionary analyses of emotion', *Psychophysiology*, **23**, 123–45.

Öhman, A. 1999. 'Distinguishing Unconscious from Conscious Emotional Processes: Methodological Considerations and Theoretical Implications', In T. Dalgleish and M. J. Power (eds), *Handbook of Emotion and Cognition* (pp. 321–52). (Chichester: John Wiley and sons).

Öhman, A. 2002. 'Automaticity and the amygdala: Nonconscious responses to emotional faces', *Current Directions in Psychological Science*, **11**(2), 62–6.

Öhman, A. and Soares, J. J. F. 1994. Unconscious anxiety: phobic responses to masked stimuli. *Journal of Abnormal Psychology*, **102**, 121–32.

Parkinson, B. 1995. *Ideas and Realities of Emotion* (London and New York: Routledge).

Prinz, J. (Forthcoming). *Emotional Perception* (Oxford: Oxford University Press).

Rozin, P. 1976. 'The evolution of intelligence & access to the cognitive unconscious', In J. M. Sprague and A. N. Epstein (eds), *Progress in Psychobiology & Physiological Psychology* (Vol. 6, pp. 245–81). (New York: Academic Press).

Salovey, P., Bedell, B. T., Detweiler, J. B. and Mayer, J. D. 2000. 'Current Directions in Emotional Intelligence Research', In M. Lewis and J. M. Haviland-Jones (eds), *Handbook of Emotions* (2 ed., pp. 514–520). (New York: Guildford Press).

Sartre, J. P. 1962. *Sketch for a Theory of the Emotions* (P. Mairet, Trans.). London: Methuen.

Scherer, K. R. 1999. 'Appraisal Theory', In T. Dalgleish and M. J. Power (eds), *Handbook of Emotion and Cognition* (pp. 637–63). (Chichester: New York).

Solomon, R. C. 1993. 'The philosophy of emotions', In M. Lewis and J. M. Haviland (eds), *Handbook of Emotions* (pp. 3–15). (New York: Guildford).

Stein, N. L., Trabasso, T. and Liwag, M. (1993). 'The representation and organization of emotional experience: unfolding the emotion episode', In M. Lewis and J. M. Haviland (eds), *Handbook of Emotions* (pp. 279–300). (New York: Guildford Press).

Stich, S. 1983. *From Folk Psychology to Cognitive Science* (Cambridge, U.K.: M.I.T. Press).

Teasdale, J. D. 1999. 'Multi-level Theories of Cognition-Emotion Relations', In T. Dalgleish and M. J. Power (eds), *Handbook of Cognition and Emotion* (pp. 665–81). (Chichester: John Wiley and sons).

Tinbergen, N. 195). 'Derived activities: their causation, biological significance, origin and emancipation during evolution', *Quarterly Review of Biology*, **27** (1), 1–32.

Basic Emotions, Complex Emotions, Machiavellian Emotions

Whiten, A. and Byrne, R. W. (eds), 1997. *Machiavellian Intelligence II: Extensions and Evaluations* (Cambridge: Cambridge University Press).
Wollheim, R. 1999. *On the Emotions* (Yale University Press).
Zajonc, R. B. 1980. 'Feeling & thinking: preferences need no inference', *American Psychologist*, **35**, 151–75.
Zajonc, R. B. 1984a. 'On the primacy of affect', In K. Scherer & P. Ekman (eds), *Approaches to Emotion* (pp. 259–70). (Hillsdale, N.J: Lawrence Erlbaum Assoc).
Zajonc, R. B. 1984b. 'The interaction of affect and cognition', In K. Scherer & P. Ekman (eds), *Approaches to Emotions* (pp. 239–46). (Hillsdale, NJ: Lawrence Erlbaum Associates).

IV. Emotion, Psychosemantics, and Embodied Appraisals

JESSE PRINZ

1. Two Theoretical Approaches to Emotion

There seem to be two kinds of emotion theorists in the world. Some work very hard to show that emotions are essentially cognitive states. Others resist this suggestion and insist that emotions are noncognitive. The debate has appeared in many forms in philosophy and psychology. It never seems to go away. The reason for this is simple. Emotions have properties that push in both directions, properties that make them seem quite smart and properties that make them seem quite dumb. They exemplify the base impulses of our animal nature while simultaneously branching out into the most human and humane reaches of our mental repertoires. Depending on where one looks, emotions can emerge as our simplest instincts or our subtlest achievements. This double nature makes emotions captivating, but also confounding. Researchers find themselves picking one side at the expense of the other, or packaging seemingly disparate components into unstable unions. I will defend a more integrative approach. For a more thorough treatment, see Prinz (forthcoming).

1.1 Noncognitive Theories

As I will use the terms, a cognitive theory of the emotions is a theory that maintains that all true emotions involve cognitions essentially. Noncognitive theories maintain that emotions do not necessarily involve cognitions. It is no easy matter to say what cognitions are. A failure to define this key term can easily lead to unproductive cross-talk. Despite that caveat, I will proceed without a definition. One can capture the difference between cognitive and noncognitive theories by considering some examples.

An especially simple form of noncognitive theory would be a pure feeling theory. Pure feeling theories identify emotions with qualitative feelings and nothing more. It is not clear whether any one has ever seriously defended such an account. In folk psychology, we sometimes employ a pure feeling theory of twinges and pangs. A pure feeling theory of the emotions would regard emotions as analogous to these. Other relevant examples include the feeling of a buzz, glowing feelings, or unlocated pains. Freud is prone to describe emotions in this way. He insists that emotions cannot be unconscious because they are nothing but feelings (Freud, 1915). Hume (1739) can be read in this way as well, as when he insists that emotions do not represent things. A closer look at Hume, however, with his detailed taxonomy of emotion types, reveals a position that is far more sophisticated. Emotions are feelings, but they are individuated by the impressions and ideas that they have as causes and effects.

It is easier to find defenders of another class of noncognitive theories. In the 1880s William James and Carl Lange independently hit upon the suggestion that emotions are responses to patterned changes in the body. In this sense, emotions are embodied. For Lange (1885), emotions are principally responses to vascular changes. For James (1884), they are responses to more complex somatic states, including changes in skeletal muscles and visceral organs. Depth of inhalation, blood vessel dilation, heart rate acceleration, muscle tension, facial expression, and even instrumental actions can all factor into an emotional state. Fear might be an internal state that registers constricted vessels, blood flow to the extremities, a frowning open mouth, and flight behaviour. For James, the internal states are feelings, but they are not the *mere* feelings of a pure feeling theory. Emotions are feelings of the body. They are somatic feelings.

In recent times, Damasio (1994) has resuscitated the James-Lange theory, with a few alterations. Among the relevant bodily states Damasio now includes changes in the internal milieu, including changes of hormone levels. Damasio also denies that emotions are feelings, allowing that an unconscious state that registers a bodily change would qualify as an emotional response. And finally, Damasio argues that emotional responses can bypass the body. Our brains can respond as if our bodies had undergone a characteristic pattern of changes in the absence of such changes. For the brain, it can be 'as-if' the body had changed. This too would count as an emotion. James makes a similar claim in passing, but Damasio develops the idea much more extensively (1884: note 4).

Somatic theories enjoy considerable support. It is a commonplace that emotions are associated with actions, and the bodily response implicated by somatic theories can be viewed as response preparations. Increased blood flow in fear facilitates the flight or fright response. For James and Lange these changes are not consequences of our emotions, but antecedents. Emotional feelings, at least, are feelings of the body preparing for action. To make this case, James and Lange both offer mental subtraction arguments. Imagine feeling an emotion as vividly as you can, and then subtract away each part of the feeling that owes to a bodily change. When the subtraction is complete, there is nothing left that would be recognized as the emotion.

Contemporary defences of the somatic approach emphasize empirical findings. Neural circuits that are associated with emotional response include structures that are independently associated with monitoring and maintaining bodily changes. Insular cortex and anterior cingulate cortex, for example, appear to be active in most functional neuroimaging studies of emotion (Damasio *et al.*, 2000). People with brain damage that prevents them from accurately monitoring bodily changes report a diminution of affective response (Critchley *et al.*, 2001).

These sources of evidence are suggestive, but far from decisive. A noncognitive theory must maintain that emotions are exhausted by noncognitive states. None of the evidence just mentioned rules out the possibility that the bodily concomitants of emotions may come along with cognitive states. Indeed, the evidence does not even show that emotions must have bodily components. Perhaps the evidence derives from sampling errors: placing too much emphasis on emotions that are especially primitive and intense. Even in these cases, a cognitive theorist could claim, for all the evidence thus far presented, that bodily responses are not components of emotions but mere accompaniments. The subtraction argument shows that bodily perturbations contribute to emotional feelings, but feelings may be contingent effects of emotions rather than essential features. Results from neuroimaging and self-reports from people with brain damage may, likewise, be picking up on emotional feelings. What pressure is there to think such feelings are constitutive of emotions? More to the point, what pressure is there to think that emotions can be exhaustively comprised by responses to bodily perturbations, be they felt or unfelt? Noncognitive theorists owe us more.

1.2 Cognitive Theories

The demand for further support is especially acute because noncognitive theories are seriously impoverished on the face of it. Emotions play central roles in our lives. They are ends (as when we seek pleasure, attachment, or amusement) and they are means (as when an emotion compels us to act). Emotions interact with thought and reasons. Thinking about injustice can make a person angry and sadness can lead to thoughts about one's diminished prospects in life. Emotions also have intentional objects. One can be frustrated that P, afraid of a, delighted by b. In fact, emotions typically have intentional objects in two senses: particular and formal (Kenny, 1966). Each instance of an emotion is about some particular individual, situation, or event. Jones might be mad that her new camera is defective or mad that her husband is late again. In both cases, her anger has the same formal object; it concerns an offence against her. Sadness, in each normal instance, concerns loss, fear concerns danger, guilt concerns harmful transgressions. As Pitcher (1965) and others have pointed out, this contrasts markedly with twinges and pangs.

These kinds of considerations lead many to conclude that emotions are cognitive. One can easily explain why emotions interact with thoughts if one assumes that they *are* thoughts. Suppose, to take a simple view, that each emotion is comprised by a thought about some general property that bears on well-being. Anger may be the thought that there has been an offence against me. Sadness may be the thought that there has been a great loss. These thoughts directly explain why emotions have formal objects, because each explicitly refers to such an object. The particular objects of emotions are explained by combining thoughts. Suppose my dog Fido dies. I might first think that Fido is dead and then infer that this death is a loss. The inferred thought *constitutes*, on the simple cognitive view, the emotion.

Most cognitive views are not this simple. Solomon (1976) says that the judgment comprising an emotion cannot be separated from the judgment pertaining to the particular object. Anger that P is better rendered 'anger-that-p'. It is an evaluative judgment that construes an event as offence, rather than a reaction to an event that has been independently construed in a neutral way. Nussbaum (2001) says that having an emotion is a matter of assenting to a judgment that something important to personal well-being has transpired. Assenting can be regarded as a kind of judgment in its own right. In assenting, one evaluates a judgment pertaining to well-being as appropriate. If I feel sad, it is not just that I recognize a loss; I also judge that my sense of loss is warranted.

Both Solomon and Nussbaum contend that emotions can exist without any bodily concomitants. Their theories are purely cognitive. I come back to pure theories below. But first, I want to consider impure theories. Many cognitive theorists believe that emotions are thoughts plus some noncognitive component. One might define emotions as evaluative judgments plus responses to bodily states. Appraisal theories in psychology are like this. Lazarus (1991) is a leading exponent (see also Arnold, 1960; Scherer 1984; Roseman, 1984). Emotions, he claims, involve feelings or action tendencies triggered by appraisal judgments. Each emotion involves the same appraisal 'dimensions.' There are six of these. We ask ourselves: has something relevant to my goals occurred? Is it congruent with goals? How is my ego involved? Who deserves credit or blame? What coping options are available? And What can I expect for the future? Emotions are distinguished by the different ways in which these questions can be answered. Anger involves the judgments that goals have been violated, that someone else is to blame, and that aggression is an available coping option. Every collection of answers can be summarized by what Lazarus calls a 'Core Relational Theme.' The appraisals constituting anger correspond to the theme that there has been a demeaning offence against me and mine. This is not an explicit judgment, but a way of capturing the gist of six more specific judgments answering to each dimension of appraisal.

Lazarus differs from Solomon and Nussbaum in allowing that emotions have noncognitive constituents. But, like them, he regards judgments essential. So we can ask all these researches the same question, Do all emotions necessarily involve judgments?

1.3 The Zajonc/Lazarus Debate

Zajonc (1980; 1984) is responsible for one of the most systematic critiques of cognitive theories in psychology. In his second article, Zajonc (1984) is especially concerned to refute Lazarus's theory, and he marshals several different kinds of arguments towards that end. Lazarus (1984) has responded to these arguments, and the resulting exchange has become a focal point in the battle between cognitive and noncognitive theories. I present some highlights.

In one line of argument, Zajonc contends that emotions are phylogenetically and ontogenetically prior to cognitions. Emotions are found in simpler animals, and they emerge before cognitions in human development. The difficulty with this contention is that we have no reason to deny that such creatures make judgments. Some of the concepts that figure into Lazarus's appraisal dimensions are quite sophisticated, including a concept of the self. But is it obvious that infraverbal creatures lack concepts such as danger or loss? If not, their analogues of fear and sadness may involve judgments that bear some kinship to our own. We should resist drawing *a priori* conclusions about the kinds of judgments that infants and animals can form.

In another line of argument, Zajonc points out that a person can change her explicit appraisal judgment without changing her emotional state. Emotions can be recalcitrant. A person might continue to feel anger even after accepting the apology or believing the excuse of someone who offended her. Zajonc complains that Lazarus has not done enough to establish the link between emotion and appraisal.

In response, Lazarus (1984) points to decades of research showing that judgments can influence our emotional states. In an early series of studies, for example, Lazarus and colleagues (Speisman, *et al.*, 1965) induced different emotional responses to the same film-clip by altering the accompanying narrative. In more recent studies, he has obtained correlations between emotion labels and specific appraisal judgments (Smith and Lazarus, 1993, see discussion in Prinz, forthcoming). With regard to emotional recalcitrance, Lazarus has two available strategies. First, since he claims emotions contain noncognitive components, he can identify recalcitrant emotions with those whose accompanying feeling happen to out last the precipitating judgments. Second, he can claim that explicit changes in judgment do not always reverse incongruent unconscious judgments. There is ample independent evidence for this in social psychology. Once a false belief or prejudice has been planted, new evidence may fail to erase the initial judgment (Ross, *et al.*, 1975).

Zajonc calls on his own research in making a third argument against cognitive theories. He has been able to demonstrate a 'mere exposure effect' in preference formation. When subjects are briefly presented with unfamiliar stimuli (such as Chinese ideographs), they often perform at chance levels when given a subsequent recognition test. A previously presented stimulus may be judged as new. But preferences are effected by prior exposure. The more times a stimulus is presented, the more likely it is to be regarded favourably. For example, when American subjects were asked to speculate about which Chinese characters have a positive meaning, they were more likely to select the characters to which they had been most exposed, even if they had no explicit recall of seeing those characters (Zajonc, 1968). Zajonc draws two conclusions: subjects' judgments are informed by (possibly unconscious) affective responses, and those responses are noncognitive.

Both these conclusions are open to debate, but the later is especially relevant. If we grant that emotions factor into the mere exposure effect, should we conclude that emotions can occur without cognition? We simply don't know. It is perfectly possible that subjects are performing unconscious appraisals. They may be unconsciously registering that the stimulus is novel. In our ancestral past, familiar stimuli that hadn't harmed us in the past would have been regarded as safer than entirely novel stimuli. Forced to choose between a familiar and a novel stimulus, subjects may form the appraisal that the familiar stimulus is more goal congruent, and a positive emotion will result. If this process is going on unconsciously, then the mere exposure effect is perfectly consistent with Lazarus's theory. Lazarus does not assume that his appraisals are conscious. To insist that appraisals must be conscious in order to count as cognitive would beg the question, construct a straw man, and depart from the orthodoxy within cognitive science (see, e.g., Nisbett and Wilson, 1977).

Zajonc's next batch of arguments is more convincing. He points to cases in which emotions are induced by direct physical means, as when the brain is stimulated by taking drugs, or reconfiguring facial muscles. The latter refer to the phenomenon of facial feedback. Making an emotional expression can give rise to the emotion itself even when one does not realize one is making an emotional expression (Zajonc, *et al.*, 1989). In one study, Strack, *et al.* (1988) asked subjects to fill out a questionnaire holding a pen in their mouths. Some subjects were asked to hold the pen between puckered lips and the other subjects were asked to hold it between their teeth with parted lips (conforming to a sour grimace and a smile-like facial configuration, respectively). In one part of the questionnaire subjects had to rate the amusement level of comic strips. Subjects in the teeth condition (who were unwittingly smiling) rated the comics as more amusing. Zajonc thinks there is a simple mechanism that mediates between facial change and emotional response. There is no need for the mediation of appraisals. Likewise, when we induce emotions through drugs.

Unfortunately, Lazarus (1984) does not offer a response to these kinds of cases. It would be desperate for him to propose that appraisals mediate facial feedback. There is no reason to think that appraisals are involved. There is nothing to appraise. We might take a smile as evidence that things are going well, but, in the Strack, *et al.* experiment, subjects do not even realize they are smiling. And, in any case, appraisals are unnecessary. Feedback effects could be achieved through direct wiring between brain states that register facial change and brain states that trigger the bodily responses associated with the corresponding emotion. There is one possibility available to Lazarus, however. Rather than postulating mediating appraisals, he could deny that the feelings caused by facial feedback are emotions. He could say that they are recognisably *similar* to emotional feelings, but without appraisals, they fail to qualify as emotions themselves (see Clore, 1994). Likewise for feelings brought on by drugs. When probed about the giddy feeling brought on by a smile, one might respond, 'I feel as if I were happy, but I am not really happy; I have nothing to be happy about.'

To my mind, the most convincing evidence for emotions without cognitions comes from neuroanatomy. Zajonc argues that there are direct pathways from the most rudimentary perceptual centres to centres that initiate the bodily responses associated with an emotion. If so, those responses can begin before a person has had time to form an appraisal judgment. Zajonc (1984) mentions pathways from the retina to the hippocampus. These are no longer thought to be involved in emotions (they may be involved regulating the sleep cycle as a function of light), but other subcortical pathways exist. There is, for example a pathway from the superior colliculus and the pulvinar to the amygdala, which plays a central role in mediating between perception and the physiological aspects of some emotions. The superior colliculus and pulvinar are very rudimentary perceptual structures that convey information to the amygdala before the neocortex has gotten involved. Appraisal judgments of the kind Lazarus imagines—judgments involving such concepts as 'ego' and 'loss'—are likely to be implemented in the neocortex. If emotional somatic responses can be induced before the neocortex comes on line, then Lazarus is wrong to claim that appraisals must precede those responses.

On the face of it, the anatomical evidence could be dismissed in the same way that I suggested Lazarus respond to facial feedback. Perhaps responses caused by the subcortical pathway to the amygdala should not qualify as true emotions. Perhaps they are just emotion-like. This objection is considerably less plausible here. In the case of facial feedback, one is tempted to say that the responses are not true emotions, because they are not playing typical emotion roles. In contrast, subcortically induced emotions are often quite typical. LeDoux (1996) has argued that the subcortical path to the amygdala underlies speedy fear responses to simple stimuli. Imagine seeing a snake. Before you can recognize it as such, your earliest perceptual centres have discerned the characteristic coiled shape and they have sent emotion centres into action. It is a short-cut that allows us to save time in situations where time is of the essence. Now why call this an emotional response? The reason has to do with the stimulus. As in facial feedback, the end-state feels like an emotion. But here, the elicitor is a paradigmatic emotion elicitor. Snakes are dangerous. And snakes are not the only stimulus that can travel the subcortical path. Sudden noises, angry faces, sudden loss of support, creeping bugs, looming objects, and total darkness, are among the many things that may be able to spark an emotion without the cortical assistance. If you find yourself in a state that feels just like fear after seeing something that really is threatening, there is no reason to deny that you are really experiencing fear. All this happens without the need for appraisals. Appraisals might come into the picture after the bodily response. But this won't help Lazarus. His theory requires that appraisals come first. If a state that plays the right emotion role can be initiated without appraisal, then appraisals are not essential for some emotions.

Lazarus tries to dismiss Zajonc's appeal to neuroanatomy on the grounds that our interpretation of the brain depends on our psychological theories. Perhaps there are subcortical appraisals. It is good to exercise caution when arguing about the brain, but the caution is misplaced here. There is no reason to locate appraisals in the superior colliculus or the amygdala. These structures are fairly well understood. We know how their cells respond and how they are wired. No viable interpretation could assign the concepts comprising Lazarus's dimensional appraisals or core themes to the networks in these parts. The colliculus responds to raw perceptual signals and the amygdala serves as a bridge between these and structures that control basic bodily states. The brain shows how we can move from an image to a racing heart without bringing in concepts of ego, blame, expectancy, or goals. The simplest perception can trigger the bodily perturbations that we experience as emotions.

1.4 The Emotion Problem

The preceding two subsections ended with contradictory results. First we saw that noncognitive theories are explanatorily anaemic. They cannot explain the rich interactions between emotions and reasoning, nor can they account for the two senses in which emotions can be said to have intentional objects. In a word, noncognitive theories fail to capture the fact that emotions are meaningful.

Cognitive theories are well suited to capture the meaningfulness of emotions. They identify emotions with judgments or with more complex mental episodes that include judgments as parts. But there is empirical evidence that emotions can arise in the absence of judgments. Elementary perceptions of external stimuli can send us reeling without cognitive mediation. And when this occurs, the emotion seems no less meaningful than it would in other cases. Fear caused by seeing a snake lunge towards you is surely significant. It is not like an undirected and inexplicable pang.

So we have a serious puzzle. The fact that emotions are meaningful, reason sensitive, and intentional suggests that they must be cognitive. The fact that some emotions arise without the intervention of the neocortex suggests that emotions cannot *all* be cognitive. The emotions that arise in this way seem to be meaningful. This suggests that being meaningful does not require being cognitive. Noncognitive states are explanatorily anaemic and cognitive states are explanatorily superfluous. Noncognitive theories give us too little, and cognitive theories give us too much. Call this the Emotion Problem.

2. Embodied Appraisals

2.1 Psychosemantics

The Emotion Problem is essentially a problem about getting meaning on the cheap. To solve it, we need a way of showing how emotions can have the semantic properties that they seem to have without claiming that emotions are judgments. If we are seek out a explanation of how mental states can have semantic properties without being judgments, we do not need to look very far. Prevailing theories of intentionality that have been developed within the philosophy of mind are well suited to this end. These theories were not devised to explain the emotions. They were devised to explain how concepts refer. If such theories do a reasonable job with concepts, then they may apply to mental states quite broadly. If they help explain the semantic properties of the emotions, then we may have an independently motivated solution to the Emotion Problem.

I think that informational theories are especially promising (Dretske, 1981; Fodor, 1990). These theories begin with the principle that representation involves law-like dependencies. A mental state refers to things that would cause that state to be tokened. Dretske (1988) combines this idea with a teleological component. Mental states refer to those reliable causes that they have the function of detecting. More succinctly, a mental state refers to what it is set up to be set off by. The second condition (being set off) captures the informational component of the theory. If a mental state is reliably set off by some class of things, then it carries the information that some item in the class is present (in much the way the smoke carries the information that a fire is present). But this condition is too permissive on its own. Many things cause our mental states to be tokened. It would be a mistake to say that a mental state refers to anything that causes it. This would make error impossible. The first condition (being set up) is recruited to narrow down the content. All mental states are acquired in some way, usually by inheritance or learning. Of the many things that reliably cause a mental state to be tokened only those things for which it was initially generated fall within its extension. Dretske likes to make his case by appeal to simple artefacts. If you light a match near a smoke detector it will beep, but it was set up to detect smoke caused by fires, not the flames from a match. Likewise, a concept of water refers to water, even though it is occasionally set off by encounters with other clear liquids. It was created in the context of water detection.

It is beyond the scope of this discussion to defend informational semantics. I will assume that some version will work for concepts (see Prinz, 2002). Here, I want to show that it also explains how emotions get their contents. According to Jamesian theories, emotions are the internal states that register bodily changes. On the face of it, these states represent bodily changes if they represent anything at all. This is not inconsistent with informational semantics. Such states are reliably set off by patterned changes in the body. But is it their function to detect such changes? Why did we develop minds that detect *patterned* bodily changes? Why do body-pattern detecting states get set up and why do they persist? An obvious answer is that these patterns happen to occur under conditions that are important to us. The patterns associated with fear (such as flight preparation or freezing) happen to occur when we are facing immediate physical dangers. Danger is, thus, another reliable cause of the inner states that registers fleeing or freezing patterns. And it is a cause that has especially good claim to being the one for which such states are attained in the first place. We come to be good body-pattern detectors (through evolution and learning), because body patterns co-occur with matters of grave concern. States that *register* body changes may *represent* the more abstract relational properties that induce those changes in us.

2.2 A Theory of Emotion

This suggests the following theory of emotions. Emotions are, as James suggested, inner responses to bodily changes. They are, in that sense, embodied. But emotions represent matters of concern.

They represent things like danger and loss—the core relational themes emphasized by cognitive theorists. The embodied states represent core themes because they have the function of being reliably caused by core themes. If we define an appraisal as any mental state that represents an organism-environment relation that bears on well-being, then the embodied states in question qualify as appraisals. They are embodied appraisals.

Notice that embodied appraisals do not *describe* the states that they represent. One can have an embodied state that represents an immediate physical danger without having concepts of immediacy, physicality, or danger. This is just a consequence of informational semantics. Such theories do not require highly structured representations. The beep emitted by smoke detector might be said to represent 'smoke from fire here now,' but it does not decompose into meaningful sub-beeps. It is semantically primitive. Complex contents do not need complex representations. Defenders of cognitive theories assume that emotions can only designate core relational themes if emotions are judgments, thoughts, or some other kind of concept-laden, structured states. This simply isn't true. To represent appraisal core relational themes, emotions need only occur, reliably, when those themes occur.

Cognitive theorists might raise an objection at this point. Surely emotions can reliably co-occur with core relational themes only if they contain judgments. How else could they reliably coincide with dangers, losses, offences, and all the rest? LeDoux's snake case points towards an answer. When we see a snake, our bodies enter into characteristic patterns that are registered by the embodied states that I have identified with emotions. There is no judgment involved, just a snake image in the early visual system. Now suppose that the same body pattern is innately triggered by several other kinds of images as well, such as bugs, looming objects, darkness, threatening faces, and blood. Suppose these things cause the same body pattern via direct links from perception to body control centres. The state that registers that body pattern is reliably caused by each of these things, but they have this common effect in virtue of the fact that they all instantiated a common property. They are all dangers. The embodied state is a danger detector, because danger is the property that gets the items in this hodgepodge to have an impact. Snakes, spiders, and darkness cause our hearts to race and palms to sweat in virtue of the fact that they were hazards to our ancestors.

In this initial state, judgments play no role. Danger detection is entirely noncognitive. Later we may come to recognize that bodily patterns in question are occurring in dangerous situations. We may acquire a danger concept, and that concept may come to be deployed in situations that would be hard to recognize by casual observation (e.g., judging that the newly elected politician is dangerous). The old body response can come to have a broader range of application in this way. After concepts are acquired, fear can be triggered by cognitive appraisals. But these cases are derivative. Explicit judgments come after a meaningful emotion already exists. Because such judgments are inessential to emotions, we should not count them as emotion constituents even when they do occur. They are no more a part of an emotion than a premise is a part of the conclusion it supports. They are causes, not components.

2.3 Solving the Emotion Problem

The embodied appraisal theory offers a solution to Emotion Problem. With noncognitive theories, it says that emotions are embodied, and it denies that judgments are needed for emotion elicitation. With cognitive theories, it says that emotions represent core relational themes. This helps explain why emotions interact with thinking. If emotions represent core themes, thoughts pertaining to those themes will be rationally tied to emotions. Thoughts that provide evidence that one is in danger warrant fear, and fear warrants thoughts about strategies for coping with danger.

Emotions can be said to have intentional objects in the two required senses on the embodied appraisal theory. It is a central theme of the theory that emotions have formal objects. These are just the core relational themes that emotions have the function of reliably detecting. It would take more work to show how emotions attain particular objects. How does my fear that it will rain get connected up with my thought that it may rain? Answering this question fully would require more detail than I can provide here, but I can present the basic strategy. The emotion and the thought can be linked in three ways. Semantically, the thought that it will rain may be taken as a potential danger, which may serve to induce state of fear as an entailment. Syntactically, the fear state may be bound to the thought in whatever way that mental representations are generally bound. Imagine hearing a voice coming from a moving face. We somehow link these together. Perhaps the same method of linking (or some other independently motivated method) can bind emotions to thoughts about particular objects. Finally, there may be a counterfactual dependence between the emotion and the thought such that the emotion would not have occurred if the thought had not. Syntactic links and counterfactual dependencies could link emotions to thoughts even if emotions had no meaning. The semantic point adds to the story by explaining why emotions get linked to representations of particular objects. This simply wouldn't make sense if emotions were meaningless sensations.

In sum, the embodied appraisal theory explains how emotions bridge the gap between thoughts and feelings. They are structurally simple embodied states, but they carry the kind of information that full-blown cognitions can carry. Cognitive theories have been right about content, and noncognitive theories have been right about form.

3. Generalizing the Account

By way of conclusion, I want to consider whether the embodied appraisal theory can account for the full range of emotions we experience. Cognitive theorists sometimes claim that some emotions have no bodily concomitants. Call these disembodied emotions. Cognitive theorists also claim that some emotions must have cognitive components, in addition to any bodily components they might comprise. I briefly consider these objections in turn (see Prinz, forthcoming, for more). Faced with such objections, one might simply concede that emotions do not form a coherent class (cf. Griffiths, 1997). My hope is to show that emotions are unified. All cases can be explained in terms of embodied appraisals.

Disembodied emotions include calm passions, such as loneliness or aesthetic appreciation, and long-standing emotions, such as the enduring love one feels for a spouse. Equating emotions with brief bodily perturbations does not capture these cases. Therefore, the embodied appraisal theory does not generalize.

Alleged disembodied emotions can be handled in one of three ways. Some are not emotions at all. Harré (1996) uses loneliness as an example, but it is not obvious that loneliness is an emotion. It certainly isn't a paradigm case. A theory of emotions should begin with clear cases, and then provide a way of determining whether less clear cases qualify as emotions. The embodied appraisal theory says that loneliness is an emotion only if it represents a core relational theme *and* is embodied. If it isn't embodied, we can rule that it isn't an emotion. This would only beg the question if loneliness were a clear case. The same can be said of calm aesthetic responses and what might be termed 'polite passions' (as when one says, 'I am sorry I couldn't make it to the reception'). Other putative disembodied emotions turn out to be embodied. They involve bodily changes that are harder to detect than cases involving sympathetic responses of the autonomic nervous. If loneliness is an emotion, it probably involves a reduction of heart rate rather than an increase. Loneliness is presumably related to mild sadness, which bears such bodily marks.

The third strategy for handling disembodied emotions is to draw a distinction between dispositional and occurrent states. Most mental state types have both dispositional and occurrent forms. One can say, 'wool makes Jones itchy,' and 'wool is making Jones itchy right now.' Or, 'Jones believes that Quine was right about analyticity,' and 'Jones is using that belief right now in her reasoning.' Likewise, I regard long-standing emotions as dispositions. That I love my spouse all the time is an enduring disposition to have occurrent states of love (compare 'I detest country music' or 'I am disgusted by floral wall paper' or 'I am outraged by cinema violence'). An occurrent state of love is an embodied reaction of the kind one has when one encounters the object of one's love. In line with this, Bartels and Zeki (2000) showed brain activation in limbic areas associated with bodily response when subjects viewed pictures of their lovers. I would add that long-standing love does not count as love *unless* it carries a disposition to such embodied states. If someone says, 'I love my spouse, but I never experience flutters or giddiness or cuddly tenderness in relation to him' we would doubt her sincerity. As with itchiness, standing emotions are parasitic on their embodied manifestations.

The final objection to the embodied appraisal theory concedes that all emotions contain embodied appraisals (at least dispositionally), but asserts that some emotions contain cognitive elements as well. Certain emotions pertain to situations that can only be appreciated by creatures with command of very advanced concepts. Emotions such as jealousy, guilt, shame, and indignation come to mind. These implicate ideas of infidelity, transgression, the self, and justice. They may be uniquely human. The natural explanation of such emotions aligns with cognitive theories. Guilt, for example, might be said to involve the evaluative judgment that I have committed a transgression that wrongfully harms someone whose well-being matters to me. Unlike fear, which might be triggered by a simple percept, guilt seems to require conceptual mediation.

I can only gesture towards an account of these cases here. Theorists from Descartes to Ekman have proposed that some emotions are basic. Other emotions blend these basic emotions

Jesse Prinz

together (contempt may be anger plus disgust; thrills may be joy plus fear) and others elaborate basic emotions by bringing in other resources. Oatley and Johnson-Laird (1997) talk of elaborated emotions, which are basic emotions plus thoughts. Schadenfreude might be joy plus the thought that someone is miserable. Guilt may be sadness plus thoughts about my transgressions. Romantic jealousy may be a blend of sadness, fear, anger, and disgust plus thoughts of a lover's infidelity.

I think this approach is almost right, but I would add an important modification. Rather than viewing the cognitive elaborations as constituent parts of an emotion, I regard them as calibrating causes. A calibrating cause is a mental state that triggers an emotion under a specific set of conditions that are somewhat different than the conditions that elicited the emotion initially. Calibrating causes are external to emotions, and may be highly variable. Rather than having one single thought that triggers guilt or jealousy, we may have rich calibration files, containing many thoughts and perceptions. Jealousy can be sparked by the judgment that my lover has been unfaithful, or by the thought that she has been arriving home late, or by the smell of another's cologne on her shirt, or by the glance she makes towards a passing stranger. Guilt can be caused by the explicit judgment that I have transgressed or by recognizing that I have done something specific that, on a prior occasion, I recognized as a transgression. These disparate triggers all serve to align my embodied state with core relational themes. My jealousy calibration file places a blended embodied state under the nomic control of signs of infidelity, and that blend thereby comes to represent infidelity when it is triggered by *any* item in the file. Jealousy does not contain its calibrating causes. Which one would it contain? Jealousy represent infidelity because it is set up to be set off by infidelity, and the items in a calibration file contribute to that. But these items are no more a part of jealousy than are the eyes by which the jealous person perceives infidelity's palpable signs.

If these suggestions are right, then the embodied appraisal theory is truly general. All emotions are nothing more than embodied appraisals or dispositions to embodied appraisals. All are structurally and semantically analogous. All have embodied form and appraisal content. Embodied appraisal theory offers unity in two senses. It binds all emotions into a coherent category, and it reconciles the differences that have pushed cognitive and noncognitive theorists into such opposite directions.

Emotion, Psychosemantics, and Embodied Appraisals

Bibliography

Arnold, M. B. 1960. *Emotion and Personality* (New York, NY: Columbia University Press).
Bartels, A. and Zeki, S. 2000. 'The neural basis of romantic love', *NeuroReport*, **11**, 3829–34.
Clore, G. L. 1994. 'Why emotions require cognition', In P. Ekman and R. Davidson (eds) *The nature of emotion: Fundamental questions* (Oxford: Oxford University Press).
Critchley, H. D., Mathias, C. J. and Dolan, R. J. 2001. 'Neural correlates of first and second-order representation of bodily states', *Nature Neuroscience* 2001; **4**, 207–12.
Damasio, A. R. 1994. *Descartes' Error: Emotion Reason and the Human Brain* (New York, NY: Gossett/Putnam).
Damasio, A. R., Grabowski, T. J., Bechara, A., Damasio, H., Ponto, L. L. B., Parvizi, J. and Hichwa, R. D. 2000 'Subcortical and Cortical Brain Activity During the Feeling of Self-generated Emotions', *Nature Neuroscience*, **3**, 1049–56.
Dretske, F. 1981. *Knowledge and the Flow of Information* (Cambridge, MA, MIT Press).
Dretske, F. 1988. *Explaining Behavior* (Cambridge, MA, MIT Press).
Fodor, J. A. 1990. 'A Theory of Content, I & II', In *A Theory of Content and Other Essays* (Cambridge, MA: MIT Press).
Freud, S. 1915. 'The unconscious', In *The Standard Edition of the Complete Works of Sigmund Freud*, volume 14, James Strachey (trans.) (London: Hogarth Press).
Griffiths, P. 1997. *What emotions really are* (Chicago: University of Chicago Press).
Harré, R. 1986. 'The Social Constructivist Viewpoint', In R. Harré (ed.) *The Social Construction of Emotions* (2–14). Oxford: Blackwell.
Hume, D. 1739/1978. *A treatise of human nature*. Nidditch, P. H. (ed.) (Oxford: Oxford University Press).
James, W. 1884. 'What is an Emotion?', *Mind*, **9**, 188–205.
James, W. 1894. 'The Physical Basis of Emotion', *Psychological Review*, **1**, 516–29.
Kenny, A. 1963. *Action, Emotion and Will* (London: Routledge and Kegan Paul).
Lange, C. G. 1885. *Om sindsbevaegelser: et psyko-fysiologisk studie.* Kjbenhavn: Jacob Lunds. Reprinted in *The Emotions*, C. G. Lange and W. James (eds), I. A. Haupt (trans.) (Baltimore: Williams & Wilkins Company 1922).
Lazarus, R. 1984. On the primacy of cognition. *American Psychologist*, **39**, 124–29.
Lazarus, R. S. 1991. *Emotion and Adaptation.* (New York: Oxford University Press).
LeDoux J. E. 1996. *The Emotional Brain* (New York, NY: Simon & Schuster).

85

Jesse Prinz

Nisbett, R. E. and Wilson, T. D. 1977. 'Telling more than we can know: Verbal reports on mental processes', *Psychological Review*, **84**, 231–59.

Nussbaum, M. 2001. *Upheavals of thought* (Oxford: Oxford University Press).

Oatley, K. and P. N. Johnson-Laird 1987. 'Towards a cognitive theory of emotions', *Emotions and Cognition*, **1**, 29–50.

Pitcher, G. 1965. 'Emotion', *Mind*, **74**, 324–46.

Prinz, J. J. 2002. *Furnishing the Mind: Concepts and Their Perceptual Basis* (Cambridge, MA: MIT Press).

Prinz, J. J. (forthcoming). *Emotional Perception* (New York: Oxford University Press).

Roseman I. J. 1984. 'Cognitive Determinants of Emotion: A Structural Theory', In P. Shaver (ed.) *Review of Personality and Social Psychology, Volume 5* (11–36). (Beverly Hills, CA: Sage).

Ross, L., Lepper, M. and Hubbard, M. 1975. 'Perseverance in self-perception and social perception: Biased attributional processes in the debriefing paradigm', *Journal of Personality and Social Psychology*, 32

Scherer, K. R. 1984. 'On the Nature and Function of Emotion: A Component Process Approach', In K. R. Scherer and P. Ekman (eds) *Approaches to Emotion* (293–318). (Hillsdale, NJ: Erlbaum).

Smith, C. A. and Lazarus, R. S. 1993. 'Appraisal components, core relational themes, and the emotions', *Cognition and Emotion,* **7**, 233–69.

Solomon, R. 1976. *The Passions: Emotions and the meaning of life, Indianapolis* (IN: Hackett Publishing Company).

Speisman, J. C., Lazarus, R. S., Mordkoff, A. M. and Davison, L. A. 1964. 'The experimental reduction of stress based on ego-defense theory', *Journal of Abnormal and Social Psychology*, **68**, 367–80.

Strack, F., Martin, L.L. and Stepper, S. 1988. 'Inhibiting and facilitating conditions of facial expressions. A nonobtrusive test of the facial feedback hypothesis', *Journal of Personality and Social Psychology*, **54**, 768–77.

Zajonc, R. B. 1968. 'Attitudinal effects of mere exposure', *Journal of Personality and Social Psychology Monograph Supplement*, **9**, 1–27.

Zajonc, R. B. 1980. Feeling and thinking: Preferences need no inferences. *American Psychologist,* **35**, 151–75.

Zajonc, R. B. 1984. 'On the Primacy of Affect', *American Psychologist*, **39**, 117–23.

Zajonc, R. B., Murphy, S. T. and Inglehart, M. 1989. 'Feeling and Facial Reference: Implications of the Vascular Theory of Emotion', *Psychological Review*, **96**, 395–416.

V. Emotions and the Problem of Other Minds

HANNA PICKARD

Can consideration of the emotions help to solve the problem of other minds? Intuitively, it should. We often think of emotions as public: as observable in the body, face, and voice of others. Perhaps you can simply see another's disgust or anger, say, in her demeanour and expression; or hear the sadness clearly in his voice. Publicity of mind, meanwhile, is just what is demanded by some solutions to the problem. But what does this demand amount to, and do emotions actually meet it? This paper has three parts. First, I consider the nature of the problem of other minds. Second, I consider the publicity of emotions. And third, I bring these together to show how emotions can help to solve the problem.

Traditionally, there are two problems of other minds: one epistemological, one conceptual. The epistemological problem asks how you can know, or how you can be justified in believing, that another person has a mind at all: that there exist other subjects of experience. The conceptual problem asks how you can so much as understand that there could exist other minds or subjects of experience: how you can have the concept of another's mind or experience. But why suppose these problems exist? They both arise, in part, from the same idea. This is the idea of an ontological distinction between experience (mind) and behaviour (body): they are not the same type of thing.

   The idea is intuitive. Consider, for instance, the possibility of pretence. Another person may be carrying on as if in pain, say, grimacing and crying out, but not be in pain at all. Yet you might be wholly taken in by her performance. There may be no discernible difference between real and pretend behaviour. Now pretence is not, nor perhaps could it ever be, the norm. But what it brings to the fore is the possibility of a discrepancy between experience and behaviour. If you can know how another is behaving, yet mistake her experience, the most obvious explanation is that her behaviour is observable, while her experience is hidden from view. Thus the distinction between the two.

   The result of this distinction is that the only experience you can experience, as it were, is that which you have: your own. Even in principle, let alone in practice, you cannot get inside another's head and into her mind, as if to try to have her experience. All you can experience of another is what you can observe: not her experience, but her body and behaviour. Given this, it is relatively simple to see why there is, at least prima facie, an epistemological problem. How can observation of another's behaviour be a sufficient basis for knowing that she possesses this other, distinct, kind of thing: a mind or experience? But it is less simple to see why there is a conceptual problem. If the only experience you can experience is that which you have, then to be sure, you can only understand what experience is from your own case. But why is this insufficient to account for your understanding of another's mind or experience?

It is sometimes claimed that the problem lies in an unwarranted use of the notion of sameness of type of experience in the account. Consider the classic argument from analogy and its equally classic criticism. The argument from analogy claims that you understand what pain, say, is from your own case: because you have it. Pain is just that wretched experience you sometimes suffer. It may be that, in absence of certain general intellectual capacities, or certain behavioural effects and social surroundings, you could not come to have this concept. But these are not part of what pain itself in essence is: pain is just that wretched experience. Given this, what it is for another to be in pain is for it be the same for her as it is for you when you are in pain: for her to have the same type of experience. The primary importance of behaviour, according to this account, is that it enables you to tell whether another is in pain. But since behaviour is distinct from experience, you can make mistakes.

There is no doubt that this account of our concept of pain, and its application to others, is intuitive. But it is classically charged with begging the question. The reason given is that its answer to the question of how you understand what it is for another to be in pain makes use of the notion of it being the same for her as it is for you when you are in pain: of her having the same type of experience. But your understanding of how another could have experience, same or different from you, is precisely what the conceptual problem is supposed to be about.

This criticism itself begs the question against the question of why there is a conceptual problem. It does not explain why understanding what experience is from your own case is insufficient to account for your understanding of another's mind or experience. For if the first premise of the argument from analogy is granted, namely, that you understand what pain is from your own case, then you are perfectly entitled to say that what it is for another to be in pain is for it to be the same for her as it is for you when you are in pain. For you understand what pain is. In effect, you have a concept of pain. If there is a conceptual problem, it must be because your own case is not a sufficient basis to account for this understanding. But the question, once again, is why this should be.

There is another way of explaining what the problem is. If you understand what pain is from your own case, then pain is just that wretched experience you sometimes suffer. But when another is in pain, there is none of that wretched experience around. The most you could hope to have experience of is something different in kind: her behaviour. So how can you understand that there is pain when there is no pain to experience? It is as if you said: what it is for another to be in pain is for there to be pain, but for there not to be. Now this contradiction is, in a sense, what we want to say. For it is certainly correct that what it is for another to be in pain is for there to be pain for her, but for there not to be pain for you. But to understand this, you must have the concept of a subject of experience, applicable to yourself and to others. And there seems little prospect of possessing the concept of such a subject without also possessing the concept of a mind or experience, applicable not only to yourself but to others. But that is what is now in question. If you understand what pain is from your own case, then pain is just that wretched experience. But how then can there be pain when there is no such experience?

This way of explaining the problem brings to the fore the extent to which it presumes a kind of empiricism about concepts. The problem pushes to its limit the idea that it is through experience that you understand what there is. If only you could experience the experience of others, the problem would be solved. This is the source of the demand that the mind of others must be publicly manifest: not hidden, but open to you to experience.

But of course, you cannot have another's experience. What you can experience of others is what you can observe: their bodies and behaviour. So if the problem is to be solved in this direct, empiricist way, then the demand for a public manifestation of the mind is a demand that behaviour be a part of the mind. Our concept of mind must in some sense encompass the behaviour which we observe. The question, then, is what sense this is. Here are three possible models.

The first is the simplest. The mind can be equally and unambiguously instantiated in experience and behaviour. So the behaviour you observe, like the experience you have, just is a state of mind. You do not observe the effects of another's pain, say, or the fact that she is in pain: what you observe is nothing less than her pain. Call this 'the observational model'. According to this model, behaviour is not a way of telling another's state of mind. Observation is a way of telling another's state of mind. Her behaviour just is her state of mind thus observed. In essence, the existence of an ontological distinction between what you have and what you observe—experience and behaviour—is rejected outright. Both can be states of mind, and in this, ontologically on a par.

The difficulty with the observational model is that claiming the distinction must be rejected is not to show how it can be. Certainly your own experience is a paradigm instance of a mind. And certainly there is no problem, at least for present purposes, understanding how another could exhibit behaviour. So if we could understand how experience and behaviour could be the same type of thing, then we could understand how another could have a mind. But how to understand this? How could experience and behaviour be the same type of thing?

The second model shies away from the rejection of the distinction. Behaviour is not a state of mind, but it can constitute 'logically adequate criteria' for the ascription to others of states of mind. Call this 'the critierial model'. So what are logically adequate criteria?

Sometimes they are defined negatively. Peter Strawson, for instance, claims that if we do not conceive of behaviour as logically adequate criteria, we should need to conceive of it as '*signs* of the presence, in the individual concerned, of this different thing, viz. the state of consciousness' (1959, 105–6). But to conceive of behaviour thus is to have no escape from the conceptual problem. Hence we must conceive of behaviour as logically adequate criteria.

As it stands, this negative definition faces a dilemma. Either behaviour is a state of mind, or it is not and the two are distinct. If it is, then the criterial model collapses into the observational model. Indeed, when Strawson feels forced to put his point 'with a certain unavoidable crudity' he appears to advocate the observational model (108). Taking depression as his example, Strawson proposes that 'X's depression *is* something, one and the same thing, which is felt, but not observed, by X, and observed, but not felt, by others than X' (109). On the other hand, if behaviour is distinct from experience, then it can be at most a way of telling what another is experiencing. What the criterial model claims is that this way of telling is 'logical'. One question is how there could be a logical connection between two distinct things. Another is why this should matter.

Emotions and the Problem of Other Minds

In relation to the first question, consider a proposal by John McDowell (1998). McDowell is a proponent of the disjunctive conception of perceptual experience. This is the view that the possibility of perceptual illusion must not be taken to show that there is, ontologically speaking, something in common between veridical perceptual experience and illusion: i.e. how things seem to the subject. Perceptual experience comes in two distinct varieties: veridical perception, and illusion. Just so, McDowell thinks, behaviour itself comes in two distinct varieties: veridical behaviour, and pretence and the like. The possibility of pretence—of a discrepancy between experience and behaviour—must not be taken to show that there is, ontologically speaking, something in common between veridical behaviour and pretence: i.e. how it appears to an observer. Even though you may not be able to tell whether another is deceiving you or not, that is no reason to think that the behaviour is the same in either case. Call this view 'the disjunctive conception of behaviour'. So there is a logical connection between experience and behaviour because whether a piece of behaviour counts as being of one ontological variety or another depends on the nature of the behaving subject's experience.

Consider now the second question: why should this matter? McDowell proposes that the disjunctive conception of behaviour allows us to deny that another's behaviour just is her state of mind, while yet maintaining that her behaviour 'does not fall short of' her state of mind (387). For if we accept both disjunctive conceptions, then when you veridically perceive another's veridical behaviour, your perceptual experience could not have the content it does were the other not having the experience she is. In this sense, her experience is supposed to be manifest to you.

It is possible that McDowell's proposal can help to solve the epistemological problem. This will depend on whether or not knowledge or justified belief requires that you be able to tell to which side of the disjunct your own perceptual experience, and another's behaviour, falls. But it is wholly unclear why this proposal should matter to the conceptual problem. All the disjunctive conception of behaviour achieves is the introduction of an ontological distinction within the category of behaviour. Because this distinction is drawn by appeal to experience, there is a logical connection between the two. But it is still the case that the only mind you experience is your own. What you can experience of others is only their behaviour—whichever variety of behaviour this is.

The third model seeks to steer between the claim that behaviour is a state of mind, and the claim that behaviour is a way of telling the state of mind of another. The idea is that an appreciation of a link between experience and behaviour is a constraint upon possession of the concept of experience. Only if you appreciate this link do you understand what experience, and so too the mind, is. Call this 'the behavioural-constraint model'. For our purposes, the precise nature of this link can be left open. One idea might be that you can only possess the concept of experience if you appreciate that behaviour is a way of telling about the experience of another (Davidson, 2001). Another idea might be that you can only possess the concept of experience if you appreciate that experience enables intentional behaviour directed towards the objects of experience (Peacocke, 1984).

What we need to ask about this model is why the resulting concept of experience is such that you can understand how another could have it. For it is still the case that the only experience you experience is your own. I think the intuition driving this model is as follows. The model accepts that there is a generality constraint on the possession of the concept of experience which must be respected: only if you have a concept of experience which is generally applicable, to others as much as yourself, can you have the concept at all (Evans, 1982; Strawson, 1959). Now you have experience. And you observe behaviour. So you can only possess the concept of experience if you appreciate that experience has a link to behaviour, because only then will you be able to understand that another's observed behaviour is linked to her had experience. The idea is that your possession of a general concept of experience can be manifest in your capacity to read or interpret the behaviour of others as more than crudely physical: that is, as related to a mind.

But to seek to respect this generality constraint is not to solve the problem. On the one hand, perhaps we could solve the problem, while rejecting the constraint. You might think that our concept of experience is generally applicable, and that we can explain how this can be, but reject the idea that this is how things must be. Perhaps there could be a subject whose concept of experience is utterly solipsistic. Ours is not. On the other hand, to accept the constraint is not in itself to make intelligible how our concept of experience is generally applicable: how you can so much as understand how another could have a mind or experience. The behavioural-constraint model in no way addresses this question of how. It claims only that so it must be.

The objection to both the criterial model, and the behavioural-constraint model, is really that they leave the ontological distinction

Emotions and the Problem of Other Minds

between experience and behaviour intact. No matter the philosophical nuance of these models, they accept that the only mind you can experience is your own. Contrast this with the observational model. If the mind can be equally and unambiguously instantiated in experience and behaviour, then it is perfectly intelligible how you can understand how another could have a mind. For you observe her states of mind when you observe her, just as you experience your own by having them. Certainly there are different ways of telling about someone's state of mind, depending on whether the owner is you or another. But what is ascribed in each case is the same.

But once again, the problem with the observational model is that, in this abstract form, it is utterly incredible. Not only is the ontological distinction intuitive. But there seems to be nothing in common between experience and behaviour: no respect in which they are the same, and so no prospect of explaining how they could be. Given this, the model makes another's mind so public as not to appear to be a mind at all.

This is what motivates turning to the emotions to solve the problem. If the problem is to be solved in a direct, empiricist way, then the mind must be observable. And some emotions appear to be just that.

Why should emotions be observable? The beginning of an answer is nothing more than a fact about the human species. Humans are phylogenetically endowed with what are called 'affect programmes': automatic, co-ordinated responses to an elicitor, involving distinctive facial and bodily expression and movement patterns, changes in voice tone and loudness, changes in hormone balance and level, and changes in the autonomic nervous system (Darwin, 1998; Ekman, 1992). There exist such programmes for fear, anger, disgust, joy, sadness, and possibly too contempt, sympathy, jealousy, and shame or embarrassment. Now some emotions are not associated with affect programmes: for instance, nostalgia. And some instances of emotions which are associated with affect programmes endure far longer than the duration of any one such programme, and no doubt are characterized as much or more by appeal to certain sorts of thoughts and actions: for instance, a parent's fear for a child with cancer. Nonetheless, these distinctive bodily changes prototypically do occur when humans are in the grip of the relevant emotions. And certainly they can be observed. So if emotions can be partially identified with these changes themselves, as opposed, say, to being their causes, then emotions can be observed. The question is whether it is possible to explain why this identification should be.

Hanna Pickard

Consider William James's defence of a comparable idea (1884). James notoriously claims that upon becoming aware of (or sub-personally processing) something of potential emotional significance, such as a dangerous animal, or a personal insult, '*bodily changes follow directly the* PERCEPTION *of the exciting fact, and that our feeling of the same changes as they occur* IS *the emotion*' (190–1). His defence of this is simple: 'If we fancy some strong emotion, and then try to abstract from our consciousness of it all the feelings of its characteristic bodily symptoms, we find we have nothing left behind, no "mind-stuff" out of which the emotion can be constituted, and that a cold and neutral state of intellectual perception is all that remains' (193).

James's thought has two parts. The first is that without the presence of affect, there is nothing emotional about a state at all: this is what makes a state count as an emotion, as opposed to a mere cognition. This point is fundamental. At least paradigmatically, emotions are unlike beliefs or judgments, say, but like sensations, in that they are felt. Simply believing that an animal is a threat, or judging that you have been insulted, does not suffice to make it the case that you feel fear or anger: the presence of affect is essential. The second is that the nature of this affect is bodily. James thinks that at least for us, the body, not the mind, is the right sort of domain or medium for feeling: an emotion cannot be constituted out of 'mind-stuff'.

Reflecting on what it is like to be in the grip of many a strong emotion, it is certainly intuitive that the feeling is bodily. You might, for instance, immediately imagine having certain sensations, like the feeling of a pounding heart, or a lump in the throat, or a sinking stomach. Indeed, James is classically read as identifying emotions with just such particular, located sensations. Thus interpreted, his theory is often derided. For paradigmatically, emotions are not only felt, but intentional. In this respect, they are like beliefs or judgments, and unlike sensations: they are about or directed towards objects outside of the body. For instance, you might be scared of the dangerous animal, or angry at the person who delivered the insult. Any plausible account of the emotions must be able to accommodate not only their affect, but their intentionality. If fear or anger is nothing more than, say, the feeling of a pounding heart, this can appear difficult.

But it is possible that James is correct that the affect of many emotions is bodily, without emotions being identical to particular, located sensations. We can draw a distinction between a sensation felt at a particular place in or on your body, and the way your body, as a whole, feels.

Emotions and the Problem of Other Minds

Michael Martin has drawn attention to the fact that each of us has a sort of awareness of our bodies from the inside as spatially configured one way and not another within a larger space: we enjoy conscious proprioception (1993). Consider, for instance, the experience of closing your eyes and stretching your arms in front of your body. You are aware of the span of your arms across and within a larger space. There is space between your arms, and also between your arms and your torso: space where your body is not positioned. In this way, as Martin notes, you are aware of your body as bounded, as limited, as occupying a volume of space within a larger space. This awareness of your body is awareness of it as, in a sense, located: as being placed within a larger space.

Once we recognize that we have a form of awareness of our whole bodies, we can see how a bodily feeling can be more than the feeling of particular, located sensations, however prominent these may be. On the one hand, there may be an overall feeling to the body due to a change in hormone balance or the nervous system: of energy, lethargy, anxiety, etc. Such feelings seem to encompass the body: to fill or suffuse it, as opposed to being located at discrete places within it. Yet we can still make sense of the idea that these feelings are felt to be located. They are felt to be located in that they encompass a body which is itself felt to be located. On the other hand, there may be an awareness of facial and body expressions and patterns of movement. Consider, for instance, the relevance of posture to an overall feeling of joy on the one hand, or sadness on the other. Or the feeling of tensely clenching the fists and jaw when angry. Or the feeling of shaking with fear. In these and similar cases, the feeling is literally of a bodily configuration or movement.

When in the grip of certain emotions, a slew of distinctive physiological and expressive bodily changes naturally occur: this is simply a fact about our species. But we have a form of awareness of our whole bodies from the inside. So we can explain the affect of these emotions simply: as the way your body, as a whole, feels when undergoing these changes.

This, in turn, can explain why emotions should be partially identified with bodily changes, as opposed, say, to being their causes. In contrast with 'cold and neutral' cognitions, emotions are, at least paradigmatically, affective. And affect just is the way your body, as a whole, feels when undergoing these changes. So at least some emotions are what we might think of as whole bodily states: states consisting in bodily changes which feel, or are experienced as being, a certain way from the inside.

Is it intelligible that emotions, thus conceived, could be intentional?

It is not obviously implausible that they might be. The reason is simply the intimate relation that your body bears to you. But an explanation of this bodily intentionality is yet required. I want to suggest two.

The first depends on the fact that the intentionality of many emotions is fundamentally different from the intentionality of a cognitive state like a judgment, or a belief: it can be open. On the one hand, some emotions blend into moods. They may not have an object, or their object may be anything and everything. So there may be no intentionality in need of explanation. You can just be feeling sad. On the other hand, you may know perfectly well which type of emotion you are experiencing, but neither immediately nor with authority know what the emotion is about (Pears, 1975). Consider, for instance, running into an old flame after many years, but finding to your surprise that you feel saddened as opposed to happy by the chance encounter. You might be certain that the cause of your feeling is the encounter. What you do not understand is what this feeling is about: the reason why seeing her has made you feel this way. You might run through a number of different explanations, believing each true until the next occurs. You might or might not ultimately reach the truth (Taylor, 1985).

Given this openness, one way to explain emotional intentionality is by appeal to the subject's own understanding of the reason why she is feeling as she is. For instance, when you come to realize that you are sad because you miss her still, say, that is what makes your emotion intentional: about the fact that you miss her. Of course, our understanding of many of our emotions is much easier to come by: it may be palpably apparent to you that you are angry at him because he insulted you. Nonetheless, this is a simple way to account for emotional intentionality: what makes your emotion intentional is that you understand the reason why you are in such a state, and so an emotion will not be intentional if you utterly lack understanding of the reason why you are in such a state.

Note that this suggestion does not deny that a subject's understanding of the reason why she is feeling as she is can be better or worse, right or wrong. The claim is not that the subject's understanding of this reason is constitutive of the actual reason why she is feeling as she is, but only of the feeling's intentionality. What must be denied is only that in absence of any understanding on the part of the subject, the existence of this reason itself makes an emotion intentional.

I think the intuitive objection to this explanation is that it fails to capture the phenomenology of at least some emotions. You might think, for instance, of the way adults, children, and even other mammals, have an instinctive fear of snakes. Is it really credible that the directedness of this emotion depends on an understanding, however tacit or inarticulate, of why it is felt? This seems a bit much. We might put this point by saying that there seems to be an evident or immersed intentionality to some emotions.

One way to try to accommodate this point is simply to reflect more fully on the phenomenology of bodily feeling. This is the second explanation of bodily intentionality. For when the object of the emotion is actually present, then and there in the subject's vicinity, it is possible that the body itself possesses all the intentionality which is required. In such cases, the body is likely to be spatially oriented in relation to the object. Most basically, it may be withdrawing or approaching: literally directed towards or away from the object. But within these basic modes, there are many kinds of bodily engagement. For this reason, a subject's awareness of her body from the inside can be an awareness of it as directed towards or away from objects in the world: the bodily feeling has an intrinsic intentionality. Of course, this is not a possible explanation of the intentionality of an emotion for which the object is only imagined, or exists in the remembered past or anticipated future. But for such emotions, it is much more plausible that the explanation of their intentionality can proceed via the subject's own understanding of it.

How does this help with the problem of other minds? Recall that what is needed is an understanding of how the mind could be observable. How could experience and behaviour both be states of mind, ontologically on a par, when in the abstract there seems to be nothing in common between them?

Consider now the claim that some emotions are whole bodily states consisting of bodily changes which feel, or are experienced as being, a certain way from the inside. When the body instantiating such a state is your own, you can be aware of it from the inside: you can have a feeling or experience of emotion. When the body instantiating such a state is another's, you can observe that state from the outside: you can observe another's emotion. The feeling or experience that you have, and the behaviour of another that you observe, are the same type of thing: an emotion. This is perfectly intuitive. The reason why is that, with respect to these emotions, there is something in common between experience and behaviour. Your body feels, or is experienced as being, a certain way when undergoing these bodily changes, and these bodily changes are precisely what is observable in others. Emotions can solve the conceptual problem.

There is a basic objection to this solution. Consider, for instance, how you sometimes lack all awareness of your body when in the grip of an emotion. Safe from a wild animal, say, you might comment that you had been too scared to feel scared: your attention was wholly occupied with escape. Given that the bodily changes can occur without you having a feeling or experience, there is room to drive a wedge between them. They are not, the objection claims, the same type of thing.

Note that the objection can, and indeed should, concede that the bodily changes are essential to emotions. On the one hand, it seems that what makes it the case that you are scared when escaping, as opposed to only acting on a belief that the animal is dangerous, is that your body is undergoing these changes—notwithstanding your lack of awareness. On the other hand, the bodily changes are essential to the explanation of affect: there simply cannot be any feeling or experience of your body when undergoing these changes, unless these changes occur. The objection denies only that the bodily changes, and the feeling or experience, are the same type of thing. In effect, it splits emotions into two distinct components. Certainly you can understand how another can undergo that part of an emotion consisting in bodily changes: a type of behaviour. That has never been in issue. But it is still the case that the only feeling or experience you experience is that which you have: your own. We are no better placed to solve the conceptual problem than we ever were.

In essence, the objection blocks the solution by re-introducing the ontological distinction between experience and behaviour within the account of emotions. But the difference this makes to the account itself is, in a sense, one of emphasis. We can use the notion of priority to explain what is at stake. The account of emotions I suggested begins with a basic conception of an emotion as a whole bodily state. This state consists in bodily changes which feel, or are experienced as being, a certain way from the inside: the bodily changes, and the feeling or experience, are bound together as one. Of course, we can distinguish them should we wish. But in so doing, we are distinguishing among aspects of one thing: an emotion. So the respect in which the bodily changes, and the feeling or experience, are alike has priority over the respect in which they are different. They are both equally and unambiguously aspects of an emotion, and in this way, ontologically on a par. The account of emotions suggested by the objection, in contrast, begins with a basic commitment to an ontological distinction between experience and behaviour. It then conceives of emotions as consisting in two distinct components: bodily changes, and a feeling or experience.

The bodily changes, and the feeling or experience, are certainly ontologically alike in that they are both components of an emotion. But the respect in which they are different has priority.

How can we decide between these two accounts? In principle, we can adopt either. Neither has established that we must think of emotions as it claims we in fact do. So to try to meet the objection, and solve the problem, I shall attempt two things. The first is philosophical: I shall suggest a way to develop the idea that the bodily changes, and the feeling or experience, are bound together as one thing. The second is more descriptive: I hope only to point out that, however intuitive the ontological distinction seems in the abstract, we do not obviously cleave to it in practice.

So first, how to develop the idea that the bodily changes, and the feeling or experience, are bound together as one thing? The key idea is that it is a bodily feeling or experience that is in question.

Some of the bodily changes, like a change in hormone balance, underlie certain feelings or experiences. But other of the bodily changes, like a bodily configuration or movement, are what the feeling or experience is of. Given this, one way that the bodily changes, and the feeling or experience, are bound together is that some of the bodily changes are constitutive of the content of the feeling or experience. We can make this point side-ways on, as theorists. But it is also phenomenologically salient: it is perfectly apparent to the subject.

Some emotions, like joy, are a pleasure to experience. Some, like sadness, are not. Some, like anger, can be either pleasurable or wretched: it depends, among other things, on what you are angry about. Of course, part of what is nice when you are joyful, but not nice when you are sad, is whatever it is you are joyful or sad about. But still, the experience itself has a particular valence. In this, emotions are similar to sensations like pleasure and pain. And just as it is apparent to the subject that whether she has received a loving caress or a blow to the head is not incidental to the pleasurable or painful nature of her sensations, so too it is apparent to the subject that the changes her body undergoes are not incidental to her emotional feeling or experience. This is why, for instance, you might try to 'keep smiling', as we say, in order to stay feeling cheery; or you might try to control your shakes and sobs, and calm your breathing, in order to diminish your feeling of upset. So the bodily changes, and the feeling or experience, are bound together because the bodily changes are what is felt or experienced: they are encompassed by the feeling or experience.

This idea may seem too simple to carry much weight. Compare, for instance, seeing an object. According to some realist theories of perception, the object is what is seen, and so constitutive of the content of the visual experience: it is encompassed by the visual experience. But even if this allows us to make sense of the idea that the experience and the object are bound together as one thing—a seeing of an object—it is not likely to make us think that the object seen, and the experience of seeing it, are the same type of thing.

But body awareness is importantly different from visual experience. In vision, the object seen is presented as located relative to, and so as distinct from, the subject or origin of the visual experience: the experience is perspectival. Moreover, the experience clearly belongs to the subject or origin of the experience, not to its object. This is not so in body awareness. The object of body awareness is not presented as located relative to, and so as distinct from, the subject or origin of the awareness: the experience is not perspectival. Through body awareness, you experience particular bodily changes and sensations as happening to, and located in, your body, and overall feelings as encompassing it. Phenomenologically, the feeling or experience is presented as belonging not just to the subject of the feeling or experience, but also to the object: the body itself. So the feeling or experience of an emotion is bodily in two senses. It is of the body, and it is in the body.

This can help to develop the idea that the bodily changes, and the feeling or experience, are the same type of thing. For they are bound together not only because some of the bodily changes are what the feeling or experience is of. They are bound together because both the bodily changes, and the feeling or experience, are presented as belonging to the body: both are properties of the body. In this sense, they are ontologically on a par: aspects of the state the subject's body is in.

Second, is it correct that, in practice, we apply the ontological distinction to our own emotions? Even if our use of our bodies in pretence suggests that we do, there is another, arguably more basic, dimension of our practice that suggests that we do not: our use of our bodies to communicate our emotions to others.

Sometimes your body communicates your emotions unbeknownst to you. You may be paying no attention to how your body appears to another. But sometimes you are fully aware of what your body is communicating: you can be aware of yourself as an other to others. So consider, for instance, feeling delighted at a child's spontaneous gift of a drawing. Joy comes over your body and face. You naturally smile, exclaim, and so on. But perhaps you exaggerate the expression somewhat, or turn to face the child directly, to ensure that she appreciates it. Or perhaps you try to soften your expression, or turn away slightly. You want to communicate your pleasure, but this child is always seeking attention, and must not be overly encouraged. Or perhaps you just allow your joy to run its natural course. You neither need, nor want, to do anything about it at all.

In such contexts, you communicate your emotion simply by allowing another to observe it: it is as if you literally say with your body 'This is what I'm feeling'. The idea that only one component of your emotion is observable, while the other component is kept securely hidden from view, does not occur: the ontological distinction has no place in your thinking. Needless to say, it is still the case that, in observing your emotion, another cannot have your bodily feeling or experience. Nor, at least in the normal course of affairs, can she be aware of your body from the inside. But she nonetheless appears able to observe your emotion—nothing partial, nothing less—perfectly well. That is how it is communicated.

On the one hand, we can understand how the bodily changes, and the bodily feeling or experience, could be bound together as one thing: a whole bodily state. On the other hand, in at least one dimension of our practice, we seem to think of our own emotions in just this way. Of course, the bodily changes, and the bodily feeling or experience, can be distinguished. But for both these reasons, it is open to us to hold that in the first instance, they are distinguished as the same type of thing. Both are aspects of a whole bodily state: an emotion.

But if this is right, then the objection lacks motivation. There is no reason to concede it. You conceive of the bodily feeling or experience that you have, and the bodily changes that others observe, as the same type of thing: an emotion. Given this, there is nothing problematic in understanding how the bodily feeling or experience that you have, and the bodily changes of another that you observe, could be the same type of thing: an emotion. Emotions are observational. They solve the conceptual problem.

Note that the solution requires only that emotions can, in principle, be both experienced and observed. It does not require that every emotion is observable. Nor does it require that every bodily state that appears to be an emotion, whether by design or by happenstance, genuinely is.

What, finally, is the relevance of the emotions to the epistemological problem of other minds? If emotions are observable, then it is possible to claim that you can know, or be justified in believing, that another has a mind because you observe it. But the worth of this answer will yet depend on how you can know, or be justified in

Hanna Pickard

believing, anything on the basis of perception. And there is still a practical, if not philosophical, problem about other minds in particular. Unlike inanimate objects, people are prone to pretend.

I have tried to argue that a direct, empiricist solution to the conceptual problem of other minds demands that states of mind can be either experienced or observed, and that some emotions meet this requirement. But even if this is true of these emotions, it may not be true of other states of mind. So how can this solution be extended?

When explaining the nature of the problem, I suggested that if you have the concept of a subject of experience, then no contradiction ensues from the claim that what it is for another to be in pain, say, is for there to be pain, but for there not to be. That is, if you have the concept of such a subject, then you can understand what a type of experience is from your own case alone. So perhaps we can use the emotions, in all their public manifestation, to generate the concept of a subject. We could then dispense with the demand for publicity.

Pursuing this suggestion would have the result that our basic concept of a subject is a subject of emotions. Certainly this has some developmental plausibility. But the consequences are not negligible. The emotions in question are whole bodily states consisting of naturally occurring bodily changes which feel, or are experienced as being, a certain way from the inside. If our basic concept of a subject is a subject of these emotions, then this subject is a body capable of instantiating these emotions. That is, a body which is, more or less, human—like us.

Acknowledgements

I am grateful to audiences in London, Manchester, and Oxford, as well as to Myles Burnyeat, Quassim Cassam, Naomi Eilan, Michael Martin, Matthew Nudds, Matthew Soteriou, David Velleman, and especially John Campbell, for questions and comments.

Bibliography

Darwin, Charles 1998. *The Expression of The Emotions in Man and Animals*, with an Introduction, Afterword, and Commentary by Paul Ekman (London: HarperCollins Publishers).

Emotions and the Problem of Other Minds

Davidson, Donald 2001. *Subjective, Intersubjective, Objective* (Oxford: Clarendon Press).

Ekman, Paul 1992. 'An Argument for Basic Emotions', in *Cognition and Emotion*, vol. 6.

Evans, Gareth 1982. *The Varieties of Reference* (Oxford: Clarendon Press).

James, William 1884. 'What Is An Emotion?', in *Mind*, vol. 9.

Martin, M. G. F. 1993. 'Sense Modalities and Spatial Properties', in Brewer, B., Eilan, N. and McCarthy, R., (eds) (1993) *Spatial Representation* (Oxford: Basil Blackwell).

McDowell, John 1998. 'Criteria, Defeasibility, and Knowledge', in his (1998) *Meaning, Knowledge, and Reality* (Cambridge, Massachusetts: Harvard University Press).

Peacocke, Christopher 1984. 'Consciousness and Other Minds', in *Proceedings of the Aristotelian Society*, supplementary vol. 58.

Pears, David 1975. 'Causes and Objects of Some Feelings and Psychological Reactions', in Pears, D., (ed.) (1975) *Questions in the Philosophy of Mind* (London: Duckworth).

Strawson, P. F. 1959. *Individuals: An Essay in Descriptive Metaphysics* (London: Methuen).

Taylor, Charles 1985. 'Self-Interpreting Animals', in his (1985) *Human Agency and Language: Philosophical Papers,* vol. 1 (Cambridge, England: CUP Press).

VI. Emotional Feelings and Intentionalism

ANTHONY HATZIMOYSIS

I

Emotions are Janus-faced: their focus may switch from how a person is feeling deep inside her, to the busy world of actions, words, or gestures whose perception currently affects her. The intimate relation between the 'inside' and the 'outside' seems to call for a redrawing of the traditional distinction of mental states between those that can look out to the world, and those that are, supposedly, irredeemably blind.

The phenomenology of emotional experience—(an account of) what it is like for a subject to experience an emotion—invites the question of whether we can articulate a theory of emotional feeling that could justify the claim that emotions are states in which the world is presented to the subject. That claim has been prominent in recent theories of emotion, and its importance is hard to overstate. If true, the claim that emotions are akin to perceptual states would fit nicely, and, thus, lend support to the view that emotions reveal to us a world of comforting, frightening, loveable, or unbearable persons, events and states of affairs. If emotions are indeed perceptions, and if at least some of those perceptions are not illusory, then what they attend to is real. The focus of emotion is those aspects of reality that have significance, import, a positive or negative value for us. The conclusion that could be drawn from this approach is that the world we encounter is enchanted or meaningful, or, more prosaically, that prudential, moral or aesthetic values are real.

The philosophical problem of the reality of values is as significant as it is difficult to resolve, but it is not the concern of this paper. What I shall try to achieve here is a better understanding of what is involved in the claim that emotions can be fruitfully thought of as perceptual states. My route is marked by two signposts. The first claims that 'emotions involve feelings', and the second that 'emotions are intentional states.' It might be thought that the former sign aims to keep out any 'cognitivist' intruders, while the latter hopes to exclude 'feeling-based' theorists of emotion. But that is far from the truth. Cognitivists about emotion need not deny that

105

feelings may form an important aspect of emotional phenomena; their cognitivism centres on the fact that it is not through feeling but through cognition, perception, or evaluative judgment, that the nature of emotion becomes intelligible. Feeling theorists, on the other hand, may aspire to think of emotions in a way that matches perfectly having a feeling with having an intentional state towards worldly objects. All in all, admitting the presence of emotional feelings should be part of the beginning, not the conclusion, of an inquiry into emotional intentionality.

II

What is the motivation for introducing intentionality in the analysis of emotion? A line of reasoning, that we can quickly put aside, runs as follows: all mental states are intentional; emotions are mental states; therefore, emotions are intentional. The inference is valid, but in the absence of independent grounding for the major premise, it does not deliver the intended result. We might as easily reverse the plot by arguing that: emotions are not intentional; emotions are mental states; therefore, not all mental states are intentional. Philosophical tradition might have created a tendency to think in favour of the claim that 'intentionality is the mark of the mental' but this thought might turn out to be a prejudice, if we lack the reasons for asserting that a central case of mental phenomena, such as emotions, are intentional.

Fortunately, such reasons might not be hard to come by. Ordinary language furnishes us with several examples: we can be angry *with* our neighbour, delighted *by* the news, worried *about* our friend's health. Citing phrases like these is often the main, if not the only, evidence offered in support of the intentionality of emotions. However, it is not clear precisely what these phrases show. In particular, it is not obvious whether they should be read as proving that intentionality characterizes emotional phenomena, rather than states which are closely associated, though not identical to emotion itself. Attributing intentionality to emotions on the ground that they are caused by emotionally neutral, independently conceived beliefs, identifiable irrespective of their involvement to the emotional experience, would at most endow emotion with intentionality by proxy. However, even if we establish that it is emotion itself that is directed towards intentional objects, we need to query which of the reflexive, autonomic, cognitive, or affective elements that make up an emotional experience accounts primarily for the intentionality of emotion. In order to provide a clear focus to this very general problem, I propose that we zoom in its philosophically most intriguing aspect: are emotional feelings themselves intentional?←

The standard way to answer this question has been in the negative. Feeling is commonly understood as a mental event whose nature is exhausted by its sometimes rich in nuances, and hard to describe phenomenal character; furthermore, it is often taken for granted that, however significant, the phenomenal character of an experience is neither *toward*, nor *about*, anything. It could be claimed, therefore, that as a type of feeling, emotional feelings are states that denote nothing beyond 'how it is like' for a subject to experience them, thus barring the possibility of emotional feelings having intentional objects.

III

We may try to challenge this negative view by calling upon the basic principle of philosophical intentionalism, according to which every aspect of our experience is to a larger or lesser extend representational of the way the world is. The intentional object of a state is what that state represents, namely its cause. The phenomenal properties of our experience are intentional, and their intentionality is explainable in terms of the natural properties they represent. It is worth inquiring, therefore, whether the intentionalist approach can rebut the denial of emotional intentionality, by warranting the claim that emotional feelings are directed towards the actual or imagined instantiations of properties or events of the world, which form the focus of emotional experience.

The intentionalist strategy may advance in three moves. First, we show how some basic cases of bodily feeling involve intentionality; secondly, we extend the basic cases so as to include emotional feelings; finally we establish that the intentionality of such feelings is presentative of the value properties of worldly objects.

The first move has been well worked out in the psychological literature, and so a brief reminder of its premises may suffice. A bodily feeling, such as pain, may represent a change, such as damage, stretch or disorder, in parts of one's body; the feeling of pain is a type of perception directed toward a particular point or area located within the limits of our body. The intentionalist model leaves open the question of whether pain-as-felt is a mental event exhausted by its directedness toward a particular pain-as-an-object of sensation, or whether it is required to include an account of the

Anthony Hatzimoysis

unpleasantness of pain (its very painfulness) in making sense of the experience. A full discussion of the nature of pain is beyond the scope of this paper. I would state here that what makes a bodily feeling intentional is the fact that it is directed toward a bodily event at a particular space and time, whereas what makes it a pain is a complex matter including several aspects: its representation of a bodily region or surface as one of damage or disorder (representation of a fact under a normative heading), that the feeling is unpleasant (affective reality), or one we wish it stopped (motivational dimension).

The above approach gains much of its plausibility by the fact that it is in tune with the folk ways of thinking about pain. The spatial and temporal aspects that make bodily feeling amenable to intentionalist interpretation is aptly conveyed in the ways we communicate our experience in discourse. A friend may ask 'where exactly does it hurt?' as a doctor may inquire 'where do you feel the pain?'; but neither, we trust, would ask 'where does it grieve?' or 'where exactly do you feel the shame?' In short, the specificity of spatio-temporal references to body that make intentionalism about pain plausible, is precisely what seems to render it a non-starter in the case of emotional feeling.

IV

Intentionalists may bring emotional feeling into their theory through a different route. Emotional episodes are not disembodied: they almost invariably come with changes in heart-rate, skin temperature, body posture, tightening of muscles, and so on. Information processed at a neural, sensory, perceptual, or epistemic level, on the one hand, and the goal directedness of volitional or desiderative states, on the other, may set in train autonomic responses preparatory for action (of strike in case of anger, withdrawal in case of sadness, reparation in case of guilt, etc.). The feeling of fear, according to this view, is the intentional state of sensing changes in one's body generated by the autonomic responses preparatory for fight-or-flight, caused by the, broadly construed, cognitive and conative states of the agent. The emotional feeling registers how one's body stands as a whole in a particular situation.

Intentionalism asserts that the intentional content of a feeling is what it represents, and what an emotional feeling represents is a bodily *gestalt*, a patterned web of physiological changes. This claim raises a dilemma about the relation between emotion and emotional feelings, neither horn of which is particularly attractive.

108

Emotional Feelings and Intentionalism

If emotions and emotional feelings have the same intentional object, then emotions are directed towards one's bodily state: what I dread is not the murderer catching up with me, but my pulse rate and stomach muscles. This view sounds absurd at worst, and strongly revisionary at best: absurd, because it implies that we are amused, afraid, joyous or guilty about, say, our body temperature, rather than about people, actions or events that make up our natural and social environment. At a minimum, this view demands that we understand ourselves and others as being capable of emotions with just one type of objects, namely the physiological changes that constitute our bodily gestalt. Though not logically incoherent, such a revision would require an immense effort of mental maneuvering, as it runs counter to both social scientific and folk psychological thinking about emotions.

If emotional feelings and emotions have different objects, then we are owed an explanation of why such feelings should bear the emotional title at all. The intentionalist might venture an explanation by showing what it is about certain bodily feelings that makes us identify them as emotional. The answer may invoke a chain of representation: certain feelings represent bodily changes; bodily changes represent certain of the changes in the world that impinge on the body; therefore bodily feelings represent certain changes in the world. Some of those changes in the world relate to matters of concern to us, sources of frustration or satisfaction, actual or forthcoming threats, secured or withdrawn rewards. They are precisely the kind of events that constitute the object of human emotions. Some of our bodily feelings are called emotional because they represent events in the world towards which emotions are directed.

Despite its advantages over traditional forms of naturalism about emotion, the intentionalist line of reasoning encounters some important difficulties. Starting at a rather general level, the intentionalist approach draws on the notion of a representational chain, that is made possible by the nature of representation as a relation of a state's standing in for something else. However, this contrasts sharply with the core feature of intentionality as a relation of directedness between a state and that towards which that state is. Take the simpler case of my perceiving dark clouds gathering in the sky. Clouds are caused by various chemical processes on water surfaces of the earth, and, according to the theory under consideration, clouds are thus representing such processes. However, the intentional content of my perception is that of clouds in the sky, not of chemical activities of water on earth. It is simply false to equate intentionality with representationality when the former is

Anthony Hatzimoysis

understood as a relation between a mental state and its object, and the latter as causally determined relation of entities or events that could be interpreted (for all sorts of scientific or practical purposes) as conveying information about each other.

At an explanatory level, the intentionalist approach presupposes that we posses the rather unique ability of identifying for each occasion what the object of an emotion is independently of how we feel towards it. It is not sufficient to assert that certain feelings are emotional because they unfailingly happen to co-occur with one's emotions. In order to test the explanatory power of the theory that claims that the object of feeling and emotion coincide, even though they reach their object through totally different routes, we should be in a position to state whether something is for us frightening or amusing irrespective of how we feel about it: otherwise it would be simply vacuous to claim with intentionalism that each time one experiences emotional feelings, both the feeling and the emotion are about the same thing.

Note that some of the standard positions on this issue do not face a similar problem, as they agree that what is, say, funny is that to which one responds with amusement, the projectivist claiming that it is because one feels amused that some gesture is called funny, while the realist that it is because the gesture is funny that one feels amused. Each side in this debate has attempted to appropriate the other's insights, with varying degrees of success. However, what keeps the debating parties from talking passed each other is their commitment to the view that emotional feelings are directed towards people and events in the world, rather than alterations in one's body.

It is worth noting finally, that separating the intentional object of feeling from that of emotion does not avoid the revisionist trap. According to intentionalism, to feel is to perceive changes in one's body. This implies that any locution of the form 'A feels x (an emotion) with/about/towards B', should be understood along the lines of 'A perceives y (a bodily state) and he has also x (an emotion) with/about/towards B.' Although John says that he feels angry with his neighbours, what he means is the conjunction of two contingently related things, the second of which is devoid of feeling: that he perceives his blood boil, and that he is angry with his neighbours. It might perhaps be possible for intentionalism to map ordinary thought and talk onto a two-tier model of bodily reports, and statements about one's emotion, though how this is possible in practice remains to be seen.

V

All of the above problems are symptomatic of the conflict between the phenomenology of emotional experience and its purported intentionalist explanation. Being emotionally engaged with something is experienced as a unitary state directed towards that thing. This is what makes possible the sense of seeing things as appealing or appalling, and the suggested parallel between emotional and perceptual states so apposite. The parallel, of course, is as good as the justification that supports it. Each kind of perceptual state needs its own type of content and its distinctive physiology. Those whose who support the view that emotions are perceptual states have to show both that the world is inhabited by value properties and that we are well equipped for such properties to be revealed to us. What our discussion has shown is that, in its current form, intentionalism is an example of which approach to these issues they would have to avoid.

Bibliography

Byrne, Alex 2002. 'Intentionalism Defended', *Philosophical Review*.
Carruthers, Peter 2003. *Phenomenal Consciousness* (Cambridge: Cambridge University Press).
Prinz, Jesse 2003. *Emotional Perception* (New York: Oxford University Press).
Tye, Michael 1995. *Ten Problems of Consciousness* (Cambridge, Mass: MIT Press).

VII. Emotions, Rationality, and Mind/Body[1]

PATRICIA GREENSPAN

There are now quite a number of popular or semi-popular works urging rejection of the old opposition between rationality and emotion. They present evidence or theoretical arguments that favour a reconception of emotions as providing an indispensable basis for practical rationality. Perhaps the most influential is neuroanatomist Antonio Damasio's *Descartes' Error*, which argues from cases of brain lesion and other neurological causes of emotional deficit that some sort of emotional 'marking,' of memories of the outcomes of our choices with anxiety, is needed to support learning from experience.[2]

Damasio's work has interesting connection to such issues as how to understand psychopaths, agents who lack normal feelings of guilt and other moral motives based on empathy.[3] It seems that psychopaths are not like the rational 'amoralists' of philosophic lore but rather are unable to follow through reliably on long-term plans they make in their own interests. A failure of emotional empathy—with one's own future self, in effect—apparently yields elements of practical irrationality.

On the other hand, Damasio wrongly sets up Descartes and mind/body dualism as a philosophic foil for his view.[4] His real

---

[1] Earlier versions of this paper were presented at a plenary session on emotions at the XIVth Interamerican Philosophy Conference in Puebla, Mexico, in August 1999, a conference on 'Rationality and Mental Health' of the Association for the Advancement of Philosophy and Psychiatry in May 2000, and at the Royal Institute for Philosophy conference on emotions at the University of Manchester in July 2001. Along with members of those audiences, I owe thanks, for comments, to Erich Diese, Scott James, Stephen Leighton, and Kathleen Wallace.

[2] Antonio R. Damasio, *Descartes' Error: Emotion, Reason, and the Human Brain* (New York: G. P. Putnam's Sons, 1994).

[3] Cf. Damasio, pp. 178–79. I take these suggestions further in 'Responsible Psychopaths' (unpublished).

[4] See Damasio, pp. 247ff., for an explanation, towards the end of the book, of what he takes Descartes' error to be.

target seems to be Fodorian computationalism and similar views in cognitive science ('the mind as software program').[5] He even implicitly recognizes, at one point toward the end of the book, that his announced target, Descartes' *cogito*, does include emotions, or at any rate their mental aspect ('suffering'), and he cites Descartes' detailed account of emotions in *The Passions of the Soul*.[6] But Descartes' explanation of emotions in that work in terms of 'animal spirits' (essentially an outdated predecessor of neurological impulses) seems to bridge body and mind (or soul), despite his official dualism. The title of both books—Damasio's and Descartes'—may be somewhat unfortunate.

More generally, the recent neuroscientific work on emotions seems to take all but neurophilosophy and similar approaches within philosophy as necessarily opposing the project of recognizing the cognitive or rational role of emotion. In a rough-and-ready way, emotions are assumed to fall entirely on the 'body' side of the 'mind/body' distinction for anyone who would allow that much talk in mentalistic terms.

There are other recent popular works dealing with evolutionary psychology and related subjects that do make use of some philosophic literature for insight into the moral role of emotion. These essentially follow Darwin's attempts to explain the development of the "moral sense" in terms of social emotions in animals.[7] A particular focus is eighteenth-century British moral philosophy, with its attempts to base ethics on human emotional nature. Sometimes the approach is put to conservative political uses, by 'sociobiologists' and others, and sometimes it is dismissed on just those grounds by political opponents, especially feminists. A current popular book that attempts something less ideological (though still committed to a basis in the mind's innate structure, on a version of the view derived from Chomsky) is Stephen Pinker's *How the Mind Works*.[8]

One thing many of these discussions seem to have in common is an importance assigned to emotions in rational terms specifically for

[5] See ibid., e.g. p. 250; cf. p. 248.

[6] See *The Philosophical Works of Descartes*, Vol. I, trans. by E. S. Haldane and G. R. T. Ross (Cambridge: Cambridge University Press, 1970), pp. 331–99.

[7] See esp. ch. 3 in Charles Darwin, *The Descent of Man and Selection in Relation to Sex* (New York: Modern Library, n.d. [1871], chs. 4 and 5.

[8] See Steven Pinker, *How the Mind Works* (New York: W. W. Norton, 1997), esp. ch. 6. For one of the more emotion-based versions of the sociobiological argument cf. Julius Q. Wilson, *The Moral Sense* (New York: Free Press, 1993).

resistance to full rational control. Emotions are treated as cases of 'rational irrationality': They are of use to us rationally, in promoting our long-term ends, in part because they function as barriers to rational deliberation.[9] They protect us from the need or the tendency to reason things out from scratch at every stage or in every respect, often to the detriment of rapid response or reliable follow-through or the ability to form relationships of mutual trust. In social terms, they serve as 'commitment devices,' making it demonstrably difficult for us to act as we otherwise would on the basis of narrow self-interest.[10] The extreme case of uncontrolled anger, for instance, communicates a 'hell-bent' retaliatory urge in a way analogous to throwing the steering wheel out the car window in a game of 'chicken'—Schelling's classic game-theoretic case, with two cars hurtling toward each other, about to crash unless one of them swerves.[11]

Just because emotions are somewhat recalcitrant to reason, then, they are accorded a crucial role in rational design—in creating a human nature (or a range of human natures) that is up to the human task—whether the design in question is evolutionary, cultural/political, or pedagogical. There are other recent works from a psychological or psychiatric perspective marshalling evidence for the role of emotional development in early childhood as a foundation for normal cognitive learning.[12] A further area of application to individual cases is psychotherapeutic redesign: there is a huge collection of psychological self-help and related literature (some of it theoretically respectable) dealing with emotions in rational terms. For that matter, the general line of thought here fits easily with self-developmental approaches within philosophy stressing Aristotelian notions of character-building or habituation in virtue.

However, there is still a kind of disconnection from contemporary philosophy (outside cognitive science) in the treatment given in many

[9] Cf. Derek Parfit, *Reasons and Persons* (Oxford: Clarendon Press, 1984), esp. p. 14.

[10] See Robert H. Frank, *Passions Within Reason: The Strategic Role of the Emotions* (New York: W. W. Norton, 1988); cf. my 'Emotional Strategies and Rationality', *Ethics* 110 (2000), 469–87.

[11] Cf. Thomas C. Schelling, *The Strategy of Conflict* (Cambridge, Mass.: Harvard University, 1980) esp. pp. 22ff.

[12] See esp. Stanley I. Greenspan, M.D. [no relation to the author] with Beryl Lieff Benderly, *The Growth of the Mind and the Endangered Origins of Intelligence* (Reading, Mass.: Perseus, 1997).

Patricia Greenspan

of these works to understanding the nature of emotions, what emotions are. From within philosophy Paul Griffiths' informative book, *What Emotions Really Are*, exploits and widens this gap to the extent that it caricatures the main philosophical alternative and sweeps aside one of the central questions the latter attempts to deal with, essentially a normative version of Damasio's question of the bearing of emotions on practical reasoning.[13] It is what philosophy has to teach on that subject that needs to be brought out in response to Damasio's error (and also, I think, Griffiths') of confusing ongoing attempts to understand emotions in mentalistic terms with a certain competing research program in cognitive science.

The effect of much contemporary philosophy of emotion has been to identify a rational or potentially rational (rationally assessable) content of emotions, at any rate in paradigmatic cases of developed human response. Griffiths calls this the 'propositional attitudes' approach. Emotions can be viewed as having a content expressible propositionally, or in terms of what they 'say' about their objects: personal anger, for instance, registers the agent's perception of a wrong someone presumably has done; pride registers the thought that the agent is somehow praiseworthy; fear registers a thought of danger, and so on.

This approach is generally discussed under the heading of 'emotions and judgments,' since it emerged from debate over more extreme versions that simply equated emotions with a subclass of evaluative judgments, as the category of propositional attitudes that philosophers were most at home with. But more fundamentally, what is at issue is a view of emotions as registering evaluative information and thus as susceptible to some sort of rational assessment themselves—not automatically to be consigned to the 'irrational' category.

There are overlapping theories in psychology that understand emotions in terms of cognitive 'appraisals' and similar notions.[14] However, much of the current work in 'harder' areas of science (including 'cognitive science' areas of philosophy) eschews such talk

[13] See Paul E. Griffiths, *What Emotions Really Are: The Problem of Psychological Categories* (Chicago: University of Chicago Press, 1997). Cf. my 'Practical Reasoning and Emotions,' in A. Mele and P. Rawlings (eds), *Rationality* (Oxford: Oxford University Press, in progress).

[14] See, e.g., Magda B. Arnold, 'Human Emotion and Action,' in *Human Action: Conceptual and Empirical Issues*, T. Mischel (ed.), (New York: Academic Press, 1969); cf. Nico Frijda, *The Emotions* (Cambridge: Cambridge University Press, 1986).

in favour of a treatment of emotional states as physiological or bodily reactions or reaction-clusters ('affect-programmes') capable of causal connection with rational thought and action but not themselves capable of rationality.

There may be good heuristic or other practical reasons for adopting this nonmentalistic framework for certain purposes. Within philosophy, the aim is often to lend support to an interdisciplinary scientific research programme. Minimizing metaphysical assumptions avoids a lot of potentially divisive dispute. But of course it is the job of philosophy to inquire into assumptions. In this case, the point of doing so need not be particularly metaphysical—to push beyond the categories studiable by science—but rather, as I see it, is more concerned with specifying just how it is that practical reason puts emotions to work. The essential terminology is that of normative assessment rather than mentalistic talk per se.

Philosophers have exploited the possibility of representing the evaluative content of emotions in propositional terms since Aristotle, though not always with a distinction between content and causal accompaniments. The Stoics even made out emotions as evaluative judgments. However, unlike Aristotle they also advocated an asceticism that affects their treatment of emotions. Emotions for the Stoics amount to confused judgments, and their usual advice is to minimize confusion by cultivating more detached states of mind.

However, with all the many possibilities of confusion associated with emotions, they may sometimes embody more accurate perception of the value-laden world than we allow to affect our detached judgments. Our regard for them as quick responses resisting deliberative control is heightened by this assessment: they are not just 'quick-and-dirty' (rationally speaking) but often embody a point of view worth recording even where more reasoned judgments are to hand. There has therefore been a resurgence in recent years of a 'judgmentalist' approach with a more positive spin on the value of emotion.[15]

---

[15] For the re-entry of what I am calling 'judgmentalism' into the post-Wittgensteinian Anglo-American literature see Erroll Bedford, 'Emotions,' in *The Philosophy of Mind*, V. C. Chappell (ed.), (Englewood Cliffs, N. J. : Prentice-Hall, 1962). Robert C. Solomon, *The Passions: The Myth and Nature of Human Emotion* (Garden City, N.Y.: Anchor/Doubleday, 1976) expands the view and connects it with continental philosophy, especially Nietzsche and Sartre. A more qualified variant of the view with Jamesian physiological elements appears in William Lyons, *Emotion* (Oxford: Oxford University Press, 1980).

Patricia Greenspan

I would modify the approach with an account of emotional rationality that sets it apart from the logic of judgments by allowing for rational options, including conflicting emotional responses by the same person to the same situation—or for that matter, the suppression of emotional response.[16] I refer to this as the 'perspectival' account, meaning that rational warrant for an emotional response varies with evaluative perspective—in a way not recorded in qualifications to the content of emotion, unlike what is supposed to be the case for judgment.

On the perspectival account. what emotions register, when the mechanism is working properly, is not necessarily the 'all things considered' view of things by which we assess our beliefs. To say that an emotion is reasonable, or rationally appropriate, is to say that a certain evaluative belief that represents the content of the emotion (for anger, for instance, that someone has done me a wrong) would be warranted by a significant subset of the evidence—significant in the sense of 'worth holding in mind,' perhaps for moral or other practical purposes.

This is a loose and variable standard, adding a further level of normative assessment (of the evaluative thought content of emotion as well as by it). Rationality in the relevant sense allows for emotional options and even emotional conflict or ambivalence. It does not imply the irrationality of an emotion with the opposite content—or of no emotion, emotional suppression or indifference. As a positive evidential assessment of an emotion, 'rational' means something like 'rationally acceptable,' or adequately grounded in the situational evidence, rather than 'rationally required,' or mandated by the evidence, as on the usual standard for assessing belief. What is assessed in the case of emotional evaluation is something

¹⁶ See 'A Case of Mixed Feelings: Ambivalence and the Logic of Emotions,' in A. O. Rorty (ed.), *Explaining Emotions* (Berkeley: University of California Press, 1980), pp. 223–50; cf. my extended account in *Emotions and Reasons: An Inquiry into Emotional Justification* (New York: Routledge, Chapman and Hall, 1988). For a simpler explication of the current point see my *Practical Guilt: Moral Dilemmas, Emotions, and Social Norms* (New York: Oxford University Press, 1995), ch. 5. I should note that my term 'perspectival,' here and in the second book, is not meant to evoke Nietzsche's general perspectival theory of truth (or for that matter, various other uses of the term that apply specifically to desires and emotions). Cf. esp. the perspectival account that de Sousa opposes to Solomon's view of emotions as 'subjectivity' in Ronald de Sousa, *The Rationality of Emotion* (Cambridge, Mass.: M.I.T. Press, 1987), pp. 146–49.

118

more like attention to a prima facie belief—holding a certain thought content in mind—as distinct (in some cases) from all-things-considered assent.

Imagine letting oneself get angry about a consumer complaint for the sake of arguing more forcefully with the store.[17] The propositional content of anger here would be something like: 'The store has dealt with me unfairly.' But I could think this—in the dispositional sense relevant to belief, or even as an object of occurrent attention—without necessarily reacting to it with characteristic phenomenological symptoms of anger. I may have reasons for 'letting it go' until I have more time, say, or out of sympathy for the overburdened clerk. On the other side, I have reasons for 'letting it happen,' setting up the conditions under which my anger will emerge (for instance, by reviewing the history of my interactions with the store), in order to get some action from the clerk. So I have options here for emotional reaction—appropriate reaction, as assessed in rational terms, relative to the evidence, for a more tolerant analogue of the notion of warranted belief. Either allowing or suppressing the feeling will be appropriate, in the sense of being adequately warranted by the facts of the situation.

To make more detailed sense of the account we need to distinguish the essentially cognitive notion of emotional rationality as appropriateness—evidential or representational rationality—from strategic or instrumental rationality, the practical notion that I refer to as 'adaptiveness.' Adaptiveness would include, say, a straightforward appeal to the usefulness of feelings of anger, in my example, in getting the clerk to yield—whether or not there is a real basis for the reaction. There are two senses of rationality in play in these cases and elsewhere, and they can sometimes come apart. However, I think the strategic notion (adaptiveness) does play a background role in determining the standard of evidence applicable to a given emotion, in contrast to warrant for belief.

That is, how much we demand in the way of evidential backing for an emotion is adjusted to reflect the usual value of its consequences, both for the individual himself and for people generally.[18]

---

[17] See my 'Emotional Strategies and Rationality,' *Ethics* 110 (2000), 469–87.

[18] See Karen Jones, 'Emotional Rationality as Practical Rationality', in C. Calhoun (ed.), *Setting the Moral Compass: Essays by Women Philosophers* (Oxford University Press, forthcoming) for an argument that what is relevant here is not just type-by-type consideration of emotions, of the sort I had in mind in *Emotions and Reasons*, but also a particular individual's emotional history.

Less evidence is required, for instance, for anger seen as a healthy form of self-assertion with ameliorative effects in the long run than if we interpret it simply as arrogant and destructive. But we can still make a distinction between rational appropriateness as a kind of evidential warrant and social or moral appropriateness, the assessment of a response such as anger simply as fitting or failing to fit social or moral norms in the particular case.[19] One might reject anger as undignified or uncharitable and still recognize that there are grounds for it in a particular case as opposed to others. There is a distinction, for instance, between appropriate emotion and emotion that is normal and understandable but not really warranted, on the order of blaming the messenger of bad news.

In general, the perspectival view is able to make sense of the rational validity of conflicting reactive standpoints (as in empathetic emotions) as well as our ability to shift perspectives in a way that allows for the combination of emotional uncontrol with a degree of strategy.[20] It appeals to a notion of the propositional thought con-

[19] Cf. Justin D'Arms and Daniel Jacobson, 'The Moralistic Fallacy: On the "Appropriateness" of Emotions,' *Philosophy and Phenomenological Research*, **61** (2000), 65–90. At the Manchester conference D'Arms raised the question why emotional appropriateness should be affected by adaptiveness at all. I think the answer has to do with my interpretation of appropriateness as not just the 'truth' of emotions (a measure of success or correctness as in de Sousa, *The Rationality of Emotions*) but rather a matter of fitness to reasons. The relevant reasons are reasons for taking a given thought or state of affairs as meriting attention. My assumption is that these would naturally centre on strategic considerations, though my account is meant to make their influence indirect.

[20] I should note that Griffiths' argument often seems to take for granted (or even to represent as a product of scientific theorizing) an assumption of 'passivity,' or emotional uncontrol, that essentially erects a barrier against the recognition of emotional strategies—dismissing them as mere 'pretences' of emotion in cases where the strategy is social or cultural and involves cultivating the sense of uncontrol; see esp. pp. 155–7, pp. 233f., pp. 242ff.; cf. p. 9, p. 16, p. 118, p. 120. Cf. my 'Emotional Strategies and Rationality.' At the Manchester conference Griffiths did allow for what he called 'Machiavellian emotions,' but the term suggests a degree of calculation that makes the phenomenon seem more limited than it is. In any case, it is not clear how his argument in the book can survive this modification, as it depends on ruling out cases that do not appear to be subject to evolutionary explanation. The main moral Griffiths drew from his earlier argument at the Manchester conference was that philosophers theorizing about emotions cannot afford to ignore the one area of solid

tent of emotions, but my own inclinations in philosophy of mind are basically in the naturalist camp, if the term 'naturalist' is understood to allow for serious social influence on emotion. Though it is not set up to record the results of scientific inquiry into emotions, I would hope that the view can accommodate them.

Presumably, on a naturalist account, the full-blown or fully developed cases of human emotion that my own view takes as paradigmatic for purposes of rational assessment would ultimately be made out as involving a complex relation between cortical brain states and physiological states and events.[21] By the same token, emotion on the view I have outlined in mentalistic terms involves evaluative thought content but also an element of positive or negative affect

---

[21] Cf. the evidence in Joseph LeDoux, *The Emotional Brain* (New York: Simon & Schuster, 1996), of a subcortical pathway operating in less complex cases of fear, identified as such by a behavioural ('freezing') response, in both humans and lower animals. I take it that any feelings we have in these cases—note that LeDoux takes pains to point out that what he is discussing is fear as a behavioural system rather than a subspecies of fear experience (e.g., p. 28)—would not be subject to rational assessment, except perhaps derivatively, to the extent that they 'track' reasons applicable to a sufficiently developed organism. Hence they count as 'deficient' cases of my paradigm, but despite my somewhat stipulative use of 'emotions' in *Emotions and Reasons*, I do not object to calling them emotions. I would agree with Griffiths and others that emotions (on anything like our ordinary use of the term) do not constitute a natural kind. A different choice of paradigm would of course be appropriate for other purposes, e.g. explaining the origins of fully developed human emotions. But I take it that LeDoux and other neuroscientists working on emotions mean to allow for links between subcortical and cortical pathways. For discussion of psychological evidence on the subject, see Mohan Matthen, 'Emotion and Learning' (unpublished), which argues that even freezing (along with other anticipatory reactions) has to be explained by a kind of 'displaced conditioning' (involving instinctive causal reasoning) that is part of the process endowing emotions with cognitive content.

---

scientific evidence in the area, for 'basic' emotions as evolutionarily derived affect-programmes. I take this point but was moved to meditate on it while hiking in the Lake District after the conference: in my effort to avoid muddy patches in one area I often found myself perched on a rock that led nowhere. Griffiths himself discusses many of the difficulties one has in explaining the full range of human emotions in terms of the basic subset, and he grants that getting emotions into 'the space of reasons' raises further issues.

that can be said to have that content—to be about what the associated thought is about. This 'associated' thought need not be present as a distinct occurrence. Rather, I take the affective element of (rationally paradigmatic) emotion as a propositional attitude, an attitude with an evaluative proposition as its content. But I often drop propositional attitudes talk—to avoid the logical and metaphysical overtones that worry many readers—and just speak of evaluative attitudes.[22] Affect itself essentially evaluates something as in some respect good or bad—good or bad for the organism (to be sought after or avoided), in the most primitive cases. With cognitive development this evaluative content takes on the possibilities of semantical richness that we associate with propositions.

I think of the affective element of emotions in crude terms as comfort or discomfort—discomfort that some wrong has been done me, in the anger example, say. Discomfort here amounts to a representation in affect of the negative aspect of the emotional evaluation. It (or the various physiological feelings the term covers) can be seen as a 'marker,' to use Damasio's terms in *Descartes' Error*, of practically significant thoughts—in the sense of propositions it is 'about,' not necessarily propositional thoughts held in mind in some

[22] Many people like the term 'construals'—as suggested by Robert C. Roberts, 'What an Emotion Is: A Sketch,' *Philosophical Review* **79** (1988), pp. 183–209—but for reasons I would want to resist: a construal is not necessarily either propositional or evaluative. My broad use of the term 'affect' is meant to leave open questions about the primacy of inner and outer, or mental and bodily, reactions. Though I sometimes speak in terms of feeling, I prefer 'affect' as a term less naturally used in the plural, which makes it less tempting to think of emotions as specific introspectible contents—and also to take emotions as episodic (cf. Malcolm Budd, *Music and the Emotions*, (London: Routledge & Kegan Paul, 1985). However, I do mean to be discussing occurrent emotions as ongoing states of affective evaluation. The term 'propositional attitudes'—besides carrying suggestions of logical and semantical complexity that I mean to cancel for typical cases of emotion—is standardly used for states of mind taking a propositional object: belief that p, desire that p, and so forth. Though fear that p is also on the standard list, emotions as a general category do not fit this pattern. Love, for instance, normally just has a person as its object. In *Emotions and Reasons* I distinguished internal components of emotion—in the case of love, e.g., we might have discomfort that one is far from the love object—and applied the standard account of propositional attitudes to the affective aspect of the components, taking propositions as 'internal objects' of emotion; but the result confused many readers. I can do without object-terminology and just speak of propositional content here.

independent sense. Discomfort also adds a practical or motivational significance of its own, as a bad or aversive state for the agent to be in, that affords it a role in rational decision-making. This is definitely not meant to say that the only important property of the affective element of emotions is its positive or negative aspect; there obviously is much more to feeling than that (or in some cases, such as surprise, possibly less).[23] Other features of affect such as degree of arousal can enter into the description of an emotion as a felt quality, and for that matter its classification as the particular sort of emotion it is. Early arguments for judgmentalism exploited the inadequacy of affect as a basis for distinguishing different emotion types, but it does not follow that affect adds nothing relevant. My own simple categories are set up for the purpose of rational assessment, not to give a full account of the nature or value of emotions.

I sometimes speak of affect and evaluation as 'components' of emotion, but this is meant in an analytical sense, not implying separable parts. The two components (aspects, elements) are internally connected insofar as emotional affect has an evaluation as its content. The assumption of intentionality at this level of basic feeling can sound mysterious, but in principle it is no more so than in more familiar cases involving units of language and thought. In fact, I suspect that the historical or evolutionary account of thought would start with feelings, assigned 'meanings' by their significance for the organism in a sense that includes their role in behavioural response—meanings in a sense that becomes mental only with later cognitive development.[24] Thought content in this sense, even at later stages of development, need not be a separable mental element; it is the content of a feeling.

Even if there is a more ultimate explanation of emotional intentionality in naturalistic terms, I think we need to speak in terms of propositional content in order to address normative questions of rationality. Consider, for instance, a possible alternative approach based on appeal to the causal histories of emotions. This would involve taking an emotion as rationally appropriate on the basis of

[23] Cf. David Pugmire, *Rediscovering Emotion* (Edinburgh: Edinburgh University Press, 1998), esp. 65ff.

[24] Griffiths in some ways creates an opening for this kind of account with his defence of an alternative to propositional 'content schemata' in terms of ecological significance for the organism; cf. p. 231. Cf. the evolutionary 'functionalist' or teleological conception of intentionality defended in Ruth G. Millikan, *Language, Thought, and Other Biological Categories* (Cambridge, Mass.: M.I.T. Press, 1984).

Patricia Greenspan

its occurrence in a situation that resembles in relevant respects a situation originally associated with it—whether in early childhood, as in Ronald de Sousa's 'paradigm scenarios' account of emotional rationality, or in an earlier evolutionary environment; and whether or not the connection is socially mediated, as on 'social constructivist' views of emotion.[25]

Consider male sexual jealousy, or particularly the anger component of jealousy. Imagine someone who feels jealous anger when his wife exchanges glances with another male at a party. To use Aristotle's definition of anger in the *Rhetoric*, he is reacting to an unjustified slight—or at any rate, what he sees as a slight, or as indicating that a slight is imminent.[26] But this is a first-level normative judgement (an evaluation of the situation) that requires interoperation of past events and their natural and conventional meanings—what a glance means or can mean, what legitimate expectations a relationship confers, that a glance involves or might lead to intimacies that violate those expectations—on a level that is unlikely to correspond in any simple way to connections among brain and physiological states interpreted just with reference to a descriptively characterized situational context.

On the level of second-order normative assessment (of the emotion), jealousy might sometimes be assessed as inappropriate to the current situation—if the agent finds out, say, that his wife and the recipient of her glance, a colleague in her area, are reacting to a professional faux pas on the part of someone else at the party—even where situational cues naturally give rise to jealousy because of their resemblance to some sort of paradigm scenario. To explain which cues render an emotion appropriate, rather than merely natural or understandable, given that assessments of practical significance may have changed since the paradigm scenario was established, we seem to need at least implicit reference to the notion of a propositional content, as what the emotion still essentially 'claims' about the situation.

Even supposing that a feeling is ultimately explainable in biological terms or in terms of biology plus social learning—meaning that its occurrence is thus explainable—those are not the terms in which we assess it, or could assess it, as rational or irrational in the instrumental as well as the representational sense, for purposes of self-regulation and social life. If we got to the stage where we could treat jealousy reliably with drug therapy, say, someone would have to decide whether it should be treated, and she would have to

[25] See de Sousa, *The Rationality of Emotion*, esp. pp. 181–4.
[26] See Aristotle, *Rhetorica* 1378a31–b5.

124

deliberate on the basis of at least some assessments containing further normative elements.

For a full theoretical understanding of much that goes on in human behaviour, moreover, we need to be able to recognize cases where an agent uses emotional response for his own purposes, healthy or not. For instance, we can make sense of someone talking himself into feeling jealous on flimsy or imagined grounds just in order to provoke a kind of interaction with his spouse—to exert control, perhaps, or perhaps just an occasion to express and enhance affection. Though the jealous episode may start out as a 'pretence' of sorts, some pretences are self-fulfilling.

An account without propositional attitudes would seem to be unable to capture all the causal histories and strategic aims that are relevant to assessments of emotional rationality. But the standards of appropriate response come to be internal to an emotion (anger, for instance, gets set up as a response to some sort of perceived slight), even if its affective element is first found in infancy as a response to something more basic such as physical restraint. So propositional attitudes also affect the way we identify emotions and in that sense what they are.

However, my own emphasis is not on what emotions are but what they do. The question of what they are seems to me to lead to a non-terminating dispute in which, in one way or another, the rationality of emotion get slighted: either by assimilation to more familiar rational categories or by hasty dichotomy. To end with a 'sound bite' summing up the alternative approach I have tried to defend: *Affect evaluates!* Emotional affect is itself evaluative—and the result can be summed up in a proposition.

In short, I think we can have it both ways about judgment versus feeling or bodily response as the nature of emotion—and not by simply conjoining separable components. My own view emerged from criticism of judgmentalism, but it can be thought of as a version of the 'feeling' view with enough judgmental or propositional structure to allow for rational assessment of emotions. It does not make out emotions as thoughts with hedonic tone but rather as feelings with evaluative content. This content amounts to a 'thought,' but not in the sense of an occurrent mental event, at any rate apart from feeling. Rather, it is what feeling registers or conveys. By isolating it for analysis in the form of a proposition, I have tried to show how we can begin to understand the role of emotions in practical reasoning.

VIII. The significance of recalcitrant emotion (or, anti-quasijudgmentalism)

JUSTIN D'ARMS AND DANIEL JACOBSON

I

Sentimentalist theories in ethics treat evaluative judgments as somehow dependent on human emotional capacities. While the precise nature of this dependence varies, the general idea is that evaluative concepts are to be understood by way of more basic emotional reactions. Part of the task of distinguishing between the concepts that sentimentalism proposes to explicate, then, is to identify a suitably wide range of associated emotions. In this paper, we attempt to deal with an important obstacle to such views, which arises from the dominant tradition in the philosophy of emotion. We will be attempting to steer a middle course between the traditional view and some recent, empirically-minded criticism.

A longstanding challenge to sentimentalism, raised by Philippa Foot against Hume and his descendants, concerns the relations of priority between evaluative judgment and emotional response. Foot argued that the sentiments adduced to explicate moral concepts already involve the very content they are supposed to explain. Humean sentimentalism is a mistaken enterprise, Foot concluded, because 'the explanation of the thought comes into the description of the feeling, not the other way round.'[1]

It is widely agreed that judgments of wrongs cannot be analysed in terms of guilt and disapproval, for instance, if these sentiments already involve the thought that someone has done wrong. This would render the account circular; and, though a few philosophers deny that such circularity is vicious, most balk at this conclusion.[2]

---

[1] 'Hume on Moral Judgement', p. 76, in Philippa Foot, *Virtues and Vices* (Berkeley: University of California Press, 1978). The 20th century noncognitivists are addressed directly in 'Moral Beliefs' and 'Moral Arguments,' ibid.

[2] For an attempt to defend a version of sentimentalism that is expressly circular, see David Wiggins, 'A Sensible Subjectivism?' in *Needs, Values, Truth: Essays in the Philosophy of Value* (Oxford: Blackwell, 1987).

But circularity is not the only danger for sentimentalism. If an independent account of an emotion's content can be given, then the appeal to emotional sensibility drops out of the picture. If fear could be fully explicated in terms of danger—and danger is a concept that can be independently understood—then in order to know what is fearsome we need only learn what is dangerous; we need not consult our sense of fear. That would render a sentimentalist account of the fearsome not circular but superfluous. (We should note, in passing, that we do not take such concepts as fearsome, shameful, and funny to be dispositional concepts, whose application is settled by whatever normal people are prone to feel under standard conditions. Rather, they are evaluative concepts. To judge something funny is to think that it somehow *merits* amusement. We will say a bit more on this point presently.)

This discussion of sentimentalism is brief and schematic, but to make it adequate would require more detail than we can here afford.[3] Our point is simply that the ambitions of sentimentalism seem incompatible with the *judgmentalist* tradition in the philosophy of emotion. Judgmentalism holds that an emotional state is a combination of some cognitive component with an affect—often described as a form of pain or pleasure—and also, perhaps, with some desire. The theory thus individuates specific emotions by differences in their constitutive belief or judgment. For instance, Aristotle held that fear is (a kind of) pain felt at the thought of imminent danger, combined with a desire to flee.[4] Foot claims, similarly, that one must have certain beliefs about a thing in order to be proud of it. As she explains: 'I do not mean...that one would be illogical in feeling pride toward something which one did not believe to be in some way splendid and in some way one's own, but that the concept of pride does not allow us to talk like that.'[5] Judgmentalists typically treat such constitutive beliefs as necessary but not sufficient for being in an emotional state, since the same beliefs can also be held unemotionally, without affect or its underlying physiology.

Although not every philosophical theory of the emotions adopts

---

[3] We consider a variety of sentimentalist proposals elsewhere, in D'Arms and Jacobson, 'Sentiment and Value,' *Ethics* **110** (2000), pp. 722–48.

[4] See Aristotle, *Rhetoric*, Book II Chapter 5 (1382a20). There are grounds for doubting whether Aristotle himself was fully a judgmentalist, but this is how he has commonly been understood.

[5] Foot, 'Hume,' p. 76.

this picture, it is fair to say that judgmentalism has been the dominant account. Recently, however, an influential criticism of judgmentalism, due primarily to Patricia Greenspan, has motivated a substantial modification to the theory. The objection is that judgmentalism does not permit one's emotions to conflict with one's considered judgment; yet such conflict is a familiar psychological phenomenon. We will say that an emotion is *recalcitrant* when it exists despite the agent's making a judgment that is in tension with it. (Just what this tension amounts to is one of the central issues of this paper.) A recalcitrant bout of fear, for example, is one where the agent is afraid of something despite believing that it poses little or no danger. Anger, guilt, shame, and jealousy also supply familiar examples of emotional recalcitrance, since one can seemingly feel any of these emotions while sincerely rejecting the judgments typically associated with them. You can be ashamed of something despite judging it not to reflect badly upon you, or feel guilty despite thinking that you are not at fault.

Since traditional judgmentalism holds that the relevant belief is a necessary constituent of an emotion, the theory seems committed to denying the possibility of emotional recalcitrance. On the face of it, someone who does *not* believe that flying is particularly dangerous cannot be afraid of flying. But this claim is deeply problematic, if not patently false.[6] The judgmentalist must not attribute a belief in danger to an agent simply because she is afraid, on pain of turning the theory's central claim—about the necessity of belief—into a tautology. If judgmentalism can accommodate recalcitrant emotion, it is only through the dubious attribution of peculiarly conflicted beliefs. People who are afraid of flying are typically well aware that it is safer than activities they do not fear, such as driving to the airport. Moreover, their behaviour is deeply incoherent: they do not worry when their friends fly, or buy insurance when forced to fly

[6] Fear of flying, and perhaps other phobias, might be explicable consistently with judgmentalism and without requiring the *ad hoc* postulation of conflicting judgments. That would be so, for instance, if the phobic is best described as suffering panic attacks when faced with the prospect of flying, rather than as being straightforwardly afraid of it. Furthermore, one who is subject to panic attacks under certain predictable circumstances can, without conflict of judgment, be afraid of being put into those circumstances—where the object of this fear is the panic itself rather than the eliciting conditions per se. These are complex issues, which deserve more attention than can be afforded to them here. Suffice it to say that judgmentalism needs to do more to accommodate the phenomena of recalcitrant emotion. Our thanks to Robert Solomon for pressing us on this point.

Justin D'Arms and Daniel Jacobson

themselves.[7] When confronted with the incoherence of their behaviour, they often say things like 'I can't help being afraid' or 'fear isn't rational'; that is, they do not claim their fear to be responsive to evidence and, hence, they forego attempting to justify it rationally.[8] It seems better to say that they are afraid of flying despite believing that it is not especially dangerous. We do not expect this brief critique of judgmentalism to satisfy everyone; however, since our central argument does not require rejecting the theory on these grounds, we will not belabour it any further here.

Because of the problems that classical judgmentalism has with recalcitrant emotions, Greenspan and several other philosophers have revised the theory in a way we shall call *quasijudgmentalist*. The revised theory still type-identifies the emotions by their defining propositions, and claims that certain thoughts are partly constitutive of being in an emotional state, but it loosens the requirement that these thoughts must be affirmed by the agent.[9] Greenspan describes the distinction between her view and classical judgmentalism this way: 'instead of claiming that emotions entail evaluative beliefs I take it that they sometimes just involve evaluative thoughts held in mind by intentional states of comfort or discomfort.'[10] On Robert Roberts' formulation of the view, in order to be afraid, an agent need only *construe* or *perceive* the situation as dangerous; she need not believe it to be dangerous. We think it has not yet been adequately explained just what is meant by a construal or perception of danger. Again, if simply being afraid of something suffices

[7] The great challenge for judgmentalist accounts of recalcitrant emotion is that the behavioural evidence supporting the attribution of the evidentially suspect belief is problematic. As these brief examples show, the phobic's behaviour, taken as a whole—as it must be—is less like that of the ordinary frightened person than it appears to be if one focuses exclusively on the aversive behaviour.

[8] No doubt there is some tendency to rationalize these feelings, but it is usually weak and not long sustained.

[9] At least one self-described judgmentalist, Robert Solomon, is better considered a quasijudgmentalist in our terminology, since he does not deny the claim that one can be afraid despite believing oneself to be safe. For Solomon, emotions are 'hasty and dogmatic' judgments, which can conflict with one's considered belief or evaluation. See Solomon, 'On Emotions as Judgements,' *American Philosophical Quarterly* 25 (1988), pp. 183–91. Perhaps other philosophers conventionally thought of as judgmentalists would be more charitably construed as quasijudgmentalists. In any case, our arguments here apply against both views.

[10] Greenspan, 'Subjective Guilt and Responsibility,' *Mind* 101 (1992), p. 293.

to count as perceiving it as dangerous, then the claim that fear necessarily involves a perception of danger would be trivialized. We are tempted to suggest that quasijudgmentalists bite this bullet, drop their central theoretical claim, and re-describe their claims about the nature of specific emotions in a manner that we will presently suggest. But we do not expect this result to be forthcoming. Therefore, we will grant to quasijudgmentalism a propositional attitude short of belief which, following Roberts, we will call a construal.[11] Yet we will insist that there must be something more to construing something as dangerous or funny than just being scared or amused by it.

Quasijudgmentalists claim that their view preserves the insights of judgmentalism while offering a better account of recalcitrant emotion. Recalcitrance involves a conflict between construal and judgment; it arises when an agent emotionally construes the circumstances as being one way, despite judging otherwise. This has seemed to many philosophers to be an important advance for the judgmentalist tradition.[12] If so, then quasijudgmentalism offers a similar but more trenchant challenge to sentimentalism. It explains particular emotions in terms of independent evaluative concepts, thereby undermining the point of a sentimentalist metaethics. However, we will argue that a closer inspection of recalcitrant emotion actually tells against quasijudgmentalism, and that this modification of the theory falls prey to the same difficulties besetting the original. Our arguments will help to motivate an account of the emotions that we can only sketch here—one that is more empirically adequate, makes better sense of recalcitrance, and (not coincidentally) is friendlier to sentimentalism.

Although we are in sympathy with many of the objections raised by other recent critics of the judgmentalist tradition, such as John Deigh and Paul Griffiths, we think these critics fail to acknowledge some important insights of that tradition. Judgmentalist accounts of many specific emotions have a ring of truth that itself requires some

[11] We take it to be a burden of the quasijudgmentalist position to better explain the nature of the construals claimed to be necessary for being in an emotional state. They need to make plausible their central claim that recalcitrant episodes, which are granted not to involve belief, must nevertheless involve some other, independently specifiable propositional attitude toward the characteristic thought.

[12] See Patricia Greenspan, *Emotions and Reason: An Inquiry into Emotional Justification* (London: Routledge & Kegan Paul, 1988); Robert Roberts, 'What an Emotion Is: A Sketch,' *The Philosophical Review* (1988), pp. 183–209.

sort of philosophical explication—after all, fear certainly seems to have *something* to do with thoughts of danger. Even if we are correct in rejecting the claim that evaluative thoughts are necessary constituents of emotions, there are undeniable intimacies between such thoughts and emotions. When people are frightened they typically do believe themselves, or those they care about, to be in danger. And when people sincerely disavow the belief that there is any such danger, they typically are not afraid. (The same can be said, mutatis mutandis, for a range of other emotions and beliefs.) This is the case when things are working properly; it is the standard case. Moreover, these patterns are enshrined in norms that call for feeling various emotions only when the relevant judgment is thought to be warranted or correct. There seems to be some kind of mistake involved in being afraid where there is no danger (or evidence of it). These intimacies between thought and emotion reflect the kernel of truth in Hume's notorious claim that 'a passion must be accompany'd with some false judgment, in order to its being unreasonable.'[13] We contend that any adequate account of the emotions must make sense of these data, which have traditionally been adduced in defence of judgmentalism.

Of course, Hume was overly sanguine about the power of norms of rationality to govern our feelings. He follows the above quotation by claiming that '[t]he moment we perceive the falsehood of any supposition...our passions yield to our reason without any opposition.'[14] But the existence of recalcitrant episodes of emotion shows that this is an exaggeration. Emotions do not always yield to judgment, even when one thinks they should. On the view we favour, the thoughts that judgmentalists and quasijudgmentalists treat as constituents of emotion are better understood as a special type of normative standard for emotions. These are what we have elsewhere called norms of fittingness.'[15] Crudely put, considerations of fittingness are all and only those considerations about whether to feel shame, amusement, fear, and so forth that bear on whether the emotion's evaluation of the circumstances gets it right: whether the situation really is shameful, funny, fearsome, and so forth. Norms of fittingness are one kind of rational norm for appraising emotional responses—albeit an especially important and effective kind—and

[13] Hume, *Treatise*, p. 416.
[14] Hume, ibid., p. 416.
[15] See D'Arms and Jacobson, 'The Moralistic Fallacy: On the "Appropriateness" of Emotion,' *Philosophy and Phenomenological Research* 61 (2000), pp. 65–90. Also see D'Arms and Jacobson, 'Sentiment and Value,' *Ethics* **110** (2000), pp. 722–48.

Significance of recalcitrant emotion (or, anti-quasijudgmentalism)

they must be distinguished from other forms of appraisal. Some reasons not to be afraid of a growling dog, for instance, do not bear on whether it is fearsome: for instance, that dogs can 'smell fear' or that a good parent would set a better example of bravery. Unfortunately, such moral or strategic considerations are unlikely to alter our feelings, at least in the short term. By contrast, considerations of fittingness, such as the fact that it is just a Pug—a very small breed of dog—and hence poses no real danger, are especially likely (though by no means guaranteed) to help us control our emotional response. A full defence of our view is not possible here, but some of its advantages will emerge as we undertake the central critical project of this paper: to argue against quasijudgmentalism.

II

Our objections to quasijudgmentalism concern its methodology for type-individuating emotions by their constitutive thoughts. Since this defining-propositions methodology is inherited from classical judgmentalism, our argument here will be directed against both theories in this tradition. Some of these problems have been noted before. The claim that emotions have constitutive thoughts seems incompatible with attributing them to animals and infants, who lack the requisite concepts. Furthermore, the defining-propositions methodology allows emotions to be constructed by combining any constitutive thought with an affect—that is, a state of comfort or discomfort. Hence, as Griffiths has noted, these theories seem to have no explanation for why some such combinations are realized in the economy of human mental life and others are not.[16] Our worry is less with the potential for infinite multiplication of unrealized emotions than with the possibility of infinitesimal division between cognate emotions. This threatens to turn seemingly genuine disputes over the nature of an emotion into merely terminological quarrels.

The judgmentalist methodology seems to license exceedingly fine-grained distinctions between emotions, which can obscure their fundamental similarities. The usefulness of Roberts' distinction between friendly and invidious envy, for instance, can easily be doubted.[17] This distinction, which is motivated by the desire to

[16] Paul Griffiths, *What Emotions Really Are* (Chicago: University of Chicago Press, 1997), pp. 41–43.
[17] See Robert Roberts, 'Jealously and Anger' (MS) and 'What is Wrong with Wicked Feelings?,' *American Philosophical Quarterly* **28** (1991), pp. 13–24.

differentiate morally permissible envy from more vicious strains, does so by assimilating the benign form with mere longing. As a result, it renders mysterious the ambivalence that people notoriously feel toward their friends' unmatched successes—even people who admire their friends and genuinely wish them well. This is just one example, but it is hardly unique. There is considerable internal disagreement within the tradition: for instance, over how to differentiate guilt from remorse, and regret from (what is called) agent-regret, through the nuances of their propositional content. Sometimes these distinctions track ordinary language reasonably well, and sometimes they mark philosophically important differences. But it would not be much of an exaggeration to say that there are as many ways of differentiating guilt, remorse, regret, agent-regret, and so forth as there are judgmentalists. This is doubly problematic. In the first place, it is puzzling why there should be so much disagreement about what thoughts are required for a given emotion. Moreover, it is hard to see how these disputes are to be settled, especially because it is always open to a judgmentalist faced with counterexample to rescue his theory by drawing yet another distinction.

To illustrate, consider the dispute between Greenspan and Gabrielle Taylor over the nature of guilt. They disagree not only over whether guilt can be vicarious, but also over whether it requires that one construe oneself as morally, or merely causally, responsible. Taylor's claim that guilt 'cannot arise from the deeds or omissions of others'[18] seems vulnerable to Greenspan's counterexample of liberal guilt: guilt felt by people of a certain political persuasion toward the bad deeds of their fellow citizens, co-religionists, and the like. But Taylor could avoid refutation by adducing a different but related emotion that *can* (by definition) be held vicariously, and insisting that the term 'guilt' be reserved for her preferred cases. The defining-propositions methodology seems to ensure that counterexample can be avoided by the coining of another distinct emotion. The trouble here is familiar from other intractable disputes over conceptual analysis: that what seems like a substantive disagreement may become merely semantic. The judgmentalist tradition has trouble making sense of the many different articulations of a given emotion offered by its proponents, in a way that preserves the substance and univocity of the debate.

Even when judgmentalists agree on an intuitively plausible gloss

---

[18] Gabrielle Taylor, *Pride, Shame and Guilt: Emotions of self-assessment* (Oxford: Clarendon Press, 1985), p. 91.

of an emotion's evaluative concern, we hold that they misdiagnose their accomplishment. Understood as an account of the thoughts necessary to have a given emotion, even the best glosses either are subject to counterexample, or else succeed only because the relevant thought can be attributed to an agent simply because he is feeling the emotion. Consider again Foot's claims about pride, which we take to be about as plausible an articulation of its content as can be given. 'It may seem reasonable to say that given certain behaviour a man can be described as showing that he is proud of something, whatever that something may be,' she writes, but 'if he does not hold the right beliefs about it then whatever his attitude is it is not pride.'[19] In order for an agent to be proud of something, he must believe it to be an achievement or advantage of his; it must be 'in some way splendid and in some way [his] own.'[20] Despite its plausibility, we think this claim either is false or fails to impose the substantive constraint it is supposed to provide: an independent belief necessary in order to be proud. We will argue that this problem cannot be solved by moving from a judgmentalist to a quasijudgmentalist analysis and, moreover, that the problem does not lie with the substance of the gloss but with the theory in which it is embedded.

What should Foot say about the pride that football fans commonly take in the triumphs of the team they follow? On first glance, her analysis seems to make it logically impossible for someone to be proud of the team's achievements without believing them to be his own doing—which is to say, without delusion. But surely the typical football fan does not really believe himself responsible for the triumph; it is not 'his' in that sense. Of course, quasijudgmentalism need not ascribe any such belief to the fan. It therefore seems to have a great advantage here, similar to its advantage in cases of recalcitrance. But what advance is really made by claiming that the fan construes the triumph as his own, or that he thinks of it that way? Surely he need not have any extravagant thoughts about his own role in the outcome. This is where some of the attraction of quasijudgmentalism seems specious, inasmuch as it rests on an attribution that, in a pinch, can be made simply in virtue of the fact that someone has the relevant emotion. What sense can be made of the possessive pronouns that arise in glosses of pride, guilt, and many other emotions? We contend that by claiming thoughts of possession to be a necessary constituent of pride, the judgmentalist tradition has things backwards. The sense in which the club's

---

[19] Foot, 'Moral Beliefs,' p. 113.
[20] Foot, 'Hume on Moral Judgement,' p. 76.

accomplishments belong to the fan is simply that he is able to be proud of them. It is, after all, 'his team'—but in this sense only. Should the quasijudgmentalist fall back on the claim that the fan *feels as if* the triumph were his own, we would suggest that the only sense in which this is true is the trivializing sense: he is proud of it. Hence, neither Foot's claim nor its quasijudgmentalist variant supplies any real constraint on what counts as an episode of pride. And the same is true of guilt, shame, and other emotions.

Yet the obvious plausibility of Foot's gloss, and some others like it, seems to demand explanation. We will suggest that what these glosses capture must be reinterpreted, not as a logical requirement for what to count as pride, but as circumscribing the conditions under which that feeling is fitting. Philosophers inclined to view the fan's pride as bizarre can hold that his emotional involvement is unfitting. They can claim, with some plausibility, that it is silly to take pride in the accomplishments of a team to which you do not actually belong. Reflection on the sort of identification involved in pride might lead one to conclude that there is nothing to be proud of here; but then it might not. What is at issue between the fan and the philosopher is how to feel about the triumphs of 'your' team—not how it is advantageous or even admirable to feel, but what feeling is fitting.

The judgment that an emotion is fitting is an evaluative judgment—for instance, that something is funny, shameful, or worthy of pride. Because people must be allowed to have different standards of fittingness, these questions must be contestable; they cannot be settled by conceptual analysis or linguistic fiat. But if accounts like Foot's are reinterpreted as attempts to circumscribe the conditions under which an emotion is fitting, then these glosses must be considered rough-and-ready, even in principle. That is to say, the specific terms in which an articulation is given are provisional, open to revision, and cannot be read in a strict or literal sense. It follows that there can be no empirical fact of the matter about whether something counts as *yours*, as *dangerous*, or as *contaminated* in the sense that determines questions of the fittingness of pride, fear, and disgust. Nevertheless, some articulations of the evaluation characteristic of an emotion are better than others, for reasons yet to be explained. There are facts about pride, including not just its phenomenology but the behaviour it motivates, which vindicate Foot's gloss, properly understood. Although almost anything *can* be an object of pride, it is nevertheless much easier to take some things as splendid achievements of yours than others, and there are many things that cannot *plausibly* be so taken. We will presently suggest how it is that an emotion like pride can be understood to provide a framework for considerations of fittingness, without essentially involving any particular thoughts. Thus far, our primary aim has been to call the judgmentalist tradition into question, while gesturing at an alternative explanation of its insights.

III

Before proceeding, we should note several respects in which we grant that thoughts are typically involved in emotional experience. First, most (human) emotional episodes can be described as, in some sense, essentially involving belief. One cannot be angry that one was denied tenure, for instance, without believing that one was denied tenure. Moreover, beliefs about the granting and denial of tenure can be understood without any appeal to anger sensibilities. In general, if an episode of emotion is properly called 'anger that P,' then this is sufficient to ensure that it involves the belief P.[21] But P here specifies thoughts about the object of this particular emotional episode, rather than identifying a thought common to all instances of anger. Hence, this is no concession to the judgmentalist enterprise of analysing emotion kinds like anger in terms of logically prior concepts.

It must also be granted that mental states can be grouped together in any way one likes—though not every grouping will be equally fruitful. Someone could take all the episodes of anger-that-one-was-denied-tenure together and treat them as a type of anger. This might be called 'tenure-denial anger' or, more colourfully and simply, 'tenure rage.' Unless we wanted to quarrel over what can constitute an emotion type (which we do not), we would have to grant that tenure rage can be counted as one (which we do). Tenure rage is what we will call a *cognitive sharpening* of anger. These are types constructed by specifying a subclass of instances of an emotion, or other affective state, in terms of some thought that they happen to share. There are indefinitely many possible cognitive sharpenings, and in some cases there are already words for these states, such as homesickness, religious awe, and resentment. Hence, we grant that there are affect-laden, intentional mental states—these

---

[21] The guarantee is provided, in effect, by the logic of ascriptions of this sort. See Robert Gordon, *The Structure of Emotions* (New York: Cambridge University Press, 1987), for a detailed and helpful discussion of this logic.

Justin D'Arms and Daniel Jacobson

cognitive sharpenings—that essentially involve particular beliefs or thoughts, just as judgmentalists and quasijudgmentalists claim about emotions.[22]

Our dispute with the judgmentalist tradition thus does not concern every type of state that can be named with emotion terms. Rather, we are concerned more specifically with the paradigmatic emotion kinds, such as amusement, anger, contempt, disgust, embarrassment, envy, fear, guilt, jealousy, joy, pity, pride, shame, and sorrow. This list is provisional, and we are not crucially committed to including all its members; but we will note that it closely resembles the lists of pan-cultural emotions adduced by psychologists with disparate theoretical approaches, such as Paul Ekman, Richard Lazarus, and Tooby and Cosmides.[23] To avoid some ancillary controversies over the term 'basic emotions,' we will refer to these as natural emotion kinds. Because of its defining-propositions methodology, judgmentalism seems committed to understanding the role of thought in natural emotion kinds as analogous to its role in the states produced by cognitive sharpening. We will argue that there is a crucial disanalogy between the role played by propositional thought in these two kinds of sentiment. To make this contrast clearer, we need to say more about the natural emotions.

Consider, then, a contrasting approach. Think of the natural emotion kinds as products of relatively discrete special-purpose mechanisms that are sensitive to some important aspect of human life. Emotions evolved for their adaptive value in dealing with what psychologists have called 'fundamental life tasks,' 'universal human predicaments,' or 'recurrent adaptive situations'—especially but not exclusively social situations.[24] These include 'fighting, falling in love, escaping predators, confronting sexual infidelity, and so on,

---

[22] It is also possible to circumscribe or 'sharpen' natural emotion kinds in other ways, for instance by their causes or motivations. We are inclined to think that such attitudes as spite and vengefulness, which are sometimes included on lists of the emotions, are better understood as motivational sharpenings of one (or more) natural emotions.

[23] See Paul Ekman, 'All Emotions are Basic' and Richard Lazarus, 'Appraisals: The Long and the Short of It' in Ekman, Paul and Richard J. Davidson, *The Nature of Emotion: Fundamental Questions* (New York: Oxford University Press, 1994). See also J. Tooby and L. Cosmides, 'The Past Explains the Present: Emotional Adaptations and the Structure of Ancestral Environment,' *Ethology and Sociobiology* **11** (1990), pp. 375–424.

[24] These phrases are due to Ekman, Johnson-Laird and Oatley, and Tooby and Cosmides, respectively.

each [of which] recurred innumerable times in evolutionary history.'[25] The fear system, for instance, can plausibly be described as monitoring the environment for threats to the organism, even if (as neuroscientist Joseph LeDoux claims) there are distinct pathways into the syndrome known as fear: a syndrome of directed attention, physiological changes, affect, and motivation that can be functionally understood as constituting a kind of appraisal of the circumstances.[26] There may be no better way of articulating that appraisal than by saying that it involves construing oneself to be in imminent danger; but it does not follow that, in order to feel fear, one must deploy this or any other concept.[27]

Our general view is that all natural emotion kinds—in contrast to cognitive sharpenings and various other states one might call sentiments—are subserved by discrete, non-linguistic mechanisms. Of course, the precise nature of these mechanisms may vary, as well as the degree to which they interact with, and enlist output from, various other cognitive systems. Because it is a matter for empirical study which of the states commonly called emotions fit this account, our catalogue of the class of natural emotions is provisional. But we should note that we think it plausible to include several complex, social emotions for which there are no non-human homologues. And we are sceptical about the claims of some anthropologists that certain exotic cultures do not experience paradigm natural emotions such as anger or sadness—a scepticism shared by most (though admittedly not all) psychologists working on the emotions.

In order to show how these considerations are supposed to apply to some of the states on our list of natural emotions, let us consider a few more cases. Jealousy monitors the social environment for potential losses of affection or allegiance, especially (though not solely) from mates. Its characteristic appraisal is perhaps best interpreted in terms of *defection*. Again, though, the fact that this concept is part of the best articulation of the emotion's locus of concern does not imply that the capacity for jealousy requires possession of the concept of defection—or even that it can only be articulated in those terms. Similarly for anger and *slights*, shame and *disability of mine*, contempt and *disability of yours*, disgust and *contamination*, amusement and *incongruity*, or envy and the concept

[25] Tooby and Cosmides, 'The Past Explains the Present,' pp. 407–8.
[26] Joseph LeDoux, *The Emotional Brain* (New York: Simon & Schuster, 1996).
[27] And there are empirical reasons for doubting this, several of which are catalogued by Paul Griffiths.

139

Justin D'Arms and Daniel Jacobson

difference in possession or position between myself and a rival that is, considered in itself, bad for me.[28]

IV

To this point, we have offered some reasons for doubting whether quasijudgmentalism can succeed in identifying specific thoughts that are essential constituents of natural emotion kinds. The alternative approach we have described is sketchy and incomplete, and we cannot adequately develop or defend it here. But we can offer one further consideration in its favour, which is directly relevant to our challenge to the judgmentalist tradition. We will argue that this account of the natural emotions illuminates the phenomenon of emotional recalcitrance, which strict judgmentalism cannot easily accommodate and quasijudgmentalism cannot adequately explain. Our explanation will account for a fact that has hitherto gone unnoticed: that recalcitrance is much more familiar with respect to the natural emotions than it is for the many possible cognitive sharpenings.

A recalcitrant emotion was previously characterized as a bout of emotion that exists despite the agent's making a judgment in tension with it. This somewhat vague description was buttressed with familiar examples, primarily that of the phobic who is afraid of something despite believing it to pose little or no danger. We will now add that *stable* emotional recalcitrance is a standing disposition to have recalcitrant bouts of a particular emotion. For example, fear of flying is amenable to stable recalcitrance, since it typically exists as a long-term disposition that is relatively insensitive to contextual features of the situation, such as where one is flying and with whom. The quasijudgmentalist supposes that what is happening in cases of stable recalcitrance is that one is subject to recurring thoughts that conflict with the judgments one sincerely avows, draws inferences from, and uses in practical decision-making. This might often be true, but it is important to ask why recalcitrance should occur at all.

Our account offers a straightforward if schematic explanation: recalcitrance is the product of two distinct evaluative systems, one

[28] We suspect that envy is a natural emotion kind, in part because of the ubiquity of social hierarchy in human (and primate) groups, but whether it is best articulated in terms of *possession* or *position* will likely differ according to contingencies concerning the degree of materialism in a given culture.

emotional and the other linguistic. Because these are discrete modes of evaluation, only one of which involves the deployment of conceptual capacities, it is possible for them to diverge systematically. It is to be expected, then, that recalcitrance will be far more familiar and stable with respect to the natural emotions than to cognitive sharpenings, because only when an affective state is the product of some discrete evaluative mechanism can it compete seriously with our judgments. We can also explain why some fear responses are especially difficult to unseat, whereas others yield more readily to cognitive supervision. As Martin Seligman and Randolph Nesse have shown, the most commonly diagnosed phobias are directed at objects that plausibly reflect an evolutionary preparation to be sensitive to the dangers that faced ancestral human populations: such things as insects, snakes, and heights.[29] Of course, that fact does not make common bugs, garter snakes, or roller coasters fearsome—that is, fitting of fear—though it explains why they often elicit fear. It is because we are capable of assessing risks independently of our sense of fear, and because most of us consider risks to life and limb to be fearsome, that this evolutionary story also explains the prevalence of recalcitrant fear of such objects.[30]

For quasijudgmentalism, the phenomenon of recalcitrance is more mysterious, and stable recalcitrance is especially problematic. Why do the putatively constitutive thoughts of certain emotions continually reassert themselves despite their conflict with considered judgment? After all, people are not generally vulnerable to recalcitrant thoughts contravening their settled judgments. We are prepared to grant that occasional non-stable recalcitrant belief is

[29] Martin Seligman, 'Phobias and Preparedness,' *Behaviour Therapy* **2** (1971), pp. 307–20; Randolph Nesse, 'Evolutionary Explanations of Emotions,' *Human Nature* **1** (1990), pp. 261–89.

[30] By 'risk' here we mean something that can be studied actuarially, such as the relative probabilities of dying on a car trip and a plane trip. One could call this danger, but the cost of that semantic decision is to make certain questions senseless. We cannot then ask whether it is dangerous to take up a hobby that often proves habit-forming. The question at hand is not just the chance that one forms the habit, but whether being so habituated is something to fear (as it may appear from outside) or not (as it is likely to seem upon immersion in the activity). The crucial choice is whether to leave 'danger' as an ambiguous term, or to pin it down by associating it either with risk (the empirical concept) or with fearsomeness (the evaluative concept). To make the first choice is to forego analysing the fearsome in terms of the dangerous, whereas to make the second choice is to render such an analysis uninformative.

possible, as is stable recalcitrant perception. The Muller-Lyer lines continue to appear to be of different lengths even after we are convinced that they are equal. But persistent optical illusion has the same type of explanation that we suggested for emotional recalcitrance: it is the product of a special-purpose information processing system (the visual system), which operates with a considerable degree of independence from higher cognition and is therefore capable of persistent conflict with it.[31] Because the judgmentalist tradition is committed to defining the appraisals characteristic of emotional experience in terms of independently available concepts, it is forced to treat conflicts between an agent's emotions and her judgments as competing exercises of conceptual thought. It also renders unavailable the analogy to recalcitrant perceptual experience, such as optical and auditory illusions. This makes emotional recalcitrance a strange sort of brute fact about certain concepts: that we tend to have recalcitrant, affect-laden thoughts involving them.

Since it treats the role of thought in natural emotions as analogous to its role in cognitive sharpenings, the judgmentalist tradition also has no principled basis on which to explain why the former, and not the latter, are subject to stable recalcitrance. Why aren't people prone to recalcitrant bouts of cognitively sharpened sentiments: homesickness when they know they are really at home, religious awe though they disbelieve in God, or tenure rage when they realize they actually got tenure? These examples may seem unfair. It can be objected that while concepts such as danger, possession, and contamination are nebulous, and rest uneasily between the empirical and the evaluative, it is a simple fact that either you were granted tenure or not. After all, fear of flying is our central example of recalcitrance, but you don't find recalcitrant bouts of that emotion when someone doesn't believe that she is or will be flying. But in fact this observation bolsters our point. The form of recalcitrant fear of flying that actually exists is simply recalcitrant fear, because the judgment it is in tension with is a judgment about danger: the appraisal characteristic of fear in general. If fear of flying is considered as a distinct type of emotion, a cognitive sharpening of fear involving the thought that one is flying, then on our view it will *not* be amenable to recalcitrance. For fear of flying to be recalcitrant qua cognitive sharpening, a person would have to be in that state despite

---

[31] We are not claiming total independence, which would amount to denying that perception is to some degree theory-laden. Nevertheless, one's knowledge that the stick is straight does not keep it from appearing bent when partially submerged.

judging that she is not flying. This is psychologically implausible because the judgments conflict too directly.

But perhaps this case is too easy. Consider resentment, which we claimed earlier not to be a natural emotion but a cognitive sharpening. In fact, the term has several senses in ordinary language; it is used both to refer to moralized anger and moralized envy. Here we will focus on the moralized anger sense, the constitutive thought of which is that one has not merely been slighted but wronged. Our claim, then, is that recalcitrant anger will be much more prevalent and stable than recalcitrant resentment. Suppose you believe that because you deserve tenure, you were wronged by not getting it. This bothers you. It is resentment, not merely anger, you feel; but it is not recalcitrant resentment because you believe yourself to have been wronged. Imagine, though, that in a cooler hour (or year) you come to doubt the grounds of your complaint. You may still be disposed to *anger* at the senior members of the department, but will you be prone to recalcitrant *resentment* of them? Will you continue to resent the committee despite thinking that they made a just decision? We think not. You may waver in your judgment about whether or not you got a raw deal, but the more you judge that you have not been wronged, the more difficult it will be to understand yourself as resenting those who made the decision. Why attribute thoughts of a moral compliant to someone who does not believe them, simply because he remains angry? This seems to be a gratuitous attribution of conflicting beliefs, where a simpler explanation of the situation is available.

These observations about when stable recalcitrant emotions do and do not occur help to bolster our view that there is a fundamental distinction to be drawn here. The distinction is between the natural emotion kinds and other sentiments, including cognitive sharpenings: that is, type-identifications of emotions that can be said to have constitutive thoughts but, for that reason, are not susceptible to stable recalcitrance.

V

Our arguments offer some guidance on the initial question about the order of priority between emotions and evaluative judgments. With respect to the natural emotion kinds, the answer is that they are prior to, and partially fix the content of, the concepts used to regulate them. An experience of shame or fear involves a distinctive sort of emotional evaluation, and the judgment that something is shameful or fearsome must be understood in terms of such appraisals. But the critics of sentimentalism were not entirely wrong. There also exist a wide range of states, which we have called cognitive sharpenings, that are best understood as involving beliefs or thoughts. These states are not amenable to sentimentalism precisely because they are compatible with a judgmentalist account.

The view that the natural emotions are not well explained by the judgmentalist tradition is not new with us. We have already mentioned Deigh and Griffiths as fellow sceptics. Deigh has argued that at least some instances of irrational fear are not helpfully regarded as embodying false thoughts. He writes of such cases that: 'What makes the fear unreasonable is not that it contains a faulty belief but rather that it is felt despite a sound belief that *should have* immunized its subject from feeling this fear. What makes it unreasonable, that is, is not faulty reasoning resulting in false thoughts, but rather the persistence of a tropism that *should have* yielded to sound reasoning and firm belief.'[32] We agree. But this passage also illustrates a puzzle that has not been addressed by the contemporary critics of judgmentalism. If fear is indeed a tropism—an involuntary, reflexive reaction — then in what sense is it *unreasonable* when one knows one isn't in danger? If fear need not involve the thought that one is in danger, then why should it yield to the judgment that one is *not* actually in danger, as Deigh suggests? In what sense is it recalcitrant?

Our answer must be brief, but we hope it is suggestive. Suppose for the moment that the general picture of the natural emotions as special-purpose mechanisms of the mind is compelling. Although we have argued against the central claim of judgmentalism, we want to suggest that its critics have gone too far in repudiating that philosophical tradition. Even with respect to relatively primitive emotions, which are most plausibly shared with other animals—such as fear and disgust—occurrence in the context of human mental life involves them in complex interactions with beliefs and desires. One such complexity is that human beings are evidently able to exert some measure of rational control over their emotional responses. This forces us to think critically about the emotions and to try to interpret the significance of their concerns. Such interpretation is mandatory because we are not merely prone to emotional episodes as bouts of feeling; they also move us to action—indeed, that is their primary function. Furthermore, emotional evaluations insinuate themselves into more richly conceptualized systems of motivation,

[32] John Deigh, 'Cognitivism in the Theory of Emotions,' *Ethics* **104** (1994). pp. 850–51. Emphasis added.

evaluation, and intention. These tendencies make it imperative for us to reflect on our own emotions and those of others. In this endeavour, we have no other option but to articulate their appraisals in language. We can be assisted by reflection on the function of the mechanisms subserving them, but we must not suppose that such reflection can settle whether an emotion is fitting, for this is a normative question which must remain open to dispute.

To judge an emotion is fitting is not to think it adaptive but to endorse its evaluation as correct. This is a kind of a higher-order attitude toward the emotion, which we reify by wielding a vocabulary of regulative terms such as *fearsome*, *shameful*, and *funny*. Without knowing what guilt and shame are about, we could still identify them as painful; and we could even criticize them, in light of their behavioural manifestations, as disadvantageous or immoral. But these considerations do not speak to our assessment of the accuracy of their appraisals. Only considerations of fittingness can do that and, hence, can ground the specific force of 'should' in Deigh's claim that an unreasonable emotion should yield to sound reasoning and belief.

If we are right, then the best way to think of these necessarily rough-and-ready interpretations is not as producing thoughts that are even partly constitutive of the emotions themselves, but as providing standards of fittingness which we use to judge and criticize our emotions in a distinctive fashion. Ironically, then, it is only by rejecting the central theoretical claim of the judgmentalist tradition that its true legacy can be preserved. This legacy comes from the theory's fundamentally correct sense that there is an intimacy between emotion and judgment, and from the many sensitive and insightful things that various philosophers (as well as novelists, psychologists, and others) have noticed about the nature of particular human emotions.[33]

[33] Earlier versions of this paper were presented to the Ohio Reading Group in Ethics, the Franklin & Marshall Colloquium in Moral Psychology, and the Royal Institute of Philosophy. We wish to thank those institutions for their support, and the audiences for their comments. We are especially grateful to Talbot Brewer, Janice Dowell, Bennett Helm, Karen Jones, Sigrun Svavarsdottir and David Velleman.

IX. The Logic of Emotions

AARON BEN-ZE'EV

The issue of whether emotions are rational (or intelligent) is at the centre of philosophical and psychological discussions. I believe that emotions are rational, but that they follow different principles to those of intellectual reasoning. The purpose of this paper is to reveal the unique logic of emotions. I begin by suggesting that we should conceive of emotions as a general mode of the mental system; other modes are the perceptual and intellectual modes. One feature distinguishing one mode from another is the logical principles underlying its information processing mechanism. Before describing these principles, I clarify the notion of 'rationality,' arguing that in an important sense emotions can be rational.

Emotion as a general mode of the mental system

It is beyond the scope of this paper to discuss the nature of emotions, but I must mention a few aspects regarding this in order to clarify claims concerning the logic of emotions.

An emotion is not a mental state, such as hearing a noise or having a toothache; nor is it a mere disposition, as are beliefs and desires. An emotion is also not a capacity, as are sensation, perception, memory, imagination, and thought; nor is it an intentional mode of reference, as are cognition, evaluation and motivation. It is also not a mere feeling, as is a thrill.

I have suggested that an emotion is a general mental mode of the mental system.[1] A general mental mode includes various mental elements and expresses a dynamic functioning arrangement of the mental system. The kinds of elements involved in a certain mode and the particular arrangement of these elements constitute the uniqueness of each mode. The emotional mode involves the activation of certain dispositions and the presence of some actualized states. It also includes the operation of various mental capacities and the use of different kinds of intentional references. This mode involves cognition, evaluation, motivation, and feeling.

Other possible modes are, for example, the perceptual and the

[1] Ben-Ze'ev, forthcoming.

intellectual modes. The perceptual mode is the most basic mental mode. It involves being aware of our immediate environment without being engaged in a complex intellectual activity and without being in the midst of a stormy emotional experience. Perception is the major capacity used in the perceptual mode; other capacities involved in this mode are memory and imagination. A more extensive use of the latter capacities is found in the intellectual mode, where thinking is the basic capacity.

I suggest distinguishing the various mental modes on the basis of a few categories:

(a) Basic *psychological features*;
(b) Basic types of *information-processing mechanisms*;
(c) Basic *logical principles* of information processing.

The category of psychological features may be divided into characteristics, such as complexity, instability, and intensity, and components, such as evaluation and motivation. Schematic mechanisms and deliberative mechanisms are examples of information-processing mechanisms. Logical principles are those determining the significance of events—for example, whether change or stability is of greater significance.

I focus here on the third issue. In order to have a more comprehensive picture of the emotional mode, I will say a few words about the first two issues.[2]

In describing the basic characteristics of a mental mode, we can refer to the following features: complexity of the mode, the stability and dynamism of the mode, the extent (intensity) of using the various capacities, the focus of the various modes of reference, and the duration of a typical state in such a mode. The emotional mode can be characterized as highly complex, greatly unstable, highly intense, using a partial perspective and lasting for a relatively brief period. In contrast, the intellectual mode is typically somewhat less complex, more stable, not so intense, having a broader perspective and longer duration. In comparison with the emotional mode, the perceptual mode is less complex, more stable, less intense, having more restricted perspective and can last longer.

The complexity of the emotional mode stems from the fact that it consists of elements belonging to various ontological levels; hence, its explanation requires a reference to various levels of discussion. Another feature related to the complexity of the emotional

---

[2] For a detailed discussion of these issues, see Ben-Ze'ev, (2000), chaps 2–3.

mode is its comprehensiveness. More than any other mental mode, the emotional mode involves the activation of most mental elements. Emotions indicate a transition, during which the preceding context has changed, but no new context has yet stabilized; accordingly, emotions are often tempestuous. Emotions are associated with urgency and heat, and exhibit relatively great intensity. Emotions help us to mobilize many resources in order to face the unstable situation. Emotions are partial in two basic senses: they are focused on a narrow target, such as one person or a very few people; and they express a personal and interested perspective. Typical emotions are essentially transient states with brief duration. The typical temporal structure of an emotional response involves a swift rise-time, taking less than half a minute in most cases, followed by a relatively slow decay. In addition to the above emotional characteristics, there are four basic emotional components: cognition, evaluation, motivation, and feeling. The first three components are intentional; the fourth is not.

The second feature that distinguishes various mental modes concerns their *information-processing mechanisms*. In light of the different features of each mental mode, it is plausible that each mode relies upon a different information-processing mechanism. In this regard, a distinction can be made between two major kinds of mechanisms: schematic and deliberative. Whereas a schematic mechanism is most typical of the perceptual mode, and to a lesser extent also of the emotional mode, a deliberative mechanism is most typical of the intellectual mode.

A schematic mechanism is a kind of dispositional mechanism expressing past knowledge. It typically involves spontaneous responses depending on a more tacit and elementary evaluative system. Schematic activity is typically fast, automatic, and is accompanied by little awareness. Since these schemes are part of our psychological constitution, we do not need time to create them; we simply need the appropriate circumstances to activate them. A deliberative mechanism typically involves slow and conscious processes, which are largely under voluntary control.[3]

This paper focuses on the third feature of the emotional mode of the mental system, namely, the logical principles of information processing typical of emotions. If indeed such principles can be described, we may be able to speak about the logic of emotions and hence to substantiate the rationality of emotions.

[3] For further discussion of this distinction, see, e.g., Ben-Ze'ev, (1993), chap. 4; Smith & Kirby, (2000).

Aaron Ben-Ze'ev

Two senses of rationality and intelligence

Before describing the logical principles typical of the emotional mode, I would like to clarify the notion of 'rationality.' This will enable me to claim that in certain circumstances emotions are rational.

Traditionally, something would be considered to be rational in light of one of the following two senses: (a) a descriptive sense, in that the generation of X involves intellectual calculations, and (b) a normative sense, in that X may express an appropriate response in the given circumstances.

The two senses have often been identified, although they are different: something can be rational in one sense, but not in the other. The failure to distinguish between the two senses, which underlies much of the heated dispute about the rationality of emotions, is related to a misconception of the descriptive sense. The normative sense, in light of which rationality is involved in generating appropriate responses, is not disputable; descriptions of the psychological mechanism responsible for such a response are more open to dispute.

When we arrive by chance at a certain appropriate response, the psychological mechanism involved in this response would not usually be regarded as rational. Rationality of a mechanism should express certain consistent regularities by which appropriate responses are generated. If someone tosses a coin in order to make a decision, then even if in some cases her decisions are appropriate, the agent's behaviour is not rational because the mechanism underlying it does not generate a consistent pattern of appropriate responses.

Identifying the descriptive sense of rationality with intellectual calculations stems from the assumption that only the intellect can express a consistent pattern of appropriate responses. For those hard-line rationalists who identify the laws of the intellect with the laws of reality, this assumption is natural. This assumption is also plausible for other people who consider the intellect to be the general mental capacity most able to take account of all types of circumstances.

Indeed, it would appear that intellectual calculations generate appropriate responses in a more regular and consistent manner than any other psychological mechanism. In this sense, their use may be regarded as rational in more circumstances than those of other mechanisms. Nevertheless, there are various types of circumstances where such usage typically renders responses that are not appropriate. Examples of such circumstances are cases of sudden changes—where much relevant data is missing, and speed is more important than accuracy—or when the agent is not calm enough to make the relevant intellectual calculations. In these circumstances, it is not rational (in the optimal sense) to use the intellectual capacity.

Once we admit the presence of circumstances where intellectual calculations do not generate the optimal response, the traditional identification of the descriptive and optimal senses of rationality is revealed as mistaken. This opens the door for recognizing that other types of psychological mechanisms may be regarded as rational in the sense that they generate appropriate responses in a regular and consistent manner. I believe that the emotional mechanism is such an example.

Emotions are often rational in the normative sense: frequently, they are the most appropriate response. In many cases, emotions, rather than deliberative, intellectual calculations, offer the best means to achieve our optimal response. This may be true from a cognitive point of view—emotions may supply the most reliable information in the given circumstances; from a moral point of view—the emotional response is the best moral response in the given circumstances; or from a functional point of view—emotions constitute the most efficient response in the given circumstances. Emotions are the optimal response in many circumstances associated with their generation, that is, when we face a sudden significant change in our situation but have limited and imperfect resources with which to cope with it. In these circumstances, the emotional response is often optimal, because optimal conditions for the normal functioning of the intellectual mode are absent. In such cases, it is rational (in the normative sense) to behave nonrationally (in the traditional, descriptive sense).

Emotions are essentially nonrational in the traditional descriptive sense, since they are typically not the result of deliberative, intellectual calculations. Deliberative calculations are not required for the emotional mode to process information rationally in the normative sense: reason in emotions is not simply a matter of calculation but first of all a matter of sensibility.

Abandoning the exclusivity of the traditional usage of 'rationality' enables us to admit the presence of other rational psychological mechanisms, such as the emotional one. This in turn enables a discussion about a logic that is different from the logic underlying intellectual deliberations.

A similar analysis can apply to the notion of 'intelligence.' Intelligence may be characterized as our ability to function in an

Aaron Ben-Ze'ev

appropriate (or even optimal) manner in complex situations. It has often been assumed that such ability is basically an intellectual ability. I reject this assumption as well and argue that this ability usually consists of both emotional and intellectual capacities. Hence, we may speak about emotional intelligence; that is, intelligence in which the emotional system plays a major role.

In order to avoid confusions between the normative and descriptive senses of 'rational' and 'intelligent,' I suggest using these terms only in the normative sense, i.e., referring to an appropriate or optimal response to the given circumstances.

The status of the logical principles

After indicating that behaviour and decision-making processes based upon emotional attitudes can be regarded as rational, I offer a description of the logical principles prevailing in the emotional domain. In describing the emotional principles, I compare them to corresponding intellectual principles. Since my focus is on the emotional mode, the description of the intellectual principles is brief and has mainly illustrative value; a more detailed discussion may formulate these principles in a somewhat different manner. The reference to logical principles of the perceptual mode is even more limited.[4]

Following Kant's distinction between formal and transcendental logic, we may distinguish between analytic rules of valid arguments and synthetic principles of reasoning. Formal logic consists of analytic rules of valid arguments, such as the rule of contradiction and identity. These rules are analytic, as they do not have any content; they simply indicate the formal rules that valid argumentation cannot violate. Synthetic rules of reasoning are principles dealing with content; they bestow meaning upon the events around us. In Kant's view, synthetic principles include categories such as causality and substance. The principle stating that every event has a cause is not a formal rule expressing analytic truth, as the notion of 'cause' is not part of the definition of an event. Nevertheless, scientific thinking

---

[4] For a discussion on the logic of perception, which does not necessarily reflect my own view on the issue, see Rock, 1983; see also Ben-Ze'ev, 1993. Among other investigations into the logic of thinking, see the particularly interesting discussion in Margolis (1987), which suggests many similarities between the logic of perception and that of thinking. For other discussions concerning the logic of emotions, see, e.g., Frijda, 1988; Redding, 1999.

adopts, so Kant argues, such a principle. Hence, causality is a synthetic principle of scientific reasoning. In a similar manner, I would like to describe some synthetic principles underlying emotional reasoning that are absent from intellectual reasoning. Both the intellectual and emotional principles do not violate analytic rules of formal logic—they merely refer to different ways of assigning meaning to given events.

In light of the synthetic and *a priori* nature of the principles of transcendental logic, these principles determine, in Kant's view, the type of phenomenal world we encounter. For Kant, there is only one type of transcendental logic and hence there are no alternative phenomenal worlds. If I assume that emotional reasoning has different synthetic principles than those of intellectual reasoning, then I should assume that emotional reality differs from intellectual reality. This, I believe, is indeed the case.

The logical principles described below should be conceived as principles of information processing determining the meaning of events around us. As is the case with other psychological generalizations, these principles are used by the majority of people in most, but not all, circumstances. The implementation of these principles may be influenced by personal or cultural factors.

Logical principles of information processing

I suggest dividing the logical principles underlying the emotional and intellectual modes into three groups, each concerned with a different type of information. Those types refer to (a) the nature of reality, (b) the impact of the given event upon the agent, and (c) the background circumstances of the agent.

A. The nature of reality

The emotional mode

1. The emotional world consists of the environment I actually perceive or in which I imagine myself to be;
2. Changes are more significant than stability;
3. A personal event is more significant than a non-personal event.

The intellectual mode

1. The environment that I actually perceive or in which I imagine myself to be constitutes a small portion of the intellectual world;

153

2. Changes are not more significant than stability; on the contrary, we should assume that there are stable regularities in the world;
3. A personal event is not necessarily more meaningful than a non-personal event.

B. The impact of the given event

The emotional mode

4. The perceived strength of an event is most significant in determining its impact;
5. The more real an event is perceived to be, the more significant it is;
6. Those who are relevant and close are more significant than those who are irrelevant and remote.

The intellectual mode

4. The objective strength of an event is what is most significant;
5. The significance of an event is not always connected to its perceived reality;
6. My psychological distance from a certain person is of no relevance in evaluating this person.

C. Background circumstances of the agent

The emotional mode

7. The more responsible I am for a certain event, the more significant the event is;
8. The less prepared I am for a certain event, the more significant the event is;
9. The issue of whether the agent deserves a certain event is greatly significant in evaluating this event.

The intellectual mode

7. My responsibility for a certain event is in many cases not relevant to its present significance;
8. My preparedness for a certain event is in many cases not relevant to its present significance;
9. The issue of whether the agent deserves a certain event is not always significant for evaluating this event.

A. The nature of reality

1. *The scope of reality*. Emotional and intellectual reasoning often refer to different types of realities: emotions are concerned with the immediate and personal reality perceived by the individual subject, while abstract thinking—the prototype of intellectual reasoning—is concerned with a more detached and objective world, which is common to all subjects. Sense perception and vivid imagination increase emotional significance, but are almost irrelevant for increasing intellectual significance.

The development of human cognition tends to take us further away from our immediate environment. Feelings of pain and enjoyment, which were developed first, express changes in the subject's body. The information provided by sense perception refers to an environment that is at some distance from the subject's body, but is still in the subject's immediate environment—the subject is still at the centre of this environment. Memory and imagination enlarge the subject's reality by referring to past circumstances and to those in which the subject imagines she could have been. Intellectual reasoning takes the cognitive content further away from the subject to events that the subject may not even be able to perceive—here, the subject is not necessarily at the centre of the intellectual world.

2. *Change and stability*. Emotions typically occur when we perceive positive or negative significant changes in our personal situation, or in the situation of those related to us. A positive or negative significant change is one that considerably interrupts or alters the stable continuity of a situation that is relevant to our concerns. Like burglar alarms going off when an intruder enters, emotions signal that something needs attention. When no attention is needed, the signaling mechanism can be switched off. Accordingly, change is emotionally much more significant than stability.[5]

The intellect is concerned with the general and the stable, whereas emotions are engaged with the personal and the volatile. The aim of the intellect is to see a specific event as a specific case of general stable regularities; the foundations of intellectual thinking are features common to individual cases. Change and instability are often taken to be the surface phenomena that are governed by stable regularities; the intellectual search is often a search for such regularities. Emotions prevail as long as a specific event can be seen as

[5] Ben-Ze'ev, 2000, 13–17; Frijda, 1988, 353–354; Spinoza, 1677, IIIp6; IIIdef.aff.; Vp39s.

mutable and unique. Accordingly, the intellect has difficulty in understanding change and movement, whereas emotions have difficulty in prevailing under stable and universal conditions. Indeed, Bergson's criticism of intellectual reasoning is based on its reliance on the stable and unchangeable, whereas reality encompasses, in his view, exactly the opposite attributes: instability and change.[6]

The emotional system is concerned with a change that is not merely an actual event, but also a potential event. Accordingly, the issue of the availability of an alternative is crucial for generating emotions: the more available the alternative—that is, the closer the imagined alternative is to reality—the more emotionally significant the event is. People react more strongly to those events in which it is easy to imagine a different outcome occurring. Hence, 'almost situations' or 'near misses' result in intense emotional effects. Thus, the fate of someone who dies in an airplane crash after switching flights evokes a stronger emotional reaction than that of a fellow traveler who was booked on the flight all along. A greater degree of alternative availability expresses the greater mental instability of our environment; changes are much more dominate in this reality.

In cool, intellectual thinking, the availability of an alternative should have no relevancy to the significance of an event. The fact that circumstances could have been different is of no importance in analysing the present impact of a given event. We may be sad at missing a close opportunity, but our 'objective' situation now is the same as it would be if no such opportunity had been available.

3. *Personal concerns*. Emotions are not detached theoretical states; they address a practical concern from a personal and interested perspective. This perspective may also include our consideration of those who are related to us and who can be considered as extensions of our egos. In the emotional mode, we look at the world from our own personal perspective, applying our own sense of personal importance to various events. Nussbaum rightly emphasizes that the personal nature of emotions does not make them necessarily egoistic. My personal perspective does not mean that I consider other people as merely of instrumental importance; I may consider them to have intrinsic worth.[7] Love and grief take such perspectives; other emotions, such as envy and pleasure-in-others'-misfortune, may express an egoistic stand.

Intellectual deliberations do not necessarily put the thinker at the centre of the world; nor do they necessarily address personal or

[6] Bergson, 1907, 155.
[7] Nussbaum, 2001, 1.V.

practical concerns. The thinker is more of a detached, objective observer who is looking for regularities independent of her existence. The perceiver is at the centre of the perceptual environment, but its personal characteristics have less influence upon that environment. The perceptual environment is more stable and less personal than the emotional environment.

To sum up, the nature of the world is different for the perceptual, emotional, and intellectual agents. Emotional reality consists of immediate, unstable, personal events, which could have been otherwise, whereas intellectual reality is more detached, stable, and more deterministic in nature. Perceptual reality is more stable and less personal than emotional reality, but it is more limited in its scope than the scope of the other two types of reality. The scope of perceptual reality is more limited than—although in some senses, also different from—that of emotional reality, which in turn is more limited than intellectual reality. Intellectual reality refers to information provided by thinking, imagination, memory, and perception, whereas emotional reality mainly refers to information provided by imagination, memory, and perception. Perceptual reality mainly refers to information provided by perception.

B. The impact of the given event

The different environments in which each mode prevails determine the significance of the event's impact upon the agent. This impact is determined by three major factors: the event's strength, the degree of reality, and the relevancy and closeness of the event.[8]

4. *The event's strength*. The strength of an event is an important factor in determining its significance; this is true for both the emotional and intellectual modes. However, whereas emotions are concerned mainly with perceived strength—the strength as the subject perceives it—intellectual deliberations are more often concerned with the objective strength of the event, independent of the subject's attitude toward it. This difference is in accordance with the greater role that personal concerns play in emotions. Perceived strength refers to the subject's personal perception, whereas objective strength is not related to the way a certain individual perceives it.

[8] In the emotional domain, these factors, as well as the factors referring to background circumstances, can be regarded as variables of emotional intensity; for detailed discussions of these variables, see Ben-Ze'ev, 2000: chap. 5.

157

Aaron Ben-Ze'ev

5. *The degree of reality*. The more we perceive the event as real, the more intense the emotion. In analysing the notion of 'emotional reality,' two major senses should be discerned: (a) *ontological*, and (b) *epistemological*. The first sense refers to whether the event actually exists or is merely imaginary. The second sense is typically expressed in its vividness. The degree of reality is highest when the object is real in both senses. In the emotional realm, vividness is often more significant than mere facts. Accordingly, movies often generate more intense emotions than does dry information in a newspaper

The vividness of an event is of little relevance in determining its significance in the intellectual realm. Vividness expresses the subject's personal perspective: something is vivid when it is close to the subject. In order to determine the actual reality of a certain event, the vividness of the subject's perception is of little relevance. In the emotional realm, both the ontological and epistemological senses are important, but the epistemological sense, which is expressed in the vividness of the object, has greater weight than in the intellectual realm. It also often has greater weight than the ontological sense within the emotional realm.

When emotions first evolved, there was hardly any difference between the two senses of reality: what we perceived in our immediate environment was what actually existed for us. The development of the intellectual capacity differentiates between various types of reality—usually by decreasing the degree of reality of the perceived immediate environment. Intellectual deliberations typically refer to something that is far away, while emotions refer to what is present in the here and now. This may account for the weakness of reason when opposed to the strength of emotions. One important function of emotional imagination is to transform abstract general information into concrete partial information; in the process, a strong evaluative tone is attached to the given information and the readiness to act is greater.

6. *Relevancy and closeness*. The principle of relevancy restricts the emotional impact to areas that are particularly significant to us. Not everyone and not everything is of emotional significance to us. We cannot assume an emotional state toward everyone or toward those with whom we have no relation whatsoever. The intensity of emotions is achieved by their focus upon a limited group of objects. Emotions express our values and preferences; hence, they cannot be indiscriminate. We do not envy trees for their height or lions for their strength, since these are irrelevant to our personal self-esteem.

Emotional relevance is related to emotional closeness. Events close to us in time, space, or effect are usually emotionally relevant and significant. Greater closeness typically implies greater significance and greater emotional intensity. Closeness sets the conditions for meaningful relationships and comparisons. The more that someone is detached from us, the less likely we are to have any emotional attitude toward her.

In intellectual deliberations, the distance from the observer is typically of no relevance in determining the significance of a certain event. The significance of an event is determined by analysing its properties and not by considering its distance to a certain person. Personal concerns are not a factor in such analysis.

The logical principles underlying the perceptual mode are close to the emotional mode in the sense that the strong and real event is the one that we perceive; however, as in the intellectual mode, the issue of relevancy is of little significance.

C. Background circumstances of the agent

Background circumstances of the agent are more significant in the emotional mode than in the perceptual and the intellectual modes. Such circumstances may influence to a certain degree the perceptual content, but the influence is limited: perception of a given event is quite similar among various perceivers—the similarity is much higher than in the emotional mode, where the event's significance is highly dependant on personal and background circumstances.

Background circumstances are also of little value in the intellectual mode. The intellectual negative attitude toward background circumstances is part of the more general negative attitude toward taking the past into consideration. The latter is expressed in statements such as 'No use crying over spilled milk,' 'You can't turn back the clock,' and 'What's done is done.' In a goal-oriented society, which is more typical of an intellectual than an emotional society, the past is of little concern: our gaze is directed at the future, where our goals are located. Such a negative attitude toward the past implies that it is not rational to invest resources in past events and we should rather focus our limited resources on future goals. Accordingly, repudiation of the past is a prevalent criterion of rational, intellectual decision making.

Although the past seems to be unchangeable and irremediable, our attitudes toward past events, and hence the impact of the past upon us, is significant. As Faulkner said: 'The past isn't dead. It's not even past.' Sometimes we should cry over spilled milk, otherwise how will we learn to value milk and how will we avoid spilling it again? One of the best ways to take account of the past is to take account of our emotions, as emotions are shaped by, among other things, past events. The importance of the issue of the availability of an alternative in emotions indicates the importance for emotions of background circumstances.

7. Responsibility. Responsibility (or accountability) refers to the nature of the agency generating the emotional encounter. Generally, the more responsible we are for the given change, the more available is the alternative and hence the more significant the event and the more intense our emotions. The major issues relevant in this regard are: (a) degree of controllability, (b) invested effort, and (c) intent. The greater the degree of controllability we had, the more effort we invested, and the more intended the result, the more significant the event usually is and the greater emotional intensity it generates.

In the intellectual and perceptual modes, the issue of the agent's responsibility is typically of less importance in evaluating the significance of a certain event—in those modes, the significance is derived more from present circumstances (and in the intellectual mode, from future implications as well).

8. Preparedness. Preparedness refers to the cognitive change in our mind; major factors here are unexpectedness and uncertainty. Unexpectedness, which may be measured by how surprised one is by the situation, is widely recognized as central in emotions. Since emotions are generated at times of sudden change, unexpectedness typically generates emotions and is usually positively correlated with emotional intensity, at least up to a certain point. Unexpectedness may be characterized as expressing the gap between the actual situation and the imagined alternative that we expect. A factor related to, but not identical with, unexpectedness is uncertainty. We might expect some event to happen but not be certain of its actual likelihood. Uncertainty is positively correlated with emotional intensity. The more we are certain that the eliciting event will occur, the less we are surprised at its actual occurrence and the less the emotional intensity accompanying it. In situations of certainty, the alternative to the situation is perceived as less available and hence emotions are less intense.

Like the issue of responsibility, the issue of the subject's preparedness is of little significance in the perceptual and intellectual modes, which are less concerned with past circumstances.

9. *Deservingness*. The perceived deservingness (equity, fairness) of our situation or that of others is of great importance in determining the emotional significance of a certain event. People do not want to be unjustly treated, or to receive what is contrary to their wishes. Even though people disagree about what is just and unjust, most people would like the world to be fair. Accordingly, the feeling of injustice is hard to bear—sometimes even more so than the actual hardship caused. When we perceive ourselves to be treated unjustly, or when the world in general is perceived to be unjust, this is perceived as a deviation and generates emotional reactions. The more exceptional the situation, namely, the more the situation deviates from our normal baseline, the more we consider the negative situation to be unfair or the positive situation to be lucky. In such circumstances, the issue of deservingness is crucial and emotions are intense.

The issue of deservingness, which entails considerations of the subject's past situation and rights, is again of less importance in the perceptual mode, which is mainly focused on present circumstances, and in the intellectual mode, which focuses on both the present and future implications of a certain event.

Conclusion

We have seen that emotional reasoning has a different logic to that typical of intellectual reasoning. The presence of such logic has already been acknowledged in philosophical thinking and popular culture. Thus, Blaise Pascal argued that 'The heart has its reasons which reason does not understand,' and Connie Francis had a song entitled 'My Heart has a Mind of its Own.'

The two types of logic are not entirely contradictory: they do have some common principles—both analytical principles, belonging to formal logic, and synthetic ones, belonging to transcendental logic. It should also be noted that I have described what seem to be the most general principles underlying the emotional mechanism governing information processing. There are other kinds of rules that operate at other levels.

Intellectual reasoning is broader than emotional reasoning: it refers to a broader scope of circumstances and it has more freedom in the types of perspective that it adopts when analysing given circumstances. Emotional reasoning is more limited in the types of circumstances with which it is concerned and in the types of reasoning that it employs. Accordingly, we may say that intellectual

Aaron Ben-Ze'ev

reasoning can use certain principles typical of emotional reasoning, but emotional reasoning can seldom use intellectual principles while still remaining in the emotional mode. Thus, taking a broad, detached intellectual perspective typically eliminates the emotional experience; however, taking the narrow and involved perspective typical of emotions does not necessarily eliminate the intellectual mode.

As both types of logic are useful in different circumstances, it is to the benefit of each of us to integrate them in an optimal manner. Although such integration is difficult, it is possible to achieve it, with various levels of success.

References

Ben-Ze'ev, A. 1993. *The Perceptual System: A Philosophical and Psychological Perspective* (New York: Peter Lang).

Ben-Ze'ev, A. 2000. *The Subtlety of Smotions* (Cambridge, Mass.: MIT Press).

Ben-Ze'ev, A. (forthcoming). 'Emotion as a subtle mental mode'. In R. Solomon (ed.) *Thinking about Feeling: Contemporary Philosophers on Emotion* (Oxford: Oxford University Press, forthcoming).

Bergson, H. 1907. *Creative Evolution* (New York: Holt, 1911).

Frijda, N. H. 1988. 'The laws of emotion', *American Psychologist*, **43**, 349–58.

Margolis, H. 1987. *Patterns, Thinking, and Cognition: A Theory of Judgment* (Chicago: The University of Chicago Press).

Nussbaum, M. C. 2001. *Upheavals of Thought: The Intelligence of Emotions* (Cambridge: Cambridge University Press).

Redding, P. 1999. *The Logic of Affect* (Ithaca: Cornell University Press).

Rock, I. 1983. *The Logic of Perception* (Cambridge, Mass.: MIT Press).

Smith, C. A. and Kirby, L. D. 2000. 'Consequences require antecedents: Toward a process model of emotion elicitation', In J. Forgas (ed.), *Feeling and Thinking: The Role of Affect in Social Cognition* (pp. 83–106) (Cambridge: Cambridge University Press).

Spinoza, B. (1677). *Ethics*. In E. Curley (ed.), *The Collected Works of Spinoza* (Princeton: Princeton University Press, 1985).

X. Emotion and Desire in Self-Deception

ALFRED R. MELE

According to a traditional view of self-deception, the phenomenon is an intrapersonal analogue of stereotypical interpersonal deception.[1] In the latter case, deceivers *intentionally* deceive others into believing something, *p*, and there is a time at which the deceivers believe that *p* is false while their victims falsely believe that *p* is true. If self-deception is properly understood on this model, self-deceivers intentionally deceive themselves into believing something, *p*, and there is a time at which they believe that *p* is false while also believing that *p* is true.

Elsewhere (most recently in Mele, 2001), I have criticized the traditional conception of self-deception and defended an alternative, deflationary view according to which self-deception does not entail any of the following: intentionally deceiving oneself; intending (or trying) to deceive oneself, or to make it easier for oneself to believe something; concurrently believing each of two contradictory propositions. Indeed, I have argued that garden-variety instances of self-deception do not include any of these things. On my view, to put it simply, people enter self-deception in acquiring a belief that *p* if and only if *p* is false and they acquire the belief in *a suitably biased way*.[2] Obviously, this shoulders me with the burden of showing

[1] This tradition is embraced in influential work on self-deception in philosophy, psychology, psychiatry, and biology. See, e.g., Pears, 1984, Quattrone and Tversky, 1984, Gur and Sackeim, 1979, and Trivers, 1985. *Stereotypical* interpersonal deception does not exhaust interpersonal deception.

[2] Two points should be made. First, I have never defended a statement of *necessary* and sufficient conditions of entering self-deception in acquiring a belief that *p*, but only statements of characteristic and jointly sufficient conditions. (For a recent statement, see Mele, 2001, pp. 50–1.) Second, the requirement that *p* be false is purely semantic. By definition, one is *deceived in* believing that *p* only if *p* is *false*; the same is true of being *self-deceived in* believing that *p*. The requirement does not imply that *p*'s being false has special importance for the *dynamics* of self-deception. Biased treatment of data may sometimes result in someone's believing an improbable proposition, *p*, that happens to be *true*. There may be self-deception in such a case, but the person is not self-deceived in believing

what suitable bias amounts to, and I have had a lot to say about that. The suitability at issue is a matter of kind of bias, degree of bias, and the nondeviance of causal connections between biasing processes (or events) and the acquisition of the belief that p.[3]

In Mele, 2001 (pp. 106–12), I suggested a test for relevant bias. I called it 'the impartial observer test,' and I argued that its appropriateness is underwritten by the ordinary concept of self-deception. Here is an improved version: If S is self-deceived in believing that p, and D is the collection of relevant data readily available to S, then if D were made readily available to S's impartial cognitive peers (including merely hypothetical people) and they were to engage in at least as much reflection on the issue as S does and at least a moderate amount of reflection, those who conclude that p is false would significantly outnumber those who conclude that p is true.[4] This is a test for the satisfaction of a necessary condition of being self-deceived in believing that p. One requirement for impartiality in the present context is that one neither desire that p nor desire that ~p. Another is that one not prefer avoidance of either of the following errors over the other: falsely believing that p and falsely believing that ~p. The kind of bias at issue may broadly be termed 'motivational or emotional bias.' Although I have discussed biasing causes and processes—especially motivational ones—at length, I have left it open that a motivationally biased treatment of data is not required for self-deception and that emotions sometimes do the biasing work without motivation's playing a biasing role. This is one of the two possibilities that I explore in this essay. The other is a more moderate thesis about the place of emotion in self-deception.

1. Background: Biased Belief and Self-Deception

In the present section, after briefly describing some mechanisms relevant to the production of motivationally biased belief of a sort

---

[3] On deviant and nondeviant causation in this connection, see Mele, 2001, pp. 121–23.

[4] Cf. Mele, 2001, p. 106. The improvement is the 'reflection' clause. An issue may be so boring to one's impartial cognitive peers that they do not reflect on it and reach no conclusion about it.

---

that p, nor in acquiring the belief that p. On a relevant difference between being deceived *in* believing that p and being deceived *into* believing that p, see Mele, 1987, pp. 127–8.

appropriate to self-deception, I sketch a general account of such belief. My primary aim is to prepare the way for my discussion of emotionally biased belief in Section 2. I have reviewed empirical evidence of motivationally biased belief elsewhere (most recently in Mele, 2001) and I will not do so again here.

Attention to some phenomena that have been argued to be sources of unmotivated or 'cold' biased belief sheds light on motivationally biased belief. A number of such sources have been identified in the psychological literature, including the following two.

1. Vividness of information. A datum's vividness for a person often is a function of the person's interests, the concreteness of the datum, its 'imagery-provoking' power, or its sensory, temporal, or spatial proximity (Nisbett and Ross, 1980, p. 45). Vivid data are more likely to be recognized, attended to, and recalled than pallid data. Consequently, vivid data tend to have a disproportional influence on the formation and retention of beliefs.

2. The confirmation bias. People testing a hypothesis tend to search (in memory and the world) more often for confirming than for disconfirming instances and to recognize the former more readily (Baron, 1988, pp. 259–65; Klayman and Ha, 1987; Nisbett and Ross, pp. 181–82). This is true even when the hypothesis is only a tentative one (as opposed, e.g., to a belief one has). People also tend to interpret relatively neutral data as supporting a hypothesis they are testing (Trope et al., 1997, p. 115).

Although sources of biased belief apparently can function independently of motivation, they may also be triggered and sustained by desires in the production of particular motivationally biased beliefs.[5] For example, desires can enhance the vividness or salience of data. Data that count in favour of the truth of a proposition that one hopes is true may be rendered more vivid or salient by one's recognition that they so count. Similarly, desires can influence which hypotheses occur to one and affect the salience of available hypotheses, thereby setting the stage for the confirmation bias.[6] Owing to a desire that p, one may test the hypothesis that p is true

[5] I develop this idea in Mele, 1987, ch. 10 and Mele, 2001. Kunda, 1990 develops the same theme, concentrating on evidence that motivation sometimes primes the confirmation bias. Also see Kunda, 1999, ch. 6.

[6] For motivational interpretations of the confirmation bias, see Friedrich, 1993 and Trope and Liberman, 1996, pp. 252–65.

Alfred R. Mele

rather than the contrary hypothesis. In these ways and others, a desire that p may contribute to the acquisition of an unwarranted belief that p.

Sometimes we generate our own hypotheses, and sometimes others suggest hypotheses to us—including extremely unpleasant ones. If we were consistently to concentrate primarily on confirmatory instances of hypotheses we are testing, independently of what is at stake, that would indicate the presence of a cognitive tendency or disposition that uniformly operates independently of desires. For example, it would indicate that desires never play a role in influencing the proportion of attention we give to evidence for the falsity of a hypothesis. However, there is powerful evidence that the 'confirmation bias' is much less rigid than this. For example, in one study (Gigerenzer and Hug, 1992), two groups of subjects are asked to test 'social-contract rules such as "If someone stays overnight in the cabin, then that person must bring along a bundle of firewood ..."' (Friedrich, 1993, p. 313). The group asked to adopt 'the perspective of a cabin guard monitoring compliance' showed an 'extremely high frequency' of testing for disconfirming instances. The other group, asked to 'take the perspective of a visitor trying to determine' whether firewood was supplied by visitors or a local club, displayed the common confirmation bias.

An interesting recent theory of lay hypothesis testing is designed, in part, to account for motivationally biased belief. I examined it in Mele, 2001, where I offered grounds for caution and moderation and argued that a qualified version is plausible.[7] I named it the 'FTL theory,' after the authors of the essays on which I primarily drew, Friedrich, 1993 and Trope and Liberman, 1996. I will offer a thumbnail sketch of the theory shortly. First, an explicit application of it to self-deception should be noted.

On James Friedrich's PEDMIN—'primary error detection and minimization'—model of lay hypothesis testing, 'detection and minimization of crucial errors is ... the central organizing principle' in this sphere (1993, p. 299). Regarding self-deception, Friedrich writes:

> a prime candidate for primary error of concern is believing as true something that leads [one] to mistakenly criticize [oneself] or lower [one's] self-esteem. Such costs are generally highly salient and are paid for immediately in terms of psychological discomfort. When there are few costs associated with errors of self-deception (incorrectly preserving or enhancing one's self-image),

---

[7] See Mele, 2001, pp. 31–49, 63–70, 90–91, 96–98, 112–18.

mistakenly revising one's self-image downward or failing to boost it appropriately should be the focal error. (p. 314)

The basic idea of the FTL theory is that lay hypothesis testing is driven by a concern to minimize making costly errors. The errors in question are false beliefs. The cost of a false belief is the cost, including missed opportunities for gains, that it would be reasonable for the person to expect the belief—if false—to have, given his desires and beliefs, if he were to have expectations about such things. A central element of the FTL theory is the notion of a 'confidence threshold'—or a 'threshold,' for short. The lower the threshold, the thinner the evidence sufficient for reaching it. Two thresholds are relevant to each hypothesis: 'The acceptance threshold is the minimum confidence in the truth of a hypothesis,' p, sufficient for producing a belief that p; and 'the rejection threshold is the minimum confidence in the untruth of a hypothesis,' p, sufficient for producing a belief that ~p (Trope and Liberman, 1996, p. 253). Acquiring the belief terminates hypothesis testing. The two thresholds often are not equally high, and the acceptance and rejection thresholds respectively depend 'primarily' on 'the cost of false acceptance relative to the cost of information' and 'the cost of false rejection relative to the cost of information.' The 'cost of information' is simply the 'resources and effort' required for gathering and processing 'hypothesis-relevant information' (p. 252).

Confidence thresholds are determined by the strength of desires to avoid specific costly errors together with information costs. Setting aside the latter costs, the stronger one's desire to avoid falsely believing that p, the higher one's threshold for belief that p. These desires influence belief in two ways. First, because, other things being equal, lower thresholds are easier to reach than higher ones, belief that ~p is a more likely outcome than belief that p, other things being equal, in a hypothesis tester who has a higher acceptance threshold for p than for ~p. Second, the desires at issue influence how we test hypotheses, not just when we stop testing them (owing to our having reached a relevant threshold). Recall the study in which subjects asked to adopt 'the perspective of a cabin guard' showed an 'extremely high frequency' of testing for disconfirming instances whereas subjects asked to 'take the perspective of a visitor' showed the common confirmation bias.

It might be claimed that if avoidance desires of the kind under discussion function in the second way, they function in conjunction with beliefs to the effect that testing-behaviour of a specific kind will tend to help one avoid making the costly errors at issue. It might be claimed, accordingly, that the pertinent testing-behaviour is performed for a reason constituted by the desire and an instrumental belief of the kind just mentioned and that this behaviour is therefore performed with the intention of trying to avoid, the pertinent error. The thrust of these claims is that the FTL theory accommodates the confirmation bias, for example, by invoking a model of intentional action.

This is not a feature of the FTL model, as its proponents understand it. Friedrich claims that desires to avoid specific errors can trigger and sustain 'automatic test strategies' (p. 313), which supposedly happens in roughly the nonintentional way in which a desire that p enhances the vividness of evidence for p. A person's having a stronger desire to avoid falsely believing that ~p than to avoid falsely believing that p may have the effect that he primarily seeks evidence for p, is more attentive to such evidence than to evidence for ~p, and interprets relatively neutral data as supporting p, without this effect's being mediated by a belief that such behaviour is conducive to avoiding the former error. The stronger desire may simply frame the topic in a way that triggers and sustains these manifestations of the confirmation bias without the assistance of a belief that behaviour of this kind is a means of avoiding a certain error. Similarly, having a stronger desire that runs in the opposite direction may result in a sceptical approach to hypothesis testing that in no way depends on a belief to the effect that an approach of this kind will increase the probability of avoiding the costlier error. Given the stronger desire, sceptical testing is predictable independently of the agent's believing that a particular testing style will decrease the probability of making a certain error. So at least I have argued elsewhere (Mele, 2001, pp. 41–49, 61–67).

I will not defend this thesis again here. Nor am I claiming that the FTL theory is acceptable without qualification. The theory may accurately describe what happens in some or many cases of lay hypothesis testing that results in belief, and in many or all cases of self-deception.

One more piece of background is in order. Elsewhere, I have distinguished between 'straight' and 'twisted' self-deception (Mele, 1997b; 1999; 2000; 2001, pp. 4–5, 94–118). In straight instances, we are self-deceived in believing something that we want to be true. In twisted instances, we are self-deceived in believing something that we want to be false (and do not also want to be true). Twisted self-deception may be exemplified by an insecure, jealous husband who believes that his wife is having an affair despite possessing only relatively weak evidence for that proposition and unambivalently wanting it to be false that she is so engaged.[8]

The FTL theory applies straightforwardly to twisted self-deception. Whereas, for many people, it may be more important to avoid acquiring the false belief that their spouses are having affairs than to avoid acquiring the false belief that they are not so engaged, the converse may well be true of some insecure, jealous people. The belief that one's spouse is unfaithful tends to cause significant psychological discomfort. Even so, avoiding falsely believing that their spouses are faithful may be so important to some people that they test the relevant hypothesis in ways that, other things being equal, are less likely to lead to a false belief in their spouses' fidelity than to a false belief in their spouses' infidelity. Furthermore, data suggestive of infidelity may be especially salient for these people. Don Sharpsteen and Lee Kirkpatrick observe that 'the jealousy complex'—that is, 'the thoughts, feelings, and behaviour typically associated with jealousy episodes'—can be regarded as a mechanism 'for maintaining close relationships' and appears to be 'triggered by separation, or the threat of separation, from attachment figures' (1997, p. 627). It certainly is conceivable that, given a certain psychological profile, a strong desire to maintain one's relationship with one's spouse plays a role in rendering the potential error of falsely believing one's spouse to be innocent of infidelity a 'costly' error, in the FTL sense, and more costly than the error of falsely believing one's spouse to be guilty. After all, the former error may reduce the probability that one takes steps to protect the relationship against an intruder. The FTL theory provides a basis for a plausible account of twisted self-deception (see Mele, 1999 and 2001, ch. 5).

2. Emotions in Self-Deception

I turn to possible roles for emotions in self-deception. Insofar as emotions are causes of belief-biasing desires or are partially constituted by such desires, they have a clear bearing on self-deception, if the FTL theory is on the right track. Consider Bob, who is self-deceived in believing that his wife, Ann, is not having an affair. Bob's love for Ann, or his fear that he cannot get along without her, may be a partial cause of his desire that she is not having an affair

[8] On this case, see Barnes, 1997, ch. 3; Dalgleish, 1997, p. 110; Lazar, 1999, pp. 274–77; and Pears, 1984, pp. 42–4. Also see Mele, 1987, pp. 114–18.

and, thereby, of his being self-deceived about this. If that desire increases the salience of his apparent evidence of her fidelity or helps shape his relevant confidence thresholds, emotions that contribute to the desire play an indirect part in this. Furthermore, Bob may fear that Ann is guilty of infidelity, and if a constituent of his fear is a desire that she is innocent, then the role the desire plays in his self-deception may be attributed to the fear, insofar as the fear encompasses the desire.[9]

There are additional possibilities. Obviously, people are averse to anxious feelings. Such feelings may be caused by reflection. In some cases, a desire that one's anxiety subside may play a role in attenuating or halting reflection on an unpleasant hypothesis, thereby decreasing the likelihood of one's undermining a contrary hypothesis to which one is attracted. Anxiety is an emotion: here, again, an emotion has an indirect role in potential self-deception. Some emotions may also help to explain some instances of self-deception by weakening one's motivation to assess evidence carefully (see Forgas, 1995, p. 50), thereby increasing the probability that one's beliefs will be unduly influenced by one's desires. Grief may do this.

Do emotions figure more prominently in some cases of self-deception? In the remainder of this essay, I explore two hypotheses about this.[10]

1. The solo emotion hypothesis. In some instances of entering self-deception in acquiring a belief, an emotion, but no desire, makes a biasing contribution to the production of that belief.

2. The direct emotion hypothesis. In some instances of entering self-deception in acquiring a belief, an emotion makes a biasing contribution to the production of that belief that is neither made by a desire nor causally mediated by a desire.[11]

My primary aim is to convey a sense of what may be said for and against these hypotheses and of difficulties involved in investigating

[9] Fear that ~p is plausibly understood as being partly constituted by desire that p. See, e.g., Davis, 1988.

[10] Elsewhere (Mele, 2000, pp. 125–29), I criticized a third hypothesis, what I called 'the anxiety reduction hypothesis'—the thesis that the function of self-deception is to reduce present anxiety (Barnes, 1997, Johnston, 1988; cf. Tesser *et al.*, 1989).

[11] To simplify discussion, I formulated both hypotheses in terms of entering self-deception in acquiring a belief. Entering self-deception in retaining a belief and remaining in self-deception in continuing to believe something also require attention.

them. As I will explain, the second, more modest hypothesis is plausible, and our knowledge about emotion is too thin to warrant a confident rejection or endorsement of the first hypothesis.

Regarding an instance of twisted self-deception, Tim Dalgleish writes: 'it is inappropriate to suggest that jealous persons desire or are motivated to find that their partners are unfaithful; rather, their emotional state is priming the relevant processing systems to gather evidence in a biased fashion' (1997, p. 110). Dalgleish's contention is that, in cases of this kind, emotion plays biasing roles of the sort I attributed to desires in straight self-deception. For example, jealousy may prime the confirmation bias by prompting a jealous man to test the hypothesis that his wife is unfaithful, and it may increase the salience of apparent evidence of infidelity. There is evidence that emotions operate in these ways. As Douglas Derryberry reports, there is evidence that 'emotional states facilitate the processing of congruent stimuli' and that 'attentional processes are involved in [this] effect' (1988, pp. 36, 38), and Gordon Bower and Joseph Forgas review evidence that emotions make 'emotionally congruent interpretations of ambiguous stimuli more available' (2000, p. 106).[12] For example, Jed's jealousy may make him highly attentive to rare memories of Jane's seemingly being flirtatious or secretive and help generate jealousy-congruent interpretations of relatively neutral data.

The jealous Jed scenario is unlikely to confirm the solo emotion hypothesis. Sharpsteen and Kirkpatrick, suggest, plausibly, that 'the jealousy complex' is 'a manifestation of motives reflecting both sexual and attachment concerns' (1997, p. 638). Jealousy is intimately bound up with desires that jealous people have concerning their relationships with the people of whom they are jealous. It is a truism that indifference about one's relationship with a person precludes being jealous of that person.[13] (Being envious of someone is another matter.) Indeed, it is plausible that if a desire for close romantic attachment is not a constituent of paradigmatic romantic jealousy, it is at least a significant, partial cause of such jealousy. If this plausible proposition is true, then if Jed's being jealous of Jane affects the hypotheses he frames about her, the vividness of his

[12] Reviews of the 'mood congruence effect' include Bower and Forgas, 2000 and Forgas, 1995.

[13] If a woman is jealous because her date is flirting with another woman, is she jealous of her date or the other woman? Ronald de Sousa expresses the proper usage succinctly: 'the person one is jealous *of* plays an entirely different part in one's jealousy from that of the rival *because of whom* one is jealous' (1987, p. 75).

Alfred R. Mele

evidence, and the focus of his attention, it is very likely that an attachment desire plays a biasing role.[14]

Again, 'the jealousy complex' can be regarded as a mechanism 'for maintaining close relationships' and appears to be 'triggered by separation, or the threat of separation, from attachment figures' (Sharpsteen and Kirkpatrick, p. 627). This suggests that the effects of jealousy are partly explained by a desire for the maintenance of a close relationship. That desire may be at work in Jed's biased cognition. The desire may contribute to Jed's having a stronger desire to avoid falsely believing that Jane is faithful than to avoid falsely believing that she is unfaithful and, accordingly, contribute to his having a lower acceptance threshold for the hypothesis that she is having an affair than for the contrary hypothesis. The desire, given its psychological context, including, importantly, the jealousy associated with it, may also help enhance the salience of evidence of threats to the maintenance of his relationship with Jane, help prime the confirmation bias in a way favouring the belief that she is having an affair, and so on.

Defending the solo emotion hypothesis is a challenging project. Owing to the tight connection between emotions and associated desires, testing empirically for cases of self-deception in which emotion, and not desire, biases belief is difficult. Constructing compelling conceptual tests also is challenging. For example, if all emotions, or all emotions that might plausibly bias beliefs, are partly constituted by desires, it is difficult to show that there are beliefs that are biased by an emotion, or by some feature of an emotion, but not at all by desires, including desires that are constituents of the biasing emotions. Even if there is a conceptual connection between types of emotions and types of desires as partial causes, rather than between types of emotions and types of desires as constituents, it would have to be shown that emotions sometimes contribute to instances of self-deception to which the desires involved in producing the emotions make no belief-biasing contribution. Furthermore, even if some emotions are neither partially constituted nor partially caused by a relevant desire (typical instances of surprise are like this), the solo emotion hypothesis requires that such an emotion's biasing contribution to self-deception not be causally mediated by a desire either and, more generally, that the emotion not contribute to

[14] The conjunction of 'x affects y' and 'z is a constituent or a cause of x' does not entail 'z affects y.' The brake pedal on Smith's car is a constituent of his car and his car affected Jones. But the brake pedal did not. Smith's car fell on Jones as he was repairing a flat tire. That explains the qualification 'very likely' in the text.

172

self-deception in combination with any biasing desire. I will return to this hypothesis shortly.

The direct emotion hypothesis is more modest.[15] Perhaps in some or many instances of self-deception, biasing roles are played both by (aspects of) emotions and by desires that are intimately related to the biasing emotions—as part to whole, or as a partial cause or effect, or as responses to the emotions (as in the case of a desire to be rid of one's present anxiety).[16] In some such cases, some biasing roles played by emotions may be direct, in the relevant sense. Perhaps an emotion can prime the confirmation bias or enhance the salience of emotion-congruent data without doing so simply in virtue of a constituent desire's playing this role and without the effect's being causally mediated by a desire. One who knows only of Jed's evidence for and against the proposition that Jane is having an affair and of his desire for the maintenance of a close relationship with her is hard put to understand why Jed believes that this proposition is true. People with much stronger evidence of infidelity than Jed has often believe that their spouses are innocent of infidelity, even though they, like Jed, strongly desire the maintenance of close relationships with their spouses. Indeed, some common philosophical examples of straight self-deception feature such people. The information that Jed is jealous helps us understand why he believes what he does. His jealousy is an important, instructive part of the psychological context in which he acquires his infidelity belief. Perhaps Jed's jealousy plays a role in the production of his biased belief that is not played by the pertinent desire alone.

Consider another scenario. Ed is angry at Don for a recent offence. His anger may prime the confirmation bias by suggesting an emotion-congruent hypothesis about Don's current behaviour— for example, that Don is behaving spitefully again. Ed's anger may also increase the salience of data that seem to support that hypothesis. There is evidence that anger tends to focus attention selectively on explanations in terms of 'agency,' as opposed to situational factors (Kilter *et al.*, 1993). Perhaps Ed's anger leads him to view certain aspects of Don's behaviour as more goal-directed and more indicative of a hostile intention than he otherwise would. If anger has a desire as a constituent, it is, roughly, a desire to lash out against the target of one's anger. Possibly, anger can play the biasing roles

[15] More specifically, although, necessarily, any emotion that makes a solo biasing contribution to self-deception makes a direct biasing contribution (in the pertinent sense of 'direct'), an emotion that makes a direct biasing contribution might not make a solo one.

[16] The categories of effect and response are not mutually exclusive.

Alfred R. Mele

just mentioned without any constituent desire's playing them and in the absence of causal mediation by a desire.

If an emotion can play a direct biasing role in self-deception, perhaps an emotion may contribute to an instance of self-deception that involves no desires as significant biasing causes. Perhaps the solo emotion hypothesis is true, despite the challenges it faces. It is conceivable, perhaps, that Ed enters self-deception in acquiring the belief that Don is behaving spitefully now, that the process that results in this belief features his anger's playing the biasing roles just described, and that no desires of Ed's have a biasing effect in this case. Now, on the assumption that Ed believes that Don is behaving spitefully despite having stronger evidence for the falsity of that hypothesis than for its truth, an FTL theorist will find it natural to suppose that Ed had a lower threshold for acceptance of that hypothesis than for rejection of it, that the difference in thresholds is explained at least partly in terms of relevant desires, and that this difference helps to explain Ed's acquiring the belief he does. But this supposition is open to debate, and I will not try to settle the issue here.

I mentioned that testing the solo emotion hypothesis empirically would be difficult. This point helps to explain the limited scope that Joseph Forgas claims for his 'affect infusion model' of the effects of affective states on social judgments (1995; cf. Bower and Forgas 2000).[17] Sketching some background will enable me to say how. Forgas identifies two 'mechanisms of affect-infusion: affect-priming and affect-as-information' (p. 40). The former is a matter of the 'selective influence [of affective states] on attention, encoding, retrieval, and associative processes' during substantive information processing (p. 40). In a nice illustration of the latter, 'when subjects were asked to make off-the-cuff evaluative judgments about their happiness and life satisfaction through a telephone survey, their responses were significantly different depending on whether they were feeling good (interviewed on a pleasant, sunny day) or feeling bad (interviewed on a rainy, overcast day). Once their attention was called to the source of their mood (the weather), however, the mood effects were constrained' (p. 53).[18] Commenting on such studies, Norbert Schwarz writes: 'rather than computing a judgment on the basis of ... features of a target, individuals may ... ask themselves "How do I feel about it" [and] in doing so, they may mistake [certain] feelings ... as a reaction to the target' (1990, p. 529).

[17] Forgas uses 'affect' as 'a generic label to refer to both moods and emotions' (p. 41).

[18] This experiment is reported in Schwarz and Clore, 1983.

Forgas attempts to demonstrate that 'affect infusion is a signifi-cant and reliable source of judgmental distortions,' and his model 'predicts that affect infusion should not influence judgments based on … motivated processing strategies' (p. 51). The 'specific goals' he cites as motivators of processing are 'mood repair and mood maintenance, self-evaluation maintenance, ego enhancement, achievement motivation, and affiliation' (p. 47; cf. Bower and Forgas, 2000, pp. 130–5, 138). Forgas wants to accommodate cases in which, instead of mood-congruent processing, incongruence is found; and his explanation of such cases is partly motivational (cf. Bower and Forgas, 2000, pp. 135, 154–5). In mood repair, for exam-ple, people selectively attend to memories and thoughts that are incongruent with their unpleasant feelings, motivated by a desire to feel better.

The idea that 'goals' such as these are at work in some cases of lay hypothesis testing is easily accommodated by the FTL model. For people experiencing an unpleasant mood or emotion, or a threat to their positive self-image, certain associated errors may be especially costly. For example, in some cases in which people are feeling sad or guilty, the errors of underestimating the quality of their lives or overestimating their responsibility for a harm may be particularly costly. However, this point about the FTL model should not be taken to ground the claim that there is a strict division of labour in lay hypothesis testing between motivation to minimize costly errors and affect infusion. Return to jealous Jed. Owing partly to his jeal-ousy, the most costly error for him may be falsely believing that Jane is faithful, and his processing may be congruent with his jealousy. Similarly, the costliest error for someone who is feeling particularly proud of himself may be falsely believing something that would entail that his pride is unwarranted, and his processing may be con-gruent with his pride. The question is open whether there is both motivated processing and affect infusion in these scenarios. Forgas apparently commits himself to holding that if motivated processing is at work in them, affect infusion is not. Seemingly, a significant part of what accounts for his taking this view is the difficulty, in such scenarios, of demonstrating empirically that affective states played an infusing role—that, for example, in cases like Jed's, selec-tive attention to and retrieval of thoughts and images congruent with one's jealousy is accounted for at least partly by affect infusion rather than solely by other factors, including 'motivated processing strategies.'

Again, on Forgas's model, 'judgments based on … motivated processing strategies' are not influenced by affect infusion (p. 51). If

the FTL theory is correct, all lay hypothesis testing involves motivated processing strategies and Forgas's claim about his model, literally interpreted, leaves no room for affect infusion in that sphere.
Of course, the FTL theory may be overly ambitious, and Forgas
may have been overly restrictive in his statement of what his model
predicts. However this may be, a method for testing for the joint
influence of motivated processing and affect infusion in biased
belief would be useful.

A related issue also merits further investigation. Return again to
Jed. He wants it to be true that Jane is not having an affair, and he
presumably fears at some point that she is. Eventually, he comes to
believe that Jane has been unfaithful. Suppose that Jed's jealousy
contributed to that biased belief. Assuming that his jealousy affected his framing of hypotheses, his attention, or the salience of his
evidence in a way that contributed to his biased belief that Jane is
unfaithful, why didn't it happen instead that his fear, or a constituent desire, affected these things in a way that contributed to his
acquiring a belief that she is faithful? Alternatively, why didn't his
fear, or a constituent desire, block the relevant potential effects of
his jealousy, with the result that the balance of his evidence carried
the day?[19]

A proponent of the FTL theory might answer these questions in
a way that downplays belief-biasing roles for emotions. In a typical
case of romantic jealousy where there are some grounds for suspecting infidelity, the belief that one's romantic partner is having an
affair would cause psychological discomfort, but it might also promote one's chances of taking successful steps to save one's relationship. It may be suggested (1) that what one believes is determined
by a combination of (a) the strength of one's evidence for and
against the proposition that one's partner is having an affair and (b)
which error one more strongly desires to avoid and (2) that b is
determined by the relative strengths of one's desire to avoid the
psychological discomfort of believing that one's partner is having
an affair and of one's desire to maintain the relationship. However,
this view of things may be too simple. Perhaps distinctively emotional features of jealousy can influence what a jealous person
believes in a way that does not depend on desire. Furthermore, even

---

[19] It may be suggested that Jed's fear issued in fear-congruent processing that meshed with his jealousy-congruent processing. Even if that is so,
one wants to understand why the desire-component of his fear—his desire
that Jane is not having an affair—did not contribute to motivated processing resulting in a belief that she is innocent of infidelity, or block
effective jealousy-congruent processing.

if desire and desire-strength are relevant to what a jealous person comes to believe, that is consistent with his jealousy's having a 'direct' biasing effect on what he believes. The questions I raised about Jed are difficult ones.[20] Answers that properly inspire confidence will not, I fear, be produced by philosophical speculation. Nor, as far as I know, are such answers available in the empirical literature on emotion: we need to know more than is currently known about the effects of emotions on cognition. These observations are, of course, consistent both with the truth and with the falsity of the direct and solo emotion hypotheses. I am keeping an open mind and trying to be unbiased.[21]

Bibliography

Barnes, A. 1997. *Seeing Through Self-Deception* (Cambridge: Cambridge University Press).

Baron, J. 1988. *Thinking and Deciding* (Cambridge: Cambridge University Press).

Bower, G. and Forgas, J. 2000. 'Affect, Memory, and Social Cognition', In E. Eich, J. Kihlstrom, G. Bower, J. Forgas, and P. Niedenthal, (eds) *Cognition and Emotion* (Oxford: Oxford University Press).

Dalgleish, T. 1997. 'Once More with Feeling: The Role of Emotion in Self-Deception', *Behavioural and Brain Sciences* **20**, 110–11.

Davis, W. 1988. 'A Causal Theory of Experiential Fear', *Canadian Journal of Philosophy* **18**, 459–83.

Derryberry, D. 1988. 'Emotional Influences on Evaluative Judgements:

[20] A proponent of the direct emotion hypothesis may urge that occurrent *aversions* to specific costly mistakes do the work attributed to *desires* to avoid these mistakes in my sketch of the FTL theory, that these aversions play the role attributed to the avoidance desires in determining confidence thresholds. Such a theorist may also contend that occurrent aversions are emotions and argue that even though an aversion to falsely believing that p has a desire to avoid falsely believing that p as a constituent, the work of the aversion in biasing belief is not exhausted by the biasing work of the desire. The claim may be that some distinct, affective feature of the aversion makes a biasing contribution of its own to confidence thresholds. It may also be claimed that the aversion plays additional direct roles—for example, enhancing the salience of evidence for $\sim p$. This is another issue that requires further investigation, including conceptual spadework. Once it is suggested that occurrent aversions are emotions, the suggestion that all desires—or all desires with some felt intensity—are emotions may not be far behind.

[21] Parts of this article derive from Mele, 1987, 1997a, 2000, 2001, and 2003. I am grateful to audiences at the University of Zurich Ethics Center and the University of Manchester for fruitful discussion.

Alfred R. Mele

Roles of Arousal, Attention, and Spreading Activation.' *Motivation and Emotion* **12**, 23–55.

de Sousa, R. 1987. *The Rationality of Emotion* (Cambridge: MIT Press).

Forgas, J. 1995. 'Mood and Judgement: The Affect Infusion Model', *Psychological Bulletin* **117**, 39–66.

Friedrich, J. 1993. 'Primary Error Detection and Minimisation (PED-MIN) Strategies in Social Cognition: A Reinterpretation of Confirmation Bias Phenomena', *Psychological Review* **100**, 298–319.

Gigerenzer, G. and Hug, K. 1992. 'Domain-Specific Reasoning: Social Contracts, Cheating, and Perspective Change', *Cognition* **43**, 127–71.

Gur, R. and Sackeim, H. 1979. 'Self-Deception: A Concept in Search of a Phenomenon', *Journal of Personality and Social Psychology* **37**, 147–69.

Johnston, M. 1988. 'Self-Deception and the Nature of Mind', In B. McLaughlin and A. Rorty, (eds) *Perspectives on Self-Deception* (Berkeley: University of California Press).

Kilter, D., Ellsworth, P. and Edwards, K. 1993. 'Beyond Simple Pessimism: Effects of Sadness and Anger on Social Perception', *Journal of Personality and Social Psychology* **64**, 740–52.

Klayman, J. and Ha, Y. 1987. 'Confirmation, Disconfirmation, and Information in Hypothesis-Testing', *Psychological Review* **94**, 211–28.

Kunda, Z. 1999. *Social Cognition* (Cambridge: MIT Press).

— (1990). 'The Case for Motivated Reasoning', *Psychological Bulletin* **108**, 480–98.

Lazar, A. 1999. 'Deceiving Oneself or Self-Deceived? On the Formation of Beliefs "Under the Influence"', *Mind* **108**, 265–90.

Mele, A. 2003. *Motivation and Agency* (New York: Oxford University Press.

— 2001. *Self-Deception Unmasked* (Princeton: Princeton University Press).

— 2000. 'Self-Deception and Emotion', *Consciousness and Emotion* **1**, 115–37

— 1999. 'Twisted Self-Deception', *Philosophical Psychology* **12**, 117–37.

— 1997a. 'Real Self-Deception', *Behavioural and Brain Sciences* **20**, 91–102.

— 1997b. 'Understanding and Explaining Real Self-Deception', *Behavioural and Brain Sciences* 20: 127–34.

— 1987. *Irrationality* (New York: Oxford University Press).

Nisbett, R. and Ross, L. 1980. *Human Inference: Strategies and Shortcomings of Social Judgement* (Englewood Cliffs: Prentice-Hall).

Pears, D. 1984. *Motivated Irrationality* (Oxford: Oxford University Press).

Quattrone, G. and Tversky, A. 1984. 'Causal Versus Diagnostic Contingencies: On Self-Deception and on the Voter's Illusion', *Journal of Personality and Social Psychology* **46**, 237–48.

Schwarz, N. 1990. 'Feelings as Information: Informational and Motivational Functions of Affective States', In E. Higgins and R. Sorrentino, (eds) *Handbook of Motivation and Cognition*, vol. 2. (New York: Guilford Press).

Schwarz, N. and Clore, G. 1983 'Mood, Misattribution and Judgements of Well-Being', *Journal of Personality and Social Psychology* 45, 513–23.
Sharpsteen, D. and Kirkpatrick, L. 1997. 'Romantic Jealousy and Adult Romantic Attachment', *Journal of Personality and Social Psychology* 72, 627–40.
Tesser, A., Pilkington, C. and McIntosh, W. 1989. 'Self-Evaluation Maintenance and the Mediational Role of Emotion: The Perception of Friends and Strangers', *Journal of Personality and Social Psychology* 57, 442–56.
Trivers, R. 1985. *Social Evolution* (Menlo Park, CA: Benjamin/ Cummings).
Trope, Y., Gervey, B. and Liberman, N. 1997. 'Wishful Thinking from a Pragmatic Hypothesis-Testing Perspective', In M. Myslobodsky, (ed.) *The Mythomanias: The Nature of Deception and Self-Deception* (Mahwah, NJ: Lawrence Erlbaum).
Trope, Y. and Liberman, A. 1996. 'Social Hypothesis Testing: Cognitive and Motivational Mechanisms', In E. Higgins and A. Kruglanski, (eds.) *Social Psychology: Handbook of Basic Principles* (New York: Guilford Press).

XI. Emotion, Weakness of Will, and the Normative Conception of Agency[1]

KAREN JONES

Empirical work on and common observation of the emotions tells us that our emotions sometimes key us to the presence of real and important reason-giving considerations without necessarily presenting that information to us in a way susceptible of conscious articulation and, sometimes, even despite our consciously held and internally justified judgment that the situation contains no such reasons. In this paper, I want to explore the implications of the fact that emotions show varying degrees of integration with our conscious agency—from none at all to quite substantial—for our understanding of our rationality, and in particular for the traditional assumption that weakness of the will is necessarily irrational.

The paper has two targets: the proximal target is the claim that *in* choosing the incontinent action *rather than* the continent one, the agent necessarily does something irrational;[2] the distal target is the dominant naturalistic conception of how to justify norms of rationality. I'm taking aim at the latter through the former. The naturalist project aims to articulate and defend norms of rationality that are norms for the kind creatures we are—that is, for finite, embodied, social beings, with a specific cognitive architecture,

[1] I would like to thank David Owen, Laura Schroeter, Francois Schroeter, Sigrun Svarvarsdottir, members of the ANU weakness of the will reading group, and audiences at Hobart, Melbourne, Sydney, and the Royal Institute of Philosophy conference on the emotions, Manchester 2001 for helpful discussion of the themes in this paper.

[2] This claim must be distinguished from the stronger claim that it is always *more irrational* for an agent to act against her all-things-considered judgement as to what she should do than act on the basis of it. The claim that continence is always more rational than incontinence is a strong thesis and one not easily defended given that an agent's all-things-considered judgment can be—quite literally— crazy. The target claim is the weaker— and therefore more plausible—thesis that weakness of will always adds an element of irrationality over and above any irrationality that might be involved in the formation of a poor all-things-considered judgment. The stronger and weaker theses are distinguished by David Owen (n.d.) but not by Nomi Arpaly (2000).

Karen Jones

functioning in particular environments. On the standard way of developing that project, norms of rationality are not *a priori* knowable and none can be viewed as privileged. Even norms as well-entrenched as norms prohibiting incontinence must await empirical support and recent work on the emotions raises the possibility that they might fail to get it. I argue that reflecting on what you might be tempted to say about emotion, weakness of will, and rationality— if you take a naturalist approach towards these topics—reveals the need for naturalists to pay greater attention to our practical and epistemic *agency* and to norms grounded in our conception of ourselves as rational agents. Nonetheless, I argue, on naturalist grounds, against the view that weakness of will always adds a element of irrationality over and above any irrationality contained in the agent's all-things-considered judgment.

1. Naturalism and norms of rationality

The naturalist project of understanding what it means for the constrained finite creatures we are to be rational has been pursued in greater depth with respect to questions regarding our theoretical rationality than with respect to questions regarding our practical rationality. So let me begin by giving a quick sketch of the naturalist approach to norms of theoretical rationality before switching to issues in practical rationality.

According to the standard naturalist picture of how norms of theoretical rationality are to be justified it is an *empirical* question whether a putative norm counts as a genuine norm and so merits our allegiance or not: does following that norm, given the kind of creatures we are, operating in the kinds of environments in which we operate, advance or hinder our epistemic goals? These epistemic goals, in turn, are to be discerned through an investigation of our epistemic practices, and include, perhaps most centrally, truth-tracking, but also arguably include concern about the system among and significance of the truths that are tracked.[3] If it turns out that, given the features of the environment in which we operate and given our cognitive equipment, a norm is not truth-conducive, then that norm is no genuine norm. Thus, for example, Louise Antony argues

[3] See Antony, 1993, 2000, for exposition and defence of this naturalistic approach to the question of justifying norms. For a naturalistic discussion of epistemic virtues other than truth-tracking, see Goldman, 1986, Chapter 2.

that a norm of objectivity that enjoins us to eliminate bias in our reasoning would be a norm that fails to assist us in truth tracking: cognitive achievements, whether basic such as the ability to learn a language, or sophisticated such as the ability to produce a well-confirmed scientific theory, are made possible for finite creatures like us only on account of our having biases both native and acquired—for example, acquired as the result of participation in a going scientific research programme.[4] If such biases are central to our ability to come to know truths about the external world, then having them cannot be disparaged as irrational. Nor does the story stop with rehabilitating bias. Recent empirical research shows that 'we cannot get by epistemically without shortcuts and tricks of all kinds, many of which would not survive scrutiny by traditional epistemological lights' (Antony, 2000, 115).[5]

A naturalist inquiry into the preconditions of our cognitive abilities can thus lead to a reconception of what it takes for creatures like us to have and display theoretical rationality and there's no *in-principle* reason to think that the deliverances of this inquiry have to coincide with the deliverances of armchair inquiry into norms of theoretical rationality (and the story about bias suggests they won't). Similarly, naturalist inspired reflection on what we know about how the emotions contribute to the practical rationality of finite creatures like us might lead us to reconceive norms of practical rationality—or so it would seem.

A parallel naturalistic story about practical rationality begins by identifying the goals of practical decision-making and then offers an instrumental justification of norms of practical rationality according as they help or hinder us—again given the kinds of agents we are, operating in the kinds of environments in which we operate—in achieving those goals. There's no non-controversial and adequately determinate account of the goals of practical decision-making. But even a statement of the goals that is schematic and indeterminate enough to secure consensus across controversy, is enough to set up the problem.[6]

[4] Antony, 1993, 2000. For a discussion of the theory dependence of method and the need for presuppositions, see Boyd, 1983. An overview of these issues with selected further reading is found in Boyd, Gasper and Trout, 1991.

[5] The literature here is long, but see especially Gigerenzer, *et al.*, 1999; Stein, 1996.

[6] Thus, for the purposes of this argument, I need not take a stance on whether there are external reasons or whether all reasons are internal (Williams, 1980).

We can make progress understanding the goals of practical deci-sion-making by considering what it is that agents regret about their decisions, for regret indicates failure to do what one was trying to do. When an agent faces a practical problem, she is trying to *identify* and select an action option that responds to *all* the reason-giving considerations present in the situation, in proportion to their strength as reasons. In hard choices, there may be no action option that respects all the reason-giving considerations and the agent must select that action option that answers to the most weighty of her reasons.

When we face a practical problem, we are not just trying to act for what we *believe* to be good reasons: we are trying to act for what actually are good reasons for us (but of course the central, though not, I'll argue, the only path of access to these reasons is through our beliefs about them.) Nor are the considerations that can count as reasons limited to those that mesh with or answer to concerns that the agent *currently* values. Agents regret overlooking consider-ations that answer to currently valued concerns ('I just didn't see how my doing that could help you, I'm so sorry'), but equally they regret recognizing considerations as reason-giving on the basis of concerns that fail to survive reflective scrutiny ('I can't believe I was so worried about what he might think of me') and they regret choos-ing in ignorance of values ('I didn't appreciate the importance of family until it was too late'). As epistemic agents we are trying to latch onto truths about the world, though all we have to go on in achieving this goal are our own mechanisms and methods, reliable and otherwise, for detecting such truths, together with our own best take on the limits and liabilities of our methods and mechanisms. Likewise, as practical agents, we are trying to latch onto those con-siderations that really are reason-giving for us in a situation, yet all we have to go on in achieving this goal is nothing more than our own mechanisms and methods, reliable and otherwise, for detecting these considerations together with our own best take on the limits and liabilities of the methods we use to work out what considera-tions matter.[7] The account remains indeterminate and so minimal-ist because it leaves it open how to cash out the phrase 'really are reasons for an agent.'

---

[7] This point is not meant to imply epistemic individualism: an impor-tant method for acquiring knowledge, even knowledge about practical matters, is testimony and the task of working out the reliability of these mechanisms and methods is conducted socially, and rests on divisions of cognitive labour.

Emotion, Weakness of Will, and Normative Conception of Agency

Now, combine this minimalist account of what we are trying to do in practical decision-making with the naturalist story of how to defend norms of rationality and you get the result that it is an *empirical* question whether we are such that our all-things-considered judgments reliably help or hinder us in latching onto our reasons and thus whether those judgments should be accorded normative authority. Finally, add some observations and examples, both scientific and everyday, about the ways emotions contribute to our being able to track our reasons, not despite, but *because of* the fact that they display at most partial integration with our evaluative judgment, and one might be led to the conclusion that our all-things-considered judgment has no special normative standing and thus that acting against it is not necessarily irrational. Here are the observations and examples:

(1) Emotions exhibit varying degrees of integration with our conscious deliberative faculties and sometimes their very independence from those faculties contributes to their adaptiveness. For example, fear responses can be initiated before the stimulus is processed by the visual or auditory cortexes and the speed of response enabled by this feature of our hardwiring is unquestionably adaptive. Even brain damaged patients who are unable to form long-term memories can have functioning fear systems that enable affective learning that 'tracks' their practical reasons though without generating any higher-level understanding of that tracking. For example, Joseph LeDoux (1996) reports the case of a woman who though unable to recognize her doctors from one meeting to the next, was able to learn not to shake hands with a doctor who had previously pricked her with a tack concealed in his palm.

(2) Even emotions that cannot be had without considerable cognitive sophistication, such as resentment and indignation which require the agent to construe the situation in terms of relatively sophisticated evaluative concepts, nonetheless display only partial integration with the agent's conscious evaluative judgment. We can be resentful of persons who we sincerely judge have done nothing that merits resentment; indeed, it has been reflection on these kinds of cases, as well as cases involving phobic emotions, that has driven the current movement in philosophy of the emotions away from judgmentalist accounts that analyse the cognitive content of an emotion in terms of evaluative belief.[8] Moreover, this ability

of even sophisticated emotions to run in opposition to evaluative judgment turns out to be important for our practical rationality. Such "outlaw" (Jaggar, 1996) emotions can function as correctives to internally coherent but false and often ideologically driven views about, to mention just two examples explored in the philosophical literature, the status of women (Scheman, 1980) and of slaves (Bennett, 1974). Our efforts to make sense of outlaw emotions can provide a starting point for the critical re-examination of even quite central evaluative assumptions. Thus, emotions can function as recalcitrant data that force a change in our evaluative assumptions.

(3) In particular cases, an agent's emotions can be keyed-to her reasons in such a way that they enable the agent to track those reasons, while her all-things-considered judgment does not. Nomi Arpaly gives us the example of Emily, who has always believed that she should pursue a PhD in chemistry. Once embarked on this project, however, Emily finds herself feeling 'restless, sad, and ill-motivated' (Arpaly, 2000, 504) to stick with her studies. As Arpaly describes the case we are to suppose that Emily's affective discomfort is keying her to the reasons that she has to leave the program—her feelings are responses to the fact that the program is ill-suited to her talents, preferences, and character. Yet this evidence does not secure uptake in her judgment. She herself sees her feelings as 'groundless.' Emily acts on her feelings and leaves the program. Later she comes to understand the reasons for her feelings and 'cites them as the reasons for her quitting, and regards as irrationality not her quitting but that she held on to her conviction that the program was right for her for as long as she did.' (Arpaly, 2000, 504).

Nor are cases of this kind uncommon: often our gut-feelings key us to the presence of reasons even though we cannot, at the time,

---

[8] If we can be resentful without the conscious belief that the person has done anything to merit resentment, and if, as judgmentalists suppose, resentment is constituted in full in or in part, by an evaluative belief, then we will have to suppose that the belief in question is unconscious. But there are good reasons for not attributing such unconscious beliefs in all cases and only the very judgmentalist theory that is in dispute for supposing that there would have to be such beliefs. For an argument against attributing unconscious beliefs as promiscuously as this theory would require, see Greenspan, 1988, chapter 2. For discussion of emotions in opposition to evaluative judgment, see Calhoun, 1984, and Stocker, 1996.

articulate what those reasons are, and even though our conscious deliberative judgment tells us no such reasons obtain (you're just being silly, get a grip). Sometimes we act on these feelings against our better judgment and discover to our relief that our feelings were exactly right and that our weakness saved us from acting on the basis of a misguided all-things-considered judgment. That is, often enough our emotions and not our conscious deliberative judgment are what enables us to latch onto those reason-giving considerations that we ought to recognize. Thus, if we are committed to the naturalist project of defending norms of rationality instrumentally according as how they help or hinder us in achieving the goals of practical deliberation, then there might be real grounds for thinking that—like norms ruling out bias—norms that prohibit incontinence might not be the sort of norms that enable the kind of limited, finite, embodied agents that we are reliably to latch onto our reason-giving considerations. What normative status to accord our all-things-considered judgment becomes an empirical question and we might answer that it has no particular normative standing.

Thus, thinking about the role of emotions in keying us to our reasons might generate an account of rationality with the following features:

(i) *no necessary irrationality*: in choosing the incontinent action over the continent one, the agent does not necessarily display irrationality, as the incontinent action may be produced by a well-functioning mechanism that is reliably keying the agent to her reasons, when her all-things-considered judgment is not.

(ii) *no transparency or agential privilege*: the rationality or irrationality of an action can be very hard to discern since it will depend on whether the mechanisms that lead to the action are keying her to reasons or not. The agent may be in the *worst* position to determine this: if she chooses the incontinent action she will think she is being irrational (as Emily did) but she might be quite wrong about this.

(iii) *broad supervenience base*: the rationality of an action supervenes on a comparatively broad class of facts including most especially facts about the reliability of the mechanism that produced the action and facts about how the agent formulated her all-things-considered judgment.

(iv) *no special normative standing for all-things-considered judgment*:

a theory of rationality should not assume that there is something special about an agent's best [all-things-considered]

187

judgment. An agent's best judgment is just another belief, and for something to conflict with one's best judgment is nothing more dramatic than ordinary inconsistency between beliefs, or between beliefs and desires (Arpaly, 2000, 512)[9]

2. A problem with this picture: the normative conception of agency

I think that we should be quite worried about the picture that has emerged: to suppose, as Arpaly does, that well-functioning mechanisms capable of latching on to reasons can be sufficient for rationality and that our all-things considered judgments are normatively speaking on all fours with our other beliefs, or to suppose that whether they are on all fours normatively is an empirical question that requires further investigation as the naturalist account that's so far been on the table does, is not yet to recognize our epistemic and practical *agency*.[10]

As a reflective agent, I cannot view myself as merely a system—however well functioning—of sub-systems, that passively register and respond to environmental stimuli much as a thermostat

[9] Arpaly would assent to each of 1–4, though she is operating within a different framework from the one used here. At least for the purposes of argument, Arpaly assumes that an act is rational if it maximizes the satisfaction of the agent's desires and she takes the chief argument against the rationality of incontinence to be an argument from (in)coherence. But this is too narrow a conception of practical rationality and the main argument against incontinence is not, as we shall see, best formulated in terms of coherence. A full exploration of Arpaly's argument would take me too far from the main business of the paper to be undertaken here.

[10] For a response to my pressing this objection to the naturalist epistemological project, see Antony, 2000. My current formulation of the problem has been influenced by Louise Antony's explication of it. However, Antony puts the point in terms of 'transparency': 'Commitment to rationality involves, among other things, a norm that bids us make our reasons transparent to ourselves as we reason—arguably that is what reasoning *is*.' (114–15) I think that the point is better put in terms of a commitment to rational guidance by reasons seen as such. Some failures of transparency will be failures to guide action (belief) by reasons seen as reasons; e.g. when I'm moved by psychological forces that are mysterious and opaque to me. But framing the issues under the concept of transparency raises further issues (e.g. about the extent to which we can know about the machinery that subserves our rational processes) that seem to me orthogonal to the central issue of rational guidance.

registers and responds to changes in temperature. Nor can I view my reasoning self—that part of me that engages in conscious deliberation about what to do or what to believe—as simply one additional epistemic mechanism operating side-by-side with other mechanisms such as perceptual or emotional ones. To think of myself in this way is not to think of myself as an agent at all. It is to give up thinking of myself as rationally *guiding* my actions via reasons. Yet from the first person point of view, it seems to me that my conscious deliberative self is capable of guiding my action; moreover, it seems that I am capable of guiding my action in accordance with my best reasons, reasons not merely registered, but understood as reasons, that is, understood as *justifying* the performance of an action. Let's see if the thought can be made more precise.

Distinguish two kinds of agents differentiated by the relation in which they stand to reasons: the first kind of agent guides its action via a conception of its reasons as reasons. Agents of this kind must have the capacity for reflection, for *guiding* actions via reasons *seen as reasons* requires that the agent have a self-conception and posses the concept of a reason as something that justifies the performance of an action. Given the comparative nature of such justifications, guiding actions via reasons understood as conferring justification on the performance of one action rather than another, commits an agent to guiding actions via best reasons.[11] That is, if an agent is to have a justification for doing A *rather than* B or C, she must suppose that her best reasons support A, even though there may be something to be said for (some reasons in favour of) both B and C.

Call agents who guide their actions via reasons understood as reasons, *reason-responders*. Reason-responders must possess and exercise a complex set of capacities if they are to respond to reasons understood as reasons. Among these capacities are the capacities to step back from any actional impulse and inquire whether the desire really reflects anything choiceworthy in the action (e.g. is the desire

[11] Talk of 'best reasons' here is consistent with but by no means requires a maximizing conception of rationality according to which rational agents seek to maximize some single value which renders all values commensurable, such as happiness, or utility. I think such views make a mistake about the nature of value. My point is less controversial: that if one is to have a reason to do A *rather than* B, and one has a reason to do both (e.g. doing A would be fun, doing B would help make an important deadline) then if one is to choose A rather than B that must be because 'having fun' is in this context seen as a better reason than all its competitor reasons; that is, is seen as the best reason.

to be eliminated rather than satisfied, as are desires to smash opponents in the face with tennis rackets (Watson, 1975)). Further, the agent must be sensitive to when putative reasons are defeated and when they are outweighed. For example 'it looks green' is defeated as a reason for believing it is green the experimenter has just told me the contact lenses in my eyes will give everything a greenish hue. Thus, having sensitivity to when reasons are defeated and when they are outweighed requires the capacity to reflect on the status of the deliverances of those mechanisms that purport to latch onto reasons such as perception, emotion and desire, but also the capacity to reflect on reasoning itself—for it too can deliver false representations of the reasons that obtain. In sum, to be able to respond to reasons as reasons, an agent requires critical reflective ability, dispositions to bring that ability to bear when needed, and dispositions to have the results of such reflection control their behaviour.[12]

The second kind of agent is capable of registering reasons and behaving in accordance with them, but it need posses neither the concept of a reason nor have a self-conception. It thus need not have the higher-order reflective capacities characteristic of reason-responders. Call such agents *reason-trackers*.

Reason-responders are thus highly sophisticated reason-trackers; that is, agents capable of tracking reasons in virtue of responding to them as reasons. The advantage of being a reason-responder rather than a mere tracker is that responders will display *robustness* in their ability to track their reasons. Animals, for example can reason track through innate and learned behaviour, but a creature who lacks critical reflective capacities will not be able to display the same kind of flexibility in its action and sensitivity to the implications of changes in its environment that a reason-responder can.

With the distinction between reason-responders and reason-trackers on hand, we can now return to the task of making the thoughts about the nature of our agency, as it appears to us from the inside, at least a bit more precise. From the first person point of view, I conceive of myself as capable of being a reason-responder; that is, I *can* guide my action in accordance with reasons understood as such. Moreover, insofar as I take myself to be rational, I take

[12] A number of theorists are moving towards something like the distinction between what I'm calling reason-responders and simple animal agents, who in my terms are merely 'reason-trackers.' See Tyler Burge, 1996; Christine Korsgaard, 1996, 1997; Thomas Scanlon, 1998, Chapter 1, especially at 23; Joseph Raz, 1999; and Francois Schroeter, n.d., who offers the most extended discussion of the capacities required to act for reasons seen as such.

myself to *be* a reason-responder. Thus, any story about my rationality that is only story about whether and how my sub-systems reason-track is inadequate as a story about the kind of agent I conceive of myself as being. But, I cannot conceive of myself as a reason-responder without being committed to guiding my actions via my best reasons, for to the extent that I fail to live up to this commitment, I fail to be the *kind* of agent that I take myself to be. This commitment thus follows from my conceiving of myself as a reason-responder. In this way, it seems that not all norms of rationality are a posteriori and await empirical proof of their use-fulness: in virtue of conceiving of myself as a reason-responder I am committed to a norm that enjoins me to guide my actions via my best reasons and that says that when I fail to do so I am not rational. I can see some norms—whether norms of practical or of theoretical rationality such as the norms about bias discussed earlier—as norms that are going to help (or hinder me) in responding to my best reasons. And I can lose my allegiance to them once I see how they hinder me from latching onto my reasons, but I can't give up on this norm of rational guidance without giving up on my conception of myself as having the kind of agency I take myself to have.

It is important that this argument is phrased in terms of how I *conceive* of myself. There's a real question, and it is not immedi-ately answerable first personally, whether I actually *am* a reason-responder. Perhaps my conscious deliberation has got nothing to do with what this body that is mine subsequently does; perhaps the appearance of guidance, is just that, *appearance*. Indeed, that's what is so disquieting about empirical research showing we are skilled confabulators and about research into the determinants of our action, such as research which purports to show that, unless you select the box of cereal on the special display stand, then you will almost certainly choose the cereal on the top shelf at the end of the aisle. (When I read about that research it so happened that the cereal I buy was to be found on the top shelf at the end of the aisle, though I would have said I was buying it because it is high in fibre, and low in sugar and fat, and so it is.) Thus, there is a real question how to reconcile this normative conception of my own agency, which seems first-personally given, with third-personal accounts of the determinants of action. Moreover, by conceiving of myself as a reason-responder, and so being committed to guiding my action via best reasons, there's a chance that I might fail to be a reason-tracker. Perhaps I'd do better if I stopped attempting to guide my actions via reasons and just let my well-functioning reason-tracking mechanisms take over. I'll return to the question of

191

Karen Jones

whether we should continue to conceive of ourselves as reason-responders later in the paper.

3. Explicating the core commitment

I have claimed that if an agent is to conceive of herself as a reason-responder, then she must be committed to guiding her action via best reasons. But on one natural reading of what this commitment amounts to, it is clearly violated in cases of weakness of will: for the commitment to guide one's action via best reasons is readily understood as the commitment to guide one's action via one's all-things-considered or *best judgment* as to what one has reason to do. No doubt, it is this conception of rational guidance that explains why incontinence has been assumed to be *so* manifestly irrational that no argument for its irrationality need be given (though it is not among the many reasons Arpaly herself canvasses). Call this interpretation of the commitment, the intellectualist reading.[13] On the intellectualist reading, any agent who acts against her best judgment thereby fails to live up to this constitutive commitment. However poorly formed her all-things-considered judgment, in failing to act according to it, she adds a further failure of rationality to her failure in forming the ill-advised judgment. Moreover she adds a *failure of an especially serious kind*: she fails in respect of the very norm that defines what it is to be the kind of agent she takes herself to be. (So most often, then, it will be all-things-considered more irrational to act incontinently than continently, but—see note 1—this need not be so in every case.)

The intellectualist reading of this core commitment denies each of the four claims about rationality mentioned earlier, asserting instead:

(i) *necessary irrationality*: in choosing the incontinent action over the continent one, the agent necessarily displays irrationality; indeed, irrationality of an especially serious sort.

(ii) *transparency and agential privilege*: rationality or irrationality— insofar as these concern failure or success at guiding one's action via one's best judgment—is readily discernible and inasmuch as the agent has privileged access to her all-things-

---

[13] The intellectualist position is common: it is explicitly endorsed by Korsgaard (1997, 222); Raz, 2000, 16; Scanlon, 1998, esp. 25 and is assumed by Wallace, 1999.

considered judgment, she is in the best position to know the rational status of her action.[14]

(iii) *narrow supervenience base*: the irrationality of an action (in respect of this central norm) supervenes on a relatively narrow range of facts: what was her best judgment? What was her action? Do they match?

(iv) *privileged normative standing for all-things-considered judgment*: all-things-considered normative judgments get normative authority just in virtue of the kind of judgments they are.

On the intellectualist reading, there's a single strand to the commitment to guiding one's actions via best reasons; namely the disposition to have one's all-thing-considered judgment be *authoritative* with respect to what one subsequently does. The all-things-considered judgment is seen as having normative authority for the agent *just in virtue* of its being the deliverance of the agent's conscious reasoning self. The commitment to rational guidance is thus seen as having unique expression in acts of continence (or most perfect expression: there is a weaker position available here, but I leave it to one side as the argument goes through even against this slightly more complex position). But, to use a rather uncharitable analogy, this is much like saying that one's concern for another finds unique (or most perfect) expression in what one says. Notoriously, this is not the case.

I want to outline a third picture, distinct from both of the currently available accounts, for it seems that there should be room for an intermediate position which, like the intellectualist position, recognizes the importance of our commitment to rational guidance via reasons but which has a richer understanding of what that guidance amounts to. The alternative picture shares with the simple naturalist model the following claims:

(i) no necessary irrationality,
(ii) no transparency or agential privilege, and
(iii) broad supervenience base.

[14] The qualification, 'insofar as these concern failure or success at guiding one's action via one's best judgement' matters here (and in (iii) below). The intellectualist does not think that norms of rational guidance are the only norms of rationality, and there may be failures of transparency and privilege with respect to success at other norms. However, the intellectualist position is typically combined with epistemological internalism and thus is typically combined with the view that the agent has in principle access to the rational status of her actions and beliefs.

But, like the intellectualist account, it recognizes the centrality of the commitment to rational guidance, though it finds expression of that commitment in more activities than the intellectualist recognizes as expressive of it.

On the alternative account of rational guidance that I propose, the commitment to rational guidance is to be understood as the commitment to the on-going cultivation and exercise of habits of reflective self-monitoring of our practical and epistemic agency. That is, the commitment to rational guidance is the commitment to the on-going cultivation and exercise of whatever abilities it is that enable the agent to have and display the capacities that are characteristic of reason-responders (see section 2). It is an empirical matter what dispositions will enable agents *of the kind we are* successfully to reflect on the status of the deliverances of those mechanisms that purport to latch onto reasons—including reasoning itself. For example, there's evidence to suggest that our ability to be wise in our trust of our own judgment and of the judgment of others rests on emotional capacities such as the capacity for empathy; thus, commitment to rational guidance includes commitment to the cultivation and exercise of empathy. In this way, the dispositions that constitute the commitment to rational guidance will be many and various and they won't all be dispositions of intellect.

If the commitment is multi-stranded in the way I am suggesting it is, then it can find expression in more ways than through the agent guiding her action via her best judgment; indeed, such judgment can *fail* to express the commitment to rational guidance. On the proposed model, an all-things-considered judgment does not get normative authority for free. It has to earn such authority and it earns it in virtue of being the product of a conscious reasoning self that has itself been subject to regulation by reflective capacities.

The difference between the three models can be shown by considering what each model has to say about fast or habitual action; that is, action undertaken without deliberation, either because the situation is urgent and so deliberation is impossible, or because the situation is routine and so deliberation is unnecessary.

On the intellectualist model fast or habitual action expresses the agent's commitment to guiding her action via reasons just in case such action is the result of a reflectively endorsed policy. If I have a reflectively endorsed, for example, acting out of immediate responses of concern for my children in such and such circumstances, then action that results from those motives, even in the absence of formulating an all-things-considered judgment as to what to do nonetheless expresses my commitment to guidance via best judgment.[15] A similar story can be told about fast action: for example, I might resolve immediately to go with my gut feelings of suspicion in my work as a security guard *because*, having reflected on my track record as a detector of possibly suspicious behaviour and on the costs and consequences of deliberating under these circumstances, I judge that a context-specific policy authorizing immediate action from this affective motive is the best policy. Thus, for fast or habitual action to express an agent's commitment to rational guidance on the intellectualist account it must be the product of self-conscious policies that are themselves endorsed by judgment.

This intellectualist account of the rationality of fast or habitual action contrasts with the account that might be given by someone who thinks that well-functioning reason-tracking mechanisms are sufficient for rationality; not surprisingly, it contrasts with the account explicitly endorsed by Nomi Arpaly. According to Arpaly, no reflective policy is needed: the action is rational if produced by a reliable mechanism and that's all there is to be said. No commitment to guiding actions via reasons is recognized and thus the question of whether such action expresses that commitment does not arise. But this seems to give us the wrong answer: an agent might have a well-functioning reason-tracking mechanism and yet it not be *responsible* for her to take the deliverances of that mechanism to be reason-tracking. It's deliverances would be undermined (the parallel with belief undermining is intended). This could be the case with our security guard: she might have evidence that her suspicion fails to track and if this is so, then her continuing to act on the basis of the deliverances of her emotional sensitivities would be an irresponsible failure of rational guidance. If her self-monitoring dispositions were functioning as they should, then she would cease to trust her emotional sensitivities.

On my preferred third picture, fast and habitual action can express the commitment to rational guidance and will do so just in case the agent's dispositions to reflective self-monitoring are such that she would not rely on that first order sub-system were it reasonable for her to believe that it failed to reason-track. That is,

[15] The intellectualist need not say that agents must express their commitment to rational guidance in all domains and can allow that sometimes one should just be spontaneous (and need not have a policy about just when to be so). However, my argument does not rest on saddling the intellectualist with the further view that all action should express this commitment—the dispute is over what can express it, rather than over the domain in which it should be expressed.

her conscious reflective capacities exert *regulative guidance* over the first-order mechanism, stepping in when necessary to discount those mechanisms, and where possible, to recalibrate them into reason-tracking mechanisms through habituation. Sometimes this guidance may remain 'virtual'—that is, revealed in how the agent would behave in various counter-factual circumstances (were she to have evidence that they are unreliable, for example, but evidence she never gets since they are reliable). There's nothing mysterious about this kind of guidance: it is just one way of describing what happens when an agent's emotional responses are shaped, fine-tuned, and sometimes even radically transformed through the process of character formation so that they become reliable at latching on to the reasons that obtain for her. But we can see at once how action that results from such regulated first-order mechanisms can express the agent's commitment to rational guidance via reasons: our subsystems can reason-track because we, as agents, reason-respond.[16]

The preferred third model has implications for what we should say about the rationality of some cases of incontinence. Regulated sub-systems that reason-track because we reason-respond can be no less operative in generating action when there is an all-things-considered judgment that opposes the action so produced. That is, the functioning of such sub-systems does not stop being expressive of our commitment to rational guidance just because there is now an opposing all-things-considered judgment. In some cases that all-things-considered judgment may be such that the agent would distrust it, if her self-monitoring capacities were functioning as they should. Thus, the regulated sub-system can be more expressive of the agent's commitment to rational guidance than the all-things-considered judgment: the incontinent action can display the agent's commitment to rational guidance more fully than does the continent action.

We can generate a schema for producing examples of rational incontinence: incontinence will be rational just in case: (1) the action is produced by a sub-system that reason-tracks because the agent reason-responded, and (2) the agent would have distrusted her all-things-considered judgment were her self-monitoring

---

[16] To be precise, but at the cost of the elegance of the slogan, the 'because' should sometimes be read as an initiating because, and sometimes as a maintaining one. That is, sometimes we, as agents, initiate a method, or recalibrate a mechanism in order to latch-on to our reasons; other times, a mechanism will be maintained in place under the 'virtual' guidance of our reflective self-monitoring capacities.

dispositions operating as they should. Once you see how to construct such examples, you can find them all over the place—for example, feminist anger can undo a decision not to raise a certain topic at a meeting and subsequent reflection on what happened can reveal that the decision not to raise the issue was the product of cowardice rather than of a sober assessment of the merits of investing scarce credibility resources to fight this fight rather than some other one. Of course, it won't be easy for the agent to work out whether her action is rational and she will have no privileged access to its rationality—but that result seems to me unsurprising. Further, whether the action is rational supervenes on a complex set of facts about the dispositions that were operative in generating the action. Often these dispositions will reveal themselves in what happens *next*: any agent committed to guiding action via reasons will experience disquiet at her own incontinence. She will want to reflect on that action —and such reflection may indeed reveal that the action was irrational. I am certainly not claiming that most incontinent action is rational. Most of it is not. What I am claiming is only that such action does not necessarily fall afoul of what seems from the first person point of view to be a non-negotiable commitment, a commitment that follows from conceiving of ourselves as having a certain kind of epistemic and practical agency.

If these reflections are along the right lines, then there's another strategy open to anyone who would deny the commonly made assertion that emotions are, if not outright irrational in themselves, then frequent contributing causes of irrationality insofar as they are frequent contributing causes of incontinence. It is salutary to remind anyone who charges emotions with causing incontinence that we frequently fail to do what we judge we ought to do because we cannot summon the compassion or the anger required to do it. Thus emotions can help us to act on our all-things-considered judgment as well as hindering us from doing so. But if I'm right, then we can *also* say: sure, emotions sometimes contribute to incontinence, but that may be just what we need to get us to overcome poor all-things-considered judgment and cannot be assumed necessarily to be irrational.

The argument I've presented is conditional: if we are to conceive of ourselves as reason-responders then we must be committed to the norm of guiding action via best reasons. First personally, it seems that we do conceive of ourselves as agents of this kind, at least insofar as we think of ourselves as rational. I've argued that this self-conception gives rise to norms that do not await further instrumental justification through a demonstration of their

Karen Jones

usefulness (as all norms must on one standard naturalist account of them): you get the norm in virtue of the self-conception. But this pushes the question back one step further. Should we think of ourselves as being reason-responders, given that thinking of ourselves in this way brings with it a commitment to the cultivation and exercise of habits of reflective self-monitoring?

There's an instrumental argument to be given here: if you think of yourself this way, then, unless your reflective capacities are really deficient or unless you are unfortunate enough to inhabit some kind of demon-world in which non-reflective sub-systems reason-track while the demon makes sure you'll mess things up if you try and reflect on their reliability, the chances are you will be more nearly able to reason-track than you would if you did not. Attempting to reason-respond can bring it about that you are better able to latch-on to your reasons. And it can bring the benefits of robustness to your reason-tracking abilities. I think the instrumental argument is fine, as far as it goes: we *are* better off thinking of ourselves in this way. I'm willing to bet the farm we're not so stupid or so unlucky that this commitment is a liability. But there is more to be said here—and I think that saying it is compatible with a naturalist approach to normativity. That more is this: in affirming the value of the normative commitment to guiding action (or belief) via best reasons, we affirm the value of the kind of agency we take ourselves to have. We do not *have* to affirm the value of this kind of agency, but if we fail to affirm it, then we fail to affirm the value of something valuable. And that's a non-instrumental reason for affirming the value of this central norm.[17]

Bibliography

Antony, Louise. 1993. 'Quine as Feminist: The Radical Import of Naturalized Epistemology', In Louise Antony and Charlotte Witt (eds) *A Mind of One's Own* (Bolder, Co: Westview Press).

[17] This answer belongs in a family of answers first sketched by Louise Antony, as follows: 'Since it is the active and self-conscious consideration of reasons that makes one an epistemic agent, the norms of rationality can be said to express our conception of what it is to be an epistemic agent; and to endorse that norm is to express one's commitment to the value of such agency.' (2000, 127). Antony's formulation is neutral between a realist gloss on evaluative judgments and an expressivist one. For reasons that cannot be explored here, I have offered a self-consciously realist statement of the evaluative mistake we make if we fail to affirm the value of this kind of agency.

Antony, Louise. 2000. 'Naturalised Epistemology, Morality, and the Real World', *Canadian Journal of Philosophy*, Supplementary Volume 26, 103–37.

Arpaly, Nomi. 2000. 'On Acting Rationally Against One's Best Judgement', *Ethics* **110**, 488–513.

Bennett, Jonathan. 1974. 'The Conscience of Huckleberry Finn', *Philosophy* **49**, 123–34.

Boyd, Richard. 1983. 'On the current status of the issue of scientific realism', *Erkenntnis* **19**, 45–90.

Boyd, R. Gasper, P. and Trout, J. D. (eds). 1991. *The Philosophy of Science* (MIT Press: Cambridge).

Burge, Tyler. 1996. 'Our Entitlement to Self-Knowledge', *Proceedings of the Aristotelian Society* **96**, 91–116.

Calhoun, Cheshire. 1984. 'Cognitive Emotions?' In Calhoun and Solomon 1984, 327–42.

Calhoun, Cheshire. 1989. 'Subjectivity and Emotion', *The Philosophical Forum*, Vol. 10, 195–210.

Calhoun, Cheshire, and Robert Solomon, (eds), 1984. *What is an Emotion? Classic Readings in Philosophical Psychology* (New York: Oxford University Press).

Descartes, Rene. 1985[1649]. *The Passions of the Soul.* In John Cottingham, Robert Stoothoff and Dugald Murdoch (trans.) *The Philosophical Writings of Descartes* Vol. 1. (Cambridge: Cambridge University Press).

de Sousa, Ronald. 1979. 'The Rationality of Emotions', In Rorty 1980, 127–52.

de Sousa, Ronald. 1987. *The Rationality of Emotion* (Cambridge: MIT Press).

Elster, Jon. 1999. *Alchemies of the Mind: Rationality and the Emotions* (Cambridge University Press).

Frank, Robert. 1988. *Passions within Reason* (New York: Norton).

Gigerenzer, Gerd, Todd, Peter and the ABC Research Group. 1999. *Simple Heuristics that Make us Smart* (New York: Oxford University Press).

Goldman, Alvin. 1986. *Epistemology and Cognition* (Cambridge: Harvard University Press).

Greenspan, Patricia S. 1988. *Emotions and Reasons: An Inquiry into Emotional Justification* (New York: Routledge).

Jaggar, Allison. 1996. 'Love and Knowledge: Emotion in Feminist Epistemology', In Ann Garry and Marilyn Pearsall (eds), *Women, Knowledge, and Reality.* Second Edition. (New York: Routledge), 166–190.

Korsgaard, Christine. 1996. *The Sources of Normativity* (Cambridge University Press).

Korsgaard, Christine. 1997. 'The Normativity of Instrumental Reason', In Garret Cullity and Berys Gaut (eds) *Ethics and Practical Reason.* (Oxford: Claredon Press).

Le Doux, Joseph. 1996. *The Emotional Brain: The Mysterious Underpinnings of Emotional Life* (New York: Simon and Schuster).

Karen Jones

Moran, Richard. 1988. 'Making Up Your Mind: Self-Interpretation and Self-Constitution', *Ratio*, n.s. 1, 135–51.

Owen, David. n.d. 'The Authority of Practical Judgement'.

Raz, Joseph. 2000. 'When we are ourselves: the active and the passive', In his, *Engaging Reason* (Oxford: OUP), 5–21.

Scanlon, T. M. 1998. *What We Owe to Each Other* (Cambridge, MA: Harvard University Press).

Scheman, Naomi. 1980. 'Anger and the politics of naming', In Sally McConell-Ginet, Ruth Borker and Nellie Furman (eds) *Women and Language in Literature and Society* (New York: Praeger), 174–87.

Schroeter, Francois. 2001. 'Normative Concepts and Motivation'.

Solomon, Robert C. 1973. 'Emotions and Choice', In Rorty 1980, 251–81.

Solomon, Robert C. 1976. *The Passions* (Garden City, New York: Anchor/Doubleday Press).

Stein, Edward. 1996. *Without Good Reason* (Oxford: The Claredon Press).

Stocker, Michael with Elizabeth Hegeman. 1996. *Valuing Emotions* (Cambridge University Press).

Wallace, R. Jay 1999. 'Three Conceptions of Rational Agency', *Ethical Theory and Moral Practice* 2, 217–42.

Watson, Gary. 1975. 'Free Agency." *Journal of Philosophy* 72, 205–22.

Williams, Bernard. 1980. 'Internal and External Reasons', In his *Moral Luck: Philosophical Papers 1973–1980*, 101–13. (Cambridge: Cambridge University Press), 1981.

XII. Narrative and Perspective; Values and Appropriate Emotions

PETER GOLDIE

To the realists.—You sober people who feel well armed against passion and fantasies and would like to turn your emptiness into a matter of pride and ornament: you call yourselves realists and hint that the world really is the way it appears to you. As if reality stood unveiled before you only, and you yourselves were perhaps the best part of it ... But in your unveiled state are not even you still very passionate and dark creatures compared to fish, and still far too similar to an artist in love? And what is 'reality' for an artist in love? You are still burdened with those estimates of things that have their origin in the passions and loves of former centuries. Your sobriety still contains a secret and inextinguishable drunkenness. Your love of 'reality', for example——oh, that is a primeval 'love' ... Subtract the phantasm and every human contribution from it, my sober friends! If you can! If you can forget your descent, your past, your training—all of your humanity and animality. (F. Nietzsche, *The Gay Science*, Book Two, extract from Section 57)

I

We are reflective creatures, capable of thoughts about thoughts, feelings about feelings, and emotions about emotions. Of course, we can be unreflectively engaged in daily interaction with the world, and most of us often are. But our capacity for reflection gives rise to something of a need: a need to understand our lives though reflection on what has happened. So we can agree both with Kafka when he said that our daily life is the only life we have, and also with Kierkegaard when he said that we live our lives forward, but understand them only backwards. We find an extreme case in Leontes, who, in Act III of *The Winter's Tale*, was only able to understand his jealous rage for what it was after it was over; only then could he say 'I have too much believed my own suspicion'. But, by choosing this example, I do not intend to encourage the idea that I mean the domain of emotions to include just those short-term episodes of

Peter Goldie

occurrent emotion that immediately and patently impinge on the way we see the world. Within the category of emotions I mean also to include more enduring psychological states and sentiments, which can imperceptibly colour our view of things. As Robert Musil puts it, 'Not just the way we see red when we get angry—that too, moreover; it is only erroneously that one considers it something that is an occasional exception, without suspecting what deep and general law one has touched upon!—but rather like this: things swim in emotions the way water lilies consist not only of leaves and flowers and white and green but also of "gently lying there"' (1995: 1561).

What I want to do today is to consider what is involved when we seek to understand our own and others' lives backwards, reflecting on earlier thoughts, feelings and emotions, and responding emotionally to them. The idea I want to put forward is that everyday explanation of what we think, feel, and do is narrative in form, presenting what happened from a possible multiplicity of perspectives: not just the perspectives of those involved in what happened, but also the perspective of the narrator—the person who is giving the explanation. Seeing our everyday explanations in this light enables us also to see how emotional responses to value can be recognised in this potential multiplicity of perspectives. Things swim in emotions. In this respect, everyday explanation is extremely close to fictional narrative, and this is because they are both species of the same genus—the genus *story*.

Recently, there has been a lot of very fertile philosophical work, and work in literary theory, concerning the nature of fictional narrative, the point of view in fiction, and our emotional responses to fiction[1]. In a way, my project can be seen as an attempt to apply the fruits of this work back onto everyday explanation, in support of the more general idea that everyday explanation, like fiction, is narrative in form, and that the perspective of the narrator is essential here, just as it is in fictional narrative.

This will be my main burden. But I want to end, in disagreement with a rather fashionable view found in literary theory (and sometimes also in philosophy), by insisting that everyday explanation and fiction, although members of the same genus, differ so far as

[1] See, for example, Currie (1990 and 1997), Walton (1990), Lamarque and Olsen (1994), Genette (1980), Ricoeur (1984, 1985, 1988), Bal (1997), and the collection of papers in Hjort and Laver (1997). Accounts of what might happen in the future, or of what might have happened in the past, can also be narrative in form, but these sorts of narrative are not my concern here.

concerns the possibility of truth: in fiction, the question of truth and falsity does not arise; whereas factual narratives can be true or false, and their being narrative in form, and thus presenting what happened from a perspective, does not imply otherwise.

II

Let me begin with a very compacted summary of the central idea. Then I will get into the detail. A narrative or story is something that can be told or narrated; it need not be narrated, though: it can be just 'thought through', as when one remembers or imagines a sequence of events. It is more than just a chronicle of a bare sequence of events, but a representation of those events that is organised, shaped and coloured in a certain way, thereby giving coherence, meaningfulness, and emotional import to what happened[2]. A narrative can report or otherwise indicate the perspective or point of view—including the thoughts, feelings and emotions—of one or more of the characters internal to the narrative, of whom one might be the internal narrator—Sherlock Holmes or Watson in the *Sherlock Holmes* stories for example. This sort of perspective I will call *internal*. (Stories can sometimes be told in a way that presents no internal perspective, but I will not dwell on this type of story here.) Then, at a level that is external to the narrative, the narrator voices his or her own *external perspective*. This external perspective is necessarily distinct from the internal perspective even where, as in first-personal autobiographical narratives, the two perspectives are those of one and the same person. And the external perspective is always there, always shaping and colouring the narrative, and thereby indicating the narrator's own evaluation of what happened, and his or her emotional response thereto, as well as inviting from the audience a similar sort of response.

I should at this stage point out a complication that I will, in general, pass over, although I will briefly come back to it later. Sometimes, where we are concerned with a written narrative, the person whose narrative voice that we hear (that is, the voice of the person who in fact *reads*) might be a different person from the nar-

---

[2] Cf. Aristotle *Poetics*, and Ricoeur (1984). For a detailed discussion of the idea of perspective or point of view in literature, see Bal (1997). Bal, like Genette (1980), uses the term 'focalisation'. Although I have learnt much from Bal, I have found that I can express what I need without the use of this technical expression.

rator (that is, the person who in fact *wrote* the narrative), or it might be the same person at a significantly different time. In such a case, the narrative voice could, in effect, alter the shaping and colouring achieved by the external perspective as it emerges directly from the text. For example, I could read my childhood diary in an ironic tone of voice when I, the original author, did not intend this irony. But let me leave this complication to one side for the moment.

It follows from the fact that a narrative involves these two levels of perspective that an adequate *understanding* of a narrative requires gaining a grasp of emotional responses at both levels: those of the external narrator, and those of one or more of the people involved in the narrative. This latter sort of understanding, often going under the name of simulation or imaginative identification, is familiar from the Verstehen tradition, and, more recently, from the work of Robert Gordon, Alvin Goldman, Jane Heal and others, where simulation theory has been put forward in contrast to, or at least in addition to, what has been the more entrenched view in philosophy of mind, that understanding involves deployment of a theory of mind[3]. I do not want to take issue here with the debate between simulation theory and theory theory, nor with the debate *within* simulation theory; I suspect that there are many ways of gaining a grasp of someone's thoughts and feelings, and no single theory should seek for hegemony in this area. But what I do want to emphasise is that understanding a narrative involves more than just grasping internal perspectives—the thoughts and feelings of characters in the narrative—however that particular task is achieved. It also involves grasping at the external level the *narrator's* perspective, and this seems to me to have been neglected on all sides of the recent debate. Perhaps one reason for this neglect is that the focus in the debate has been on our ability to *predict*, and how the competing theories can

[3] See, for example, Gordon (1995) and Goldman (1992) for accounts of imaginative simulation, and Heal (1998 and 2000) for accounts of what she calls co-cognition, as a distinct sort of simulation. I do not wish to suggest that co-cognition and imaginative identification (through empathy—centrally imagining from the other's perspective—or through putting yourself in the other's shoes) are the same thing. See Heal (2000, esp. Fn 5 and 7) for a discussion of the relation between the two. Although both processes are ways of getting a grasp of the thoughts of others, co-cognition would seem to be restricted to thoughts as propositional attitudes, capable of bearing rational relations to each other, and thus cannot cover, for example, feelings or moods. In fact, I am not sure what the relation is between these two processes; perhaps co-cognition is necessary but not sufficient for imaginative identification. But nothing that I say in what follows hangs on these issues.

account for this ability. This is all very interesting, but we should not lose sight of the fact that the role of the external perspective is very different when we seek to predict from what it is when we seek to *explain* what has already happened[4]. In everyday explanation, the role of the narrator's external perspective is essential; and it is, accordingly, essential to grasp that perspective if one is adequately to understand such a narrative.

All that was by way of summary. Now let me try to bring out in more detail the role of these different levels of perspective, and the essential role of the external perspective, by considering in turn first-personal and third-personal explanations and narratives. In first-personal explanation, of course, it is human—all too human— to take one's own side. That is to say, we tend to offer explanations involving our own internal perspective on what happened and not that of the other people involved. Thus, in order to explain what we did, we tend to appeal to how the situation struck us, whereas we tend to explain the actions of others by appeal to their fixed character traits. So typically we have 'I acted as I did because my experience was terrifying' and 'She acted as she did because she is a timid person'. This tendency is known in social psychology as *agent-observer divergence*[5]. Thus, in these typical cases, the perspective of the external narrator, as expressed in the narrative voice, and the perspective that is internal to the narrative, are perspectives of one and the same person. It would, however, be seriously mistaken to think that the need to distinguish the external and internal perspectives is accordingly less important than it is in third-personal narratives, just because they are the perspectives of one and the same person. To show this, let me begin with a fairly straightforward example of an everyday explanation in the first person.

[4] See Footnote 7 below for a brief further discussion.
[5] See, for example, Storms (1973) and Regan and Totten (1975). But we can, of course, imagine ourselves as others would see us. Anyone who has seen a replay of a video of himself making a presentation will be familiar with this sort of phenomenon: we suddenly see ourselves as the audience would have seen us, and exclaim: 'I didn't know I was such a nervous person'. (Agent-observer divergence has been reversed in experimental conditions by Storms (1973).) An example of Hume's nicely captures the idea of how we can shift perspective: 'A man will be mortified if you tell him he has a stinking breath; though it is evidently no annoyance to himself. Our fancy easily changes its situation; and, either surveying ourselves as we appear to others, or considering others as they feel themselves, we enter, by that means, into sentiments which no way belong to us, and in which nothing but sympathy is able to interest us' (*Treatise*, Book III, part III, Section 1).

Peter Goldie

(1) 'Last night, in the dark, I tripped over because a suitcase had been left in the hall whilst I was out shopping.'

Here the explanation involves an external perspective, which is mine with the knowledge that I now have about the presence of the suitcase, whilst, at the internal level, the internal perspective is mine at the time of the experience of tripping over. The presence of these two distinct perspectives of mine can be seen through consideration of how I go about recreating what happened in imagination—in particular in my visual imagination—in order to be able to relate the story. What I do not do is recreate now in imagination exactly how things seemed to me then. To do this, I would have to 'abstract' the presence of the suitcase in the hall from what I now know, and then imagine myself *centrally*, or 'from the inside', unwittingly tripping over something that I did not observe. This is not so easy to do—at least in a way that is unalloyed by what I now know. In such circumstances, it is, at least typically, easier for me to imagine myself *acentrally*, that is for me-now to imagine, at this level not from a point of view within the imagined scene, me-then tripping over a suitcase which was unseen by me-then[6]. In this sense, what I do in this imaginative process is, so to speak, stand back from my earlier self, acentrally imagining the scene unfold. Accordingly, as I am myself standing back in this way, and not centrally imagining myself as I then was, the story that I relate does not invite you either to imaginatively identify with me as I then was, although this is something you could try to do. Rather, the story invites you to do what I now do, which is to acentrally imagine me-then tripping over a suitcase which was unseen by me-then. If you do this, you will have, in a sense, come to stand beside my later self, sharing the same external perspective[7].

[6] This acentral imagining is equivalent to what Currie (1995) calls impersonal perceptual imagining. (He argues, surely rightly, that impersonal perceptual imagining is what is typically involved with cinema audiences.) The contrast between central and acentral imagining is set out in Wollheim (1984).

[7] There is, I think, an asymmetry in the first-person case between thinking back over how things went and thinking forward when planning or predicting how things will go. In thinking back I tend, for the reasons I have given, to imagine myself acentrally. Whereas in thinking forward I tend to imagine myself centrally or from the inside. Contrast, for example, on the one hand going back in your imagination over a job interview which has taken place, and on the other hand, planning a job interview which is yet to take place. This point does not apply to all forward thinking though. If one tries to think forward far enough, or to think about oneself as a signif-

Narrative and Perspective; Values and Appropriate Emotions

The point generalises to other autobiographical narratives. What is typical when one is autobiographically recounting something with the benefit of hindsight is for the explanation to include things that it would not if the narration were a present-tense stream-of-consciousness account, just as the narrative of my tumble invites the audience to imagine the presence of the suitcase before imagining me tripping. And thus the explanation includes *what wasn't known then.* Nicola King, at the beginning of her book, *Memory, Narrative, Identity*, brings out the import of this last phrase with great starkness where she recounts how she heard a talk given by a survivor of Auschwitz, Leon Greenman. In the talk, she says, 'Greenman describes the moment when, after arriving at Auschwitz, he saw his wife being taken away on a truck—to the gas chamber, although, as he said, he "didn't know that then". This phrase', she continues, 'haunted his narrative, repeated several times: it marked the moments when emotion broke through what was otherwise a rather detached, dead-pan delivery. His memory of that moment seems to have been deeply affected by what he didn't know at the time of the event'[8].

I will now turn to the role of the different levels of perspective in *third*-personal explanations and stories. Consider, for example, the following third-personal account of something that, in fact, happened, where I am the narrator and you are the audience:

(2) 'Two strangers, a woman and a man, were the only passengers on a tube train late one night. The man, in a shabby Macintosh, smelling of drink, stood up, and, towering over the woman, who was frozen to the spot, began to shout at her and spray her with saliva.'

[8] King (2000: 1). A central theme of King's book is to contrast two views of the way in which the past is recollected, both of which she finds in the writing of Freud. In one view, the past is understood on an archaeological model, where the past is initially hidden, and is waiting to be rediscovered through excavation. In the other view, 'memory inevitably incorporates the awareness of "what wasn't known then"' (2000: 12); so memory is more of a reconstruction than an excavation and rediscovery. Here, in this later view, Freud's concept of *Nachträglichkeit* (translated roughly as 'afterwardsness') is to the fore.

---

icantly different sort of person, one tends to imagine acentrally. Trying to imagine being twenty years older, you see yourself in the wheelchair, with a rug on your lap and saliva trickling down your chin. You thereby feel repelled as well as ashamed. Trying to imagine being ten million pounds richer, you feel admiration as well as pride. (I have in mind here Hume's 'square' of passions; see Book II of his *Treatise*.)

Peter Goldie

This very short narrative involves perspectives on two levels: that of the woman at the level that is internal to the narrative; and that of me, the narrator, at the level that is external to the narrative. So far as concerns the internal level, it is clear from the second sentence that I, as narrator, am inviting you, the audience, to grasp the *woman's* perspective, rather than the man's, and thus to think about how things were for her, and, so far as you are able, to imaginatively identify with her feelings of fear and revulsion at the man's behaviour. Your focus of attention is drawn to her perspective through the way that the narrative is presented by me[9]: and, in this example, this effect is achieved without my directly ascribing, as part of the narration, any thoughts, feelings or emotions to the woman. One could put it like this: I, the narrator, *show* her state of mind, rather than specifically *stating it* as part of the narrative itself. Next, and distinctly, I, the narrator, invite you to share in my own external perspective on what happened, imagining what happened acentrally, and in doing this I also invite you to respond emotionally as I do, with compassion at her plight. Again, though, this is achieved without my actually stating that I feel compassion for her or that I think that compassion is deserved; no overtly emotional terms are used.

So, if the narration is successful, you, the audience, will gain a grasp of, and come to share in, emotional responses at two distinct levels of perspective: the emotional responses of the woman, internal to the narrative (namely fear and revulsion), and the emotional responses of me the narrator, external to the narrative (namely compassion). Success is a matter of degree at both levels of perspective. The extent to which you imagine feeling fear and revulsion, or even actually feel these emotions, will depend in part on how much you are like the woman, and in part on how much you imaginatively enter into the situation as it faced her. And the extent to which you feel compassion will depend in part on how compassionate an audience you are, and in part on how much you consider compassion to be appropriate in this instance. Success at both levels will also depend on how evocative of these emotions the narrative is; a longer story, better told, would have more success.

In this story, then, there is what I will call *concordance* between

---

[9] Cf Carroll (1997). Carroll rejects what he considers to be Plato's idea, that the audience identifies with the characters in the text, so that their emotions 'are transferred to the audience'; he emphasizes, in contrast, the idea that the audience has an emotional response to the text. I am in agreement with him about the latter idea, but to my mind he downplays the importance of imaginative identification; as audience one can respond emotionally in *both* ways.

208

the emotions at the two levels: between the fear and revulsion felt by the woman, which you grasp through gaining insight into her perspective, and the compassion that the narrator and audience feel towards her emotions. This need not be the case. For example, another story might be told about the incident on the tube train where the internal perspective is shifted to that of the man, so that you are invited to imaginatively identify with him rather than with the woman:

(3) 'Two strangers, a woman and a man, were the only passengers on a tube train late one night. The man had been drinking all evening, and, as sometimes happens to us when we have had too much to drink, suddenly, and for no good reason, he became very angry with the woman, and got up and began to tell her in no uncertain terms just what he thought of her disapproving glances.'

Here, the internal perspective has shifted to that of the man, so that you the audience are invited to imaginatively identify with his anger. But the external perspective remains the same, continuing to present the story in a way that invites just the same emotional response as before: compassion with her horror and not with his anger. Thus in this example we have *discordance* of emotional response between the two levels.

Equally, there might be discordance between external and internal levels in a first-personal story. In relating my own drunken behaviour one night, I might now invite you to imagine how it was for me then, in fits of hysterical laughter, trying to retrieve my keys from the gutter; but still I now invite you also to share in the embarrassment that I now feel at my earlier behaviour.

Discordance of emotions can occur between perspectives at the *same* level, as well as between internal and external levels of perspective. At the internal level, of course, there can be discordance where the perspective of more than one character is presented. For example, in Act I of *The Winter's Tale*, there was discordance between the perspective of Leontes—involving jealous rage—and that of the other characters. At the external level, there can be discordance in a number of places. First, there can be discordance between the narrator's response, which the audience is invited to grasp, and the response of the audience itself. For example, my narrative might invite compassion, yet you fail to feel compassion[10].

---

[10] Currie calls this a failure of 'emotional congruence' (1990: 213), although on his account, this is with the fictional or implied narrator, not with the actual narrator. See Livingston and Mele (1997) for a rejection of the notion of the implied narrator. I too have no need for it. Indeed, the postulation of an implied narrator without an actual author precludes the possibility of failed authorial intentions.

Peter Goldie

Second, there can be discordance amongst different members of the audience. For example, some members of the audience might respond with compassion and some with amusement. Third, there can be discordance between the perspective of the narrator of the written text and the perspective expressed through the spoken narrative voice. This is what happened in the example I gave earlier of my ironic reading of my own childhood diary. Fourth, a narrative can present an external emotional perspective that was not intended by the author. For example, I might give an account of my behaviour at a cocktail party that unintentionally reveals my arrogance and vanity. Fifth, a narrative can fail to present an emotional perspective that was intended by the external narrator. For example, I might tell the story of the woman on the tube intending to invite compassion, but failing in that intention. And finally, there can be emotional discordance where a narrative is insincere. For example, I might tell the story of the woman on the tube in a way that intentionally indicates and invites compassion, whilst myself feeling no such emotion. Perhaps I am trying to give the impression that I am compassionate in order to make a good impression on my audience; perhaps I really think she was just a silly old woman. If you, the audience, see through my insincerity, you will respond emotionally to me, and to the discordance between what I indicate that I feel and what are my real feelings. One should not forget that we tell stories with all sorts of motives in mind other than to communicate the content of the story: to curry favour, to amuse, to impress, to shock, to deceive, and so forth.

We have, then, a picture of narrative, perspective and emotional response that is at the same time quite complicated and yet, I hope, utterly familiar to each of us. In hearing a narrative related, whether fiction or everyday explanation, a member of the audience can latch on to possibly multiply divergent perspectives and thus on to possibly multiply divergent emotional responses: that of one or more of the people involved in the narrative, that of the external narrator of the written text, that of the speaker of the narration, and that of others in the audience. And we can, more or less, hold all of these perspectives in our minds pretty much at the same time—at least well enough to gain an insight into the concordant or discordant emotional responses across all of these possible locations.

How is it that narratives can be *explanations*, which can give *understanding* of why things happened as they did? Let me be brief here, reserving a fuller answer for another place. The essential idea is that a narrative can throw light on the particularity of what happened within, and beyond, the particular narrative under consideration, and it can do this without aspiring to be anything like a full

210

causal explanation. This sort of explanation is what Collingwood (1946) calls *idiographic*; as the OED defines this term, it is 'concerned with the individual, pertaining to or descriptive of single and unique facts and processes' (in contrast to *nomothetic* explanation, which is 'concerned with the study of general or scientific laws')[11]. Idiographic explanations can be replete with sentences that are, or that imply, causal statements; and causal statements will imply that there is a causal law under which these events fall. So, even though narrative explanations do not set out to be full causal explanations, the events that they describe are still part of the causal nexus, and thus can fall under general or scientific laws. For example, the narrative in (1) explains why I tripped over: the hall was dark; the suitcase was left in the hall; it was unseen by me; and so on. And the narrative in (2) would explain why, later that evening, the woman got home in tears: after hearing the explanation, one could say 'Now I understand why she was so upset!'.

How are we to explain our emotional responses to narratives, both in those instances where there is concordance amongst the diverse perspectives, and where there is discordance? The idea here is that each perspective involves not only emotions, but also evaluative thoughts, and concordance or discordance between evaluative thoughts can explain concordance or discordance between emotional responses.

III

Each perspective involved in the narration of a story potentially involves an emotional response to value[12]. To illustrate how this works, let me return to the story (2) of the encounter on the tube train between the woman and the drunken man. It is, I hope, by

[11] Thanks to Neil Mason for telling me about Collingwood here.

[12] In what follows, I will remain neutral on the metaphysics of value. I am in effect advocating what Justin D'Arms and Daniel Jacobson (2000) have recently called an 'ecumenical' stance between those who agree that there is an intimate relation between emotion and value, but who disagree on weighty metaphysical issues about value: cognitivism, non-cognitivism, realism, and projectivism; see for example Wiggins (1987), McDowell (1985), Blackburn (1998), and Gibbard (1990). Also see Goldie (2000) and Goldie (forthcoming b). The agreements in this area seem to be much more important that the disagreements: it is agreed by the contestants that value properties are anthropocentric; it is agreed that the phenomenology involves experience of value properties as monadic; it is agreed that recognition of value is related internally to certain motivations; and it is agreed that first-order ethical discourse allows talk of correctness, and of justification, and of openness of opinion to correction.

now familiar that this narrative indicates or suggests the woman's internal perspective, and thus invites you, the audience, so far as you are able, to imaginatively identify with her thoughts and feelings of fear and revulsion at the man's behaviour. But not only are you invited to do this; you are also invited to assume, still at this internal level of perspective, that the woman took her emotional response to be justified and appropriate: she considered the man's behaviour to be both frightening and revolting—that is, *to be an appropriate object of both fear and revulsion.* This need not be the case; it is possible to experience an emotion and at the same time believe that the emotional response is inappropriate; for example, I might fear the dark but believe the dark not to be an appropriate object of fear. But this is not the case in this narrative. In this narrative, we can discern, at the internal level of perspective, both her emotions (fear and revulsion) and her evaluative thought (that the man's behaviour was frightening and revolting), which makes her emotions appropriate by her lights. Then, moving to the external level, the narrator's external perspective in this case endorses her emotional response, thereby indicating that her fear and revulsion were indeed appropriate and that this is because the man's behaviour was indeed frightening and revolting. And this explains why the narrative invites the reader or audience, through acentral imagination, to join the narrator in feeling compassion for her, for she is an appropriate object of compassion. So we have emotions and evaluative thoughts at this external level too—emotions and thoughts that are, in this case, concordant with those at the internal level.

We can now see that a narrative will be appropriate only if the external emotional responses that are invited through the narrative are *really* appropriate to what happened. Other narratives, inviting other external emotional responses, will be inappropriate. For example, it would be an inappropriate narration of the incident on the tube if it suggested that compassion with the woman's horror was not appropriate, and that it was all really rather amusing and harmless.

This notion of what makes a narrative appropriate thus leaves room for the posibility that a narrative can be appropriate whilst inviting you to imaginatively identify, at the internal level, with an inappropriate emotional response of a character, one which that character mistakenly considers to be appropriate. To take a gruesome example, I might tell a story of a camp guard at Auschwitz, inviting you to imaginatively identify with his pride at a job well done as he finishes neatly sorting out all the clothes, shoes and jewellery of those who have been gassed, and you might, at least to some extent, succeed in getting inside this man's mind. Yet the narrative could still be appropriate, because, at the same time, and at the external level, my narrative could reveal that it was really a terrible and evil job well done, and thus that his pride was utterly inappropriate. Stories told in this way, inviting one to imaginatively identify with bad people who do not think they are bad, can be very upsetting to read: one feels, so to speak, torn between two perspectives.

This account of narrative and perspective, and of emotion and evaluative thought, can now be applied in principle to narrative as a genus, and thus to fiction as well as to everyday explanation. We respond emotionally to fictional stories, when we know them to be such, in two distinct ways. One mode of response, which is not my concern here, is to see the characters *as characters*, crafted by the author. We might, for example, judge Vronsky in *Anna Karenin* to be insufficiently characterized by Tolstoy for the purposes of the story. Another mode of response, which *is* my concern, is our response to the characters *as persons*. Here the question of appropriate emotional response arises just as it does in everyday explanations[13]. When we respond in this way to Vronsky, we judge him as we do a real person, and, in the fiction, we respond emotionally as we would to a real person: for example, we are genuinely shocked at his lack of feeling at the death of his horse[14].

Shared external emotional responses to fiction are, in many ways, as important to us as are shared external emotional responses to what happens in the real world. And it is largely for this reason that fiction is such a central part of a child's moral education. Children are brought up on stories, and the paradigms of moral thought that we find in fables, fairly stories, parables, and *contes moraux* provide a guide to appropriate emotional responses and to values. For example, the parent or carer, in reading the story of Cinderella to the child, guides the child towards a grasp of the values which the story illustrates, and he or she does so by guiding the child to what is, hopefully, the appropriate external emotional response. And Jesus, in narrating the parable of the prodigal son, not only invites us to identify

[13] Walton (1990) and Lamarque and Olsen (1994) discuss these two different sorts of reader response.
[14] That there is emotion, and that it is genuine, should be acceptable to all sides of the debate on the paradox of fiction. Walton (1997), for example, finds that he needs to respond to his critics of his earlier work (1990): 'It goes without saying that we *are* genuinely moved by novels and films and plays, that we respond to works of fiction with real emotion' (1997: 38). I discuss this aspect of the paradox of fiction, and other apparent contrast between our emotional responses to real life and to fiction, in Goldie (forthcoming a).

in imagination with the elder son's indignation at what he thought was his father's unfair treatment, but also invites us to see, at the external level, that this angry response really was not appropriate.

One might at this point be worried by the well-known argument that, in fiction, we surely cannot experience, as I claim we do, the same kinds of emotion as we do in real life, because in fiction there is no direct connection between the reader's or audience's emotion and action[15]. In real life the direct connection will be one where an emotion involves (I oversimplify here, but it does not affect the central point) a belief and a desire, which lead to an intention, and which in turn can explain and putatively justify the action. For example, I hear a story on the evening news of how a remote tribe is starving as a result of a drought. I feel compassion. Compassion involves a belief that someone is suffering, and a desire to do something to alleviate the suffering, and this desire in turn explains the intention to give money to Christian Aid, and this intention in turn explains the donation itself. Giving money on this occasion is what one *ought* to do—assuming, of course, that compassion really was appropriate. Whereas, if I were to read a *fictional* story of a starving tribe, I might feel compassion, but I will not reach for my cheque book, at least on *their* account. This is true, but nevertheless, in fiction there *is* a connection, albeit hypothetical and thus less direct, from emotion to action. In fiction, the hypothetical connection to action is from emotion to what one ought to do *if* the story were fact and not fiction, and *if* one could act. Thus, in reading what I know to be a fictional narrative of a starving tribe, I would determine that, if the story were factual, which it is not, and if I could act, which I cannot, then what I ought to do is give money on their account. The mere fact that there is this difference in the connection between emotional response and action is not sufficient to warrant the worry that our external emotional responses to fictional stories are radically distinct from, or less genuine than, our real life emotional responses. Moreover, to a considerable extent, a similar sort of less direct connection between emotion and action can be found in thoughts and imaginings about what is hypothetical, and the worry about emotion does not arise here[16]. For example, in wonder-

[15] Again, see Walton (1990) and (1997), and Currie (1990). This point is closely related to the so-called paradox of fiction.

[16] Currie refers in this context to what he calls *Moran's constraint*: any solution to the paradox of fiction 'should also deal with the large number of cases of what is essentially the same phenomenon that arises in other areas'; Currie (1997: 64). He names the constraint after its inventor, Richard Moran (1994).

ing whether or not to do something rather depraved in the privacy of my own bedroom, I might imagine myself being seen doing it by a neighbour through a gap in the curtains. As a result I might imagine feeling shame and embarrassment at being seen, and I might even actually *feel* shame and embarrassment at the *thought* of being seen. The connection between emotion and action in this case, then, might be for me to determine that I ought not to do this depraved act, because if I did do it I would be ashamed and embarrassed to be seen doing it. Alternatively, I might just decide that I ought to make sure that the curtains are tightly pulled.

IV

I now want to end by briefly considering another worry that might seem to be pressing. The worry is this: How can we distinguish, as distinct species of story, between, on the one hand, everyday explanation and historical explanation, and, on the other hand, the fictional story? Of course the former relate to events that took place in historical time. But are they not condemned, in virtue of what I have said is their essential narrative structure and perspectival form, to float free of the events which they seek to portray and of any possibility of truth, at best achieving some sort of internal coherence and satisfying aesthetic form? Here are some expressions of this view: Hayden White: '... there has been a reluctance to consider historical narratives as what they most manifestly are: verbal fictions, the contents of which are as much *invented* as *found* ...' (1978: 82, cited by Lamarque and Olsen 1994: 304). Christopher Nash: 'the text is so seamlessly interwoven with all utterances—from which what we call reality itself is inseparable—that questions not merely of "fictionality" versus "truth" but of referentiality versus non-referentiality dissolve altogether'... (Nash, 1990: 210, cited by Lamarque and Olsen 1994: 231). Stanley Fish: 'One might object that (my position) has the consequence of making all discourse fictional; but it would be just as accurate to say that it makes all discourse serious, and it would be better still to say that it puts all discourse on a par' (Fish 1980, cited in Walton 1990: 100)[17]. There is here, I think, a particularly post-modern sort of exaggeration—in fact, a double exaggeration, although, as with so many post-modern

---

[17] Where Richard Rorty stands on these matters is not so easy to determine, but at one point Rorty suggests that truth is 'a compliment paid to sentences that seem to be paying their way and that fit with other sentences that are doing so' (1989: xxv).

Peter Goldie

exaggerations, we should not lose sight of what might be correct in these views, once they are suitably watered down.

We should begin by noticing that what stories have in common, whether or not of the fictional kind, is their structural dimension, being narrative in form and perspectival. But where they differ is in their referential dimension, where some sorts of story and not others aspire to be true[18]. A story is fictional not in virtue of its content being false[19], but in virtue of its being narrated, and read or heard, as part of a practice of a special sort: one which invites the reader or audience to imagine or make believe that what is being narrated actually happened, even when it is known that it did not. Thus the question of reference and of truth does not arise within the 'fictive stance'[20]: it is, simply, irrelevant. Fiction, of course, can aspire to be true to life, and to be much else besides, but to aspire to be true to life is not to aspire to be true in the sense that I am concerned with here.

The contrast would disappear if one were to assimilate a narrative and what the narrative is about—for example, if one were to say that a particular life (or a particular illness) *is* a narrative. But this would be a mistaken assimilation; rather, one should say that a life *can be narrated*, so that the narrative is *about the life*, and thus there remains, in the real life case but not in the fictional case, the possibility of reference and of truth.[21]

If it is right, then, that metaphysical notions of reference and truth have no application in fiction, but do have application in historical and everyday explanation, there also arises, but only in this latter area, the epistemological notion of evidence[22]. Explanations

[18] Cf Walton (1990: 98–102).

[19] A story's being false is neither necessary nor sufficient for its being fictional. Cf Lamarque and Olsen (1994: 31).

[20] See Lamarque and Olsen: 'a reader is invited to *entertain* sense and *make-believe* truth and reference' (1994: 77). Cf Currie (1990: 30): 'The author intends that we make-believe the text (or rather the constituent propositions) and he intends to get us to do this by means of our recognition of that very intention'. Also cf Walton (1990: 70–3).

[21] This contrast does not require a substantial notion of truth: it remains in place with a minimalist notion, so, for example, the real life narrative in (1), 'Last night, in the dark, I tripped over because a suitcase had been left in the hall whilst I was out shopping' will be true if and only if last night, in the dark, I tripped over because a suitcase had been left in the hall whilst I was out shopping. And, to repeat, *this* notion of truth does not arise within the fictive stance.

[22] In what follows, I am much indebted to Richard Evans' *In Defence of History* (1997), and to Lamarque and Olsen (1994).

216

can be verified by appeal to the evidence that is evinced in their support, and competing explanations can be tested one against the other. (It will, however, not be epistemically possible in every case to establish whether a part, or even all of a particular explanation is true; but unless one is a verificationist, this does not imply that there is no room for truth in these cases.) What might evidence consist of? Well, it could consist of all sorts of thing: what others say now about what happened then; written documents that were produced at the time of what happened; tube timetables; aeroplane tickets. That is, roughly, the historian's primary sources. Now here comes the characteristically post-modern exaggeration. It goes as follows. All these documents are just more texts, multiply open to interpretation, and the historian's much-prized distinction between primary and secondary source is a distinction without a difference. This is, in fact, doubly an exaggeration. It exaggerates first the degree to which at least some evidence is open to interpretation. If someone's story is that he was in London on some particular day, and the flight tickets and hotel bills show that this person was in Paris, then the story is, simply, false in that respect. Secondly, it exaggerates in quite another direction: the implication is that we did not realise, until it was kindly pointed out to us, that evidence is indeed open to interpretation. But we already know this: we are, in effect, already epistemological holists, examining each piece of evidence with due care, and considering it only in the light of all sorts of other evidential considerations. For example, if there are minutes of the meeting, which were taken at the time, and which are put forward as evidence in support of a story about what happened that day, we know that we should enquire just who produced those minutes, and consider whether there are special reasons to doubt what they relate. Was the minute-taker unobservant, a fool, the sworn enemy of one of the protagonists, or did he have some other special 'agenda' of his own?

So, within the general constraints of interpretation, there is a perfectly good commonsense notion that there can be evidence which can be appealed to in support of those species of story that aspire to be true. The idea of perspective, and of diversity of emotional response to value, need not threaten the possibility of reference, of truth, and of evidence.

However—and here is the grain of truth in the post-modern exaggeration, suitably watered down. When we are trying to give an explanation of what happened, there is no possibility that our explanation can cease to be narrative in structure or to be perspectival.

Peter Goldie

We cannot, like Charles Dickens' Gradgrind, hope to give just the 'bare facts', an impersonal, non-perspectival chronicle of events, a schedule of comings and goings, of tube timetables and of plane tickets, 'as if', to quote Nietzsche's remarks at the beginning of this paper, 'reality stood unveiled before you only, and you yourselves were perhaps the best part of it'[23].

Bibliography

Aristotle, 1987. *Poetics*, tr. S. Halliwell, (London: Duckworth).
Bal, M. 1997. *Narratology: Introduction to the Theory of Narrative*, 2nd. Edition, (Toronto: University of Toronto Press).
Blackburn, S. 1998. *Ruling Passions: A Theory of Practical Reasoning* (Oxford: Clarendon Press).
Carroll, N. 1997. 'Art, Narrative, and Emotion', in M. Hjort and S. Laver (eds), *Emotion and the Arts* (New York: Oxford University Press), 190–211.
Collingwood, R. 1946. *The Idea of History* (Oxford: Oxford University Press).
Currie, G. 1990. *The Nature of Fiction* (Cambridge: Cambridge University Press).
Currie, G. 1995. *Image and Mind: Film, Philosophy and Cognitive Science* (Cambridge: Cambridge University Press).
Currie, G. 1997. 'The Paradox of Caring: Fiction and the Philosophy of Mind', in M. Hjort and S. Laver (eds), *Emotion and the Arts* (New York: Oxford University Press), 63–77.
D'Arms, J. and Jacobson, D. 2000. 'Sentiment and Value', *Ethics* **110**, 722–48.
Evans, R. 1997. *In Defence of History* (London: Granta Books).
Fish, S. 1980. 'How to Do Things with Austin and Searle', in his *Is There a Text in This Class? The Authority of Interpretive Communities* (Cambridge, Mass.: Harvard University Press).
Genette, G. 1980. *Narrative Discourse*, tr. J. Lewin, (Ithaca, NY: Cornell University Press).
Gibbard, A. 1990. *Wise Choices, Apt Feelings* (Cambridge, Mass.: Harvard University Press).
Goldie, P. 2000. *The Emotions: A Philosophical Exploration* (Oxford: Clarendon Press).

[23] Many thanks to audiences at The University of Hertfordshire, The Erasmus Summer School on Social Ontology in Rotterdam, and at the Royal Institute of Philosophy Conference on the emotions at Manchester University, for their comments and suggestions. Special thanks also to Matthew Kieran, Adam Morton, David Papineau, and Elisabeth Schellekens for their help. The mistakes are all mine, I am afraid.

Goldie, P. forthcoming a, 'Imagination and Emotion in Fiction', in *Imagination and the Arts*, M. Kieran and D. Lopes (eds), (London: Routledge).

Goldie, P. forthcoming b, 'Can We Trust Our Emotions?', in *Emotion, Evolution, and Rationality*, P. Cruse and D. Evans (eds), (Oxford: Oxford University Press).

Goldman, A. 1992. 'In Defence of the Simulation Theory', *Mind and Language* **7**, 104–19, reprinted in M. Davies and T. Stone (eds), *Folk Psychology: The Theory of Mind Debate* (Oxford: Blackwell), 1995.

Gordon, R. 1995. 'Simulation without Introspection or Inference from Me to You', in M. Davies and T. Stone (eds), *Mental Simulation: Evaluations and Applications* (Oxford: Blackwell), 1995.

Heal, J. 1998. 'Co-cognition and Off-line Simulation: Two Ways of Understanding the Simulation Approach', *Mind and Language* **13**, 477–98.

Heal, J. 2000. 'Other Minds, Rationality and Analogy', *Proceedings of the Aristotelian Society*, supp. vol. **74**, 1–19.

Hjort, M. and Laver, S. (eds), 1997. *Emotion and the Arts* (New York: Oxford University Press).

Hume, D. 1978, *A Treatise of Human Nature*, ed. L. A. Selby-Bigge, (Oxford: Oxford University Press).

King, N. 2000. *Memory, Narrative, Identity: Remembering the Self* (Edinburgh: Edinburgh University Press).

Lamarque, P. and Olsen, S. 1994. *Truth, Fiction, and Literature* (Oxford: Clarendon Press).

Livingstone, P. and Mele, A. 1997. 'Evaluating Emotional Responses to Fiction', in M. Hjort and S. Laver (eds), *Emotion and the Arts* (New York: Oxford University Press), 157–76.

McDowell, J. 1985. 'Values and Secondary Qualities', in T. Honderich (ed.), *Morality and Objectives: A Tribute to J. L. Mackie* (London: Routledge), 110–29.

Moran, R. 1994. 'The Expression of Feeling in Imagination', *Philosophical Review* **103**, 75–106.

Musil, R. 1995. *The Man Without Qualities*, tr. S. Wilkins and B. Pike, (New York: Alfred A. Knopf).

Nash, C. 1990. 'Literature's Assault on Narrative', in C. Nash (ed.), *Narrative in Culture: The Uses of Storytelling in the Sciences, Philosophy, and Literature* (London: Routledge).

Regan, D. And Totten, J. 1975. 'Empathy and Attribution: Turning Observers into Actors', *Journal of Personality and Social Psychology* **32**, 850–56.

Ricoeur, P. 1984. *Time and Narrative, vol. 1*, tr. K. McLaughlin and D. Pellauer, (Chicago: University of Chicago Press).

Ricoeur, P. 1985. *Time and Narrative, vol. 2*, tr. K. McLaughlin and D. Pellauer, (Chicago: University of Chicago Press).

Ricoeur, P. 1988. *Time and Narrative, vol. 3*, tr. K. McLaughlin and D. Pellauer, (Chicago: University of Chicago Press).

Rorty, R. 1989. *Contingency, Irony, and Solidarity* (Cambridge: Cambridge University Press).

Peter Goldie

Storms, M. D. 1973. 'Videotape and the Attribution Process: Reversing Actors' and Observers' Points of View', *Journal of Personality and Social Psychology* **27**, 165–75.

Walton, K. 1990. *Mimesis as Make-Believe: On the Foundation of the Representational Arts* (Cambridge, Mass.: Harvard University Press).

Walton, K. 1997. 'Spelunking, Simulation, and Slime: On Being Moved by Fiction', in M. Hjort and S. Laver (eds), *Emotion and the Arts* (New York: Oxford University Press), 37–49.

White, H. 1978. *Tropics of Discourse: Essays in Cultural Criticism* (Baltimore: John Hopkins University Press).

Wiggins, D. 1998. 'A Sensible Subjectivism', Chapter V in his *Needs, Values, Truth* (Oxford: Blackwell).

Wollheim, R. 1984. *The Thread of Life* (Cambridge, Mass.: Harvard University Press).

XIII. Passion and Politics[1]

SUSAN JAMES

The sudden resurgence of interest in the emotions that has recently overtaken analytical philosophy has raised a range of questions about the place of the passions in established explanatory schemes. How, for example, do the emotions fit into theories of action organized around beliefs and desires? How can they be included in analyses of the mind developed to account for other mental states and capacities? Questions of this general form also arise within political philosophy, and the wish to acknowledge their importance and find a space for them has led to some fruitful developments. Among these are a new sensitivity to ways in which attributions of emotion can create and sustain unequal power relations[2], an interest in the underlying emotional capacities that make politics possible[3], a concern with the kinds of emotional suffering that politics should aim to abolish[4], and analyses of the emotional traits it should foster.[5] While these and comparable explorations have enormously enriched contemporary political philosophy, a great deal of mainstream work continues to ignore or marginalize the emotions, so that their place remains uncertain and obscure. There is no consensus as to what kind of attention should be paid to them, or indeed whether they

[1] I received many helpful comments on an earlier version of this paper at the conference held in Manchester from which this book originated, from the members of the Birkbeck Graduate Philosophy Seminar, and from the members of the Departmental Philosophy Seminar at the University of Sheffield. I owe special thanks to Raymond Geuss, Lucy Selman, Robert Stern and Quentin Skinner for their probing questions.

[2] On this Nietzschian theme see for example Elizabeth Spelman's account of the way that subordinate races, and women, are not regarded as entitled to righteous anger but are dismissed as prone to childish tantrums or hysteria. 'Anger and Insubordination' in A. Garry and M. Pearsall (eds), *Women, Knowledge and Reality*, 1st edn. (London, 1996), pp. 263–73.

[3] See for example Jessica Benjamin, *The Bonds of Love* (New York, 1988); Axel Honneth, *The Struggle for Recognition* (Cambridge, 1995).

[4] See for example Richard Rorty, *Contingency, Irony and Solidarity* (Cambridge, 1989); Judith Shklar, *Ordinary Vices* (Cambridge, Mass., 1984); Avishai Margalit, *The Decent Society* (Cambridge, Mass., 1996).

[5] A notable example of this concern is Rawls's discussion of self-respect in Part III of *A Theory of Justice* (Cambridge, Mass., 1971).

deserve any systematic attention at all. This is a curious state of affairs, because it was until quite recently taken for granted that political philosophy and psychology are intimately connected, and that political philosophy needs to be grounded on an understanding of human passion. In this essay I shall first consider why political philosophers ever rejected this set of assumptions. I shall then return to the pressing issue of how we might take account of the emotions in our own political theorizing.

The view that one can resolve philosophical questions about politics only with the help of a theory of the passions derived its plausibility from the belief that political philosophy should, as Rousseau put it, 'take men as they are and laws as they might be'. Insofar as it is concerned with central values such as justice, obligation, consent or freedom, political philosophy aims to delineate principles that are better than the ones we live by (it imagines laws as they might be rather than simply justifying existing arrangements) and in this sense aims to be transformative. But at the same time, it appeals to the emotional dispositions and capacities that people ordinarily possess, rather than to ones that are found only in exceptional individuals or which arise only in unusual circumstances, and in this way tries to avoid utopianism. These restrictions are designed to deliver principles and conceptions of society that are realizable. To be sure, it will often be difficult to decide what a society is capable of realizing, either because it is unclear what 'ordinary' feelings and patterns of action its members possess, or because it is unclear what measures are needed, and may legitimately be taken, to sustain a set of 'ordinary' emotional dispositions through changing circumstances. Despite these reservations, many political philosophers have aspired to produce realizable theories, and have agreed that such theories must take account of our everyday emotions. While these may be varied and malleable, they shape what we are able to do, and a theory which ignores or goes against them is liable to be unrealizable and therefore (if judged by the standard of realizability) uninteresting.

One can get a fuller understanding of the view that political philosophies are dependent on theories of the passions by considering the work of a philosopher for whom this is an obvious truth. In his *Treatise of Human Nature*, the young David Hume argues that our passions flow from two natural dispositions: an inclination to sympathize with other people, which enables us to experience certain kinds of love, hatred and pity; and an inclination to compare ourselves with others, which accounts for our feelings of pride and humility, contempt and esteem. Each of these inclinations is further modified by a sensitivity to distance—a disposition to feel more strongly about people who are physically or figuratively close to us than about those who are far away. As Hume presents the matter, these propensities are some of the raw materials which create the problems political philosophers confront. For instance, the fact that 'our passions always plead in favour of whatever is near and contiguous' makes it difficult for us to observe the impartial laws of justice and equity.[6] Furthermore, the fixity of this natural inclination places limits on possible ways of bringing about states of affairs in which individuals behave justly. We cannot hope to change the underlying disposition that makes us partial, namely our sensibility to distance; instead, the best we can do is 'to change the circumstances and situation, and render the observation of the laws of justice our nearest interest, and their violation our most remote.'[7] We have to work with this disposition and find a way to make it function in favour of justice. Hume's point is that the particular emotions we are prone to, and the underlying mechanisms that govern them, create some of the problems that are the stuff of political philosophy and limit the ways in which they can be solved. More generally, his analysis of the passions bears on his analysis of the art of politics. As he explains, 'the utmost that politicians can perform is to extend the natural sentiments beyond their original bounds; but still nature must furnish the materials, and give us some notion of moral distinctions.'[8]

This conception of the relation between an account of the emotions and a political theory is to be found in the work of quite a range of philosophers[9], and for convenience I'll refer to it as the systematic view. It may be helpful to stress at this point that the systematic view need not see the task of politics as that of limiting 'bad' emotions and encouraging 'good' ones. It just stipulates that philosophers need to examine whatever ordinary emotional dispositions people have, and take into account their implications for political life. Nor need it posit a universal and unchanging set of emotional dispositions with which all human beings are endowed. In discussing Hume, I have focused on passions he takes to be immutable. But he also recognizes various ways in which emotions can alter, whether over an individual lifetime or with cultural

[6] David Hume, *A Treatise of Human Nature*, p. 535, p. 537.
[7] *Treatise*, p. 537.
[8] *Treatise*, p. 500.
[9] For instance Hobbes, Spinoza or Smith, to cite just a few prominent examples.

223

circumstances.[10] First and most straightforwardly, he allows that the objects of our emotions can change. For instance, indifference to a law may turn into hatred once I come to see it as threatening my interests. Secondly, we may come to feel new passions. Hume claims, for example, that once people live under rules of justice they begin to 'receive a pleasure from the view of such actions as tend to the peace of society and an uneasiness from such as are contrary to it'. This sentiment, our sense of honour or duty, only arises once the artificial rules of justice are in place, but it then follows, Hume says, naturally and of itself.[11] It brings with it two further kinds of change. The first is a modification of the normative judgments that attach to types of emotion. For example, people who value a sense of honour in themselves and others will be critical of forms of hatred or devotion that conflict with it. Along with this come changes of feeling. Where someone unacquainted with a sense of honour may feel an unalloyed delight in their partial loves and pre-occupations, an honourable person may reproach themselves for partiality, and may feel cross-pressured by shame, self-hatred or despondency. Such shifts in whatever emotional dispositions are regarded as ordinary are also relevant to political philosophy. They flesh out our conception of the types of emotional transformation that lie within our reach, and shape our understanding of political possibility.

When Hume discusses political issues such as property or justice, he treats the emotional dispositions he has identified as both obstacles and opportunities. They are obstacles insofar as they set limits to the ways in which people can reasonably be expected to live, limits of which political philosophy must in one way or another take note. At the same time they are opportunities, both because our most basic emotional dispositions create certain political possibilities, and because our emotional repertoire can be extended by political institutions. As Hume and many other writers agree, this interdependence between passion and politics makes it essential for political philosophers to pay attention to human psychology. The task is to distinguish the immutable from the mutable features of our passions, and to work out what each implies for political life.

Contemporary political philosophers—and here I am thinking mainly of authors within the analytical tradition—seem to take a different view of the relations between psychology and political

[10] See Martha Nussbaum, 'Constructing Love, Desire and Care' in David M. Estlund and Martha C. Nussbaum (eds), *Sex, Preference and Family* (Oxford, 1997), pp. 17–43.
[11] *Treatise*, pp. 533–4

philosophy. They too aim to articulate political principles that are realizable; but on the whole, and in spite of the exceptions already mentioned, they pay little or no attention to psychology or to the emotions. Judging from their practice, they disagree with the systematic view outlined so far, and believe that one can do political philosophy without an account of our everyday emotional dispositions. But what grounds might there be for this belief?

It is possible, of course, that although contemporary political philosophers do not lay out analyses of our ordinary emotional dispositions in the manner of their forebears, this is not because they regard them as irrelevant, but simply because they do not think such accounts need to be made explicit. A strong version of this position is less than persuasive. One can imagine a philosopher explaining that we know, nowadays, what emotional dispositions are most salient, and therefore know without spelling it out what dispositions political philosophers need to take account of. However, as long as the many current debates about the character and mutability of our emotions remain unresolved, it is hard to take this claim seriously. Greater plausibility attaches to a weaker version of the argument, which also harmonizes with the injunction that political philosophy should take people as they are. The starting point here is that, while we may lack systematic knowledge of our emotional dispositions and capacities, we have a certain amount of common sense knowledge about them. This is what political philosophy rightly relies on, and precisely because it is commonsensical, there is no need to make it explicit.

It is of course true that political philosophers rely on what they take to be common sense knowledge about our emotional dispositions. Theories are built around our everyday conviction that people fear punishment, yearn for security, hate their oppressors, and so on. But it does not follow that there is no need to examine these presuppositions. A first reason for doing so is that one theorist's common sense is another theorist's fantasy. (Consider, for example, the divergent assumptions employed by rational choice theorists and theorists of deliberative democracy.) A second reason, to which I shall return, is that even where the emotional dispositions that a theory presupposes are agreed to be commonplace, it may be informative to make them explicit. This type of response to our question is therefore insufficient.

A different reply claims that we have no choice but to do political philosophy without a systematic theory of our ordinary emotional dispositions. Traditional attempts to provide such theories are hopelessly flawed, and there is no reason to believe that we can avoid the pitfalls into which Hume and others tumble so innocently. The main deficiency of systematic accounts is that they are far too schematic to be credible, and amount to little more than anecdotal reportage dressed up as grand theory. When, for instance, Hume tells us that we habitually feel esteem for those whose houses are more magnificent than our own, he paints a drastically oversimplified picture of our emotional life which would be deeply misleading as the basis for a realizable political philosophy. Equally, his specification of the dispositions by which our passions are formed—for instance his view that they are sensitive to distance—is unacceptably crude. Finally, although he allows that our emotional dispositions are variable, he closes off enquiry about the extent to which they diverge. His confidence that the psychological mechanisms he identifies are as active among the ancient Romans or American Indians as among eighteenth-century Scotsmen, or his assumption that people the world over feel a profound attachment to their property, precludes consideration of whether our guiding emotions may be more diverse than he believes.

If these straightforward criticisms are just, and our emotional dispositions are far more complicated and varied than systematic theorists have allowed, we are unlikely to be able to arrive at any satisfactory equivalent of their highly general claims. However, this rather pessimistic conclusion has to coexist with the recognition that it is not open to us to do political philosophy without making assumptions about the emotional dispositions of the communities for whom our theories are intended. If people were indifferent to peace, justice or freedom, for example, political theories organized around these categories would be pointless. The decision to make such values central to our investigations is guided by the knowledge that in many circumstances we are emotionally engaged with them—afraid of war, indignant in the face of injustice, resentful when we are coerced. What we seem to require, therefore, is a way to take account of our emotional dispositions which is less demanding than the systematic approach, yet full enough to underpin judgments about whether or not political theories are realizable.

We still need, however, to consider a third reason sometimes given for supposing that we can do political philosophy without a systematic theory of the passions. If we want to know what political principles or structures are realizable, so the argument goes, we need to focus not on what a community feels, but on what it believes. This proposal gains support from cognitive accounts of the emotions which regard them as formed around a belief about an object. If, for example, I believe that the man over there with the gun is dangerous, the belief licenses my feeling of fear. But if I alter my belief, perhaps when I am told that the gun is only a toy, I will no longer be afraid. In short, where there are no complicating factors, our emotions track and are submissive to our beliefs.

If this view is correct, the important issue for a political philosopher does not concern the emotional dispositions people have, and what they are capable of feeling. Rather, it concerns their dispositions to form beliefs, and what they are capable of believing. Members of a society who find the principles embedded in a political theory incredible will be unable to form the beliefs the theory requires of them, and as a result will be unable to form the associated emotions. The theory will then be unrealizable. But as long as people are able to form the beliefs on which the theory depends, their emotions will for the most part come into line; and if there are obstacles to realizing the theory, these will hinge on the inability of the community to form the relevant beliefs, rather than on its emotional dispositions. The way to ensure that a theory is realizable, then, is to make it credible; and the way to make it credible is to provide persuasive reasons for the claims it contains. The possibilities implicit in this view are engagingly expounded by John Stuart Mill in his *Autobiography*. Discussing the attitudes he inherited from his father, Mill explains that the main aim of his own intellectual circle 'was to alter people's opinions; to make them believe according to the evidence, and know what was their real interest, which when they once knew, they would, we thought, by the instrument of opinion, enforce a regard to it upon another. While fully recognizing the superior excellence of unselfish benevolence and the love of justice, we did not expect the regeneration of mankind from any direct action on those sentiments, but from the effect of educated intellect, enlightening the selfish feelings.'

This strategy seems to answer to what many political philosophers see themselves as doing, and is undoubtedly a powerful one. The realizability of a theory does indeed depend on what we believe we have good reason to do, and our beliefs are indeed sometimes moulded by the reasons that political philosophers offer us. Furthermore, these beliefs may, as Hume observed, shape our emotions; for example, people who come to believe that slavery is unjust may also come to find it repellent. The appeal of this account of realizability derives at least in part from the widely-held view that, insofar as we are rational, our emotions are submissive to our beliefs, and that when the two diverge a rational person will work on herself to bring her emotions in line. This process may be long or short, sudden or gradual, and also allows for conflicting or ambivalent emotions when the available evidence is insufficient to resolve conflicting beliefs.

For all its strengths, however, such a picture of our mental life is insensitive to the power of what are sometimes known as recalcitrant emotions. Even when we are more or less clearly aware that our emotions and beliefs are at odds with one another, we may not feel any inclination to overcome the lack of fit by reforming our feelings. Our investment in our existing emotional dispositions is sometimes stronger than our attachment to rationality and more powerful than our ability to change, and when this is the case, our emotional attachments can generate reasons for our beliefs rather than the other way round. If, for example, a fear of Islamic fundamentalism is an important aspect of a man's life as a member of the American Republican party, a life to which he is deeply bound, he may continue to believe that fundamentalists are dangerous in the face of the evidence, and may in various ways avoid confronting the possibility that his fear is ungrounded. In everyday cases such as these, our emotions are not submissive to our beliefs. On the contrary, our beliefs are submissive to our emotions.

Recalcitrant emotions are experienced by individuals, but because they are often sustained by shared images and points of reference, a particular recalcitrant emotion may be widespread among members of a social group. As a group, American Republicans may have a fear of Islamic fundamentalists fostered by their shared experiences, their telling of their own history and the anxieties these sustain. A political philosopher may feel able to ignore the recalcitrant emotions of individuals, perhaps on the grounds that they will cancel each other out, but the recalcitrant emotions of groups are harder to dismiss. They may make us resistant to some of the principles and arguments that political philosophies offer, and too ready to accede to others. They may shape what we are prepared to accept and what we are able to do, and may thus bear on the realizability of political theories.

If this is right, the claim that the realizability of a theory depends solely or principally on the credibility of the reasons that can be given for it will only be true in special circumstances, where we are dealing with a community of individuals whose emotions are submissive to their beliefs. When, as is usual, this is not the case, realizability is a more complex matter. A realizable theory will have to answer to the emotional dispositions and capacities of a community, allowing for the fact that these may be out of line with their beliefs, or insusceptible to reasoning. Realizability, then, requires us to pay attention not only to beliefs, but to emotional dispositions as well. We need to take account of the various ways in which our epistemological and affective states can relate to one another, rather than making either subordinate to the other.

The psychological complexities that attach to the phenomenon of recalcitrant emotions should also alert us to a further difficulty with the claim that political philosophers need to concentrate on beliefs rather than emotions. The line of argument we have just been following associates rationality with belief and irrationality with emotion; but these are alliances we need to avoid. Rather than thinking of emotions as states that disrupt and are at odds with rationality, we need to remember the obvious point that they run through the whole of our lives. We assess some patterns of emotion positively, as justified, rational, virtuous or commonsensical, and others negatively, as pathological, irrational, wrong, or merely odd. Furthermore, it is partly because some emotional capacities and patterns of feeling are integral to political life that political theory cannot altogether ignore them. If a systematic theory of the emotions is not forthcoming, we can either take our emotional dispositions for granted and view them as commonsense assumptions which do not need to be made explicit, or look for an middle way— a more than merely commonsense but less than systematic analysis of the relations between the emotions and politics.

For some purposes, and some kinds of political philosophy, the first of these approaches may be sufficient. Philosophers who see themselves as articulating universal political values often aim to ensure that their claims are widely applicable by making only a few, purportedly uncontentious assumptions about the emotional dispositions of human beings, and deliberately avoiding more elaborate psychological commitments. Furthermore, they tend to devolve the task of worrying about the realizability of their theories on to political scientists, policy makers or psychologists, and to draw a sharp line between philosophical and empirical issues. If the emotional dispositions dominant in a given society make it difficult to realize a specific normative conception in that context, this does not constitute a criticism of the conception. Rather, it raises a set of empirical problems about ways in which the society might be reformed, and these are not the business of philosophers.

Theorists who are content with this summary of the task of political philosophy, which I shall call the *normative approach*, will presumably regard the question I am raising as superfluous. But their response is arguably too quick. The normative approach relies on a distinction between widespread, 'ordinary' emotional dispositions, and more specific, 'deviant' ones. It holds that a theory is realizable by virtue of the fact that it appeals only to ordinary emotional dispositions, but at the same time allows that deviant dispositions may make the theory unrealizable in at least some contexts. This is a familiar and in some ways a sensible stance, but it has significant limitations. One worry is that theories with this structure may be unduly complacent about their own interpretations of ordinary emotional dispositions. If dispositions which stand in the way of realizability can easily be dismissed as exceptional, how can we be confident that the theory captures configurations of feeling that really are commonplace? Equally, how can we be confident that these configurations are habitually powerful enough to override conflicting emotional dispositions and thus to guide action? Unless these conditions are met, the theory will be realizable only in the weak sense of 'realizable where the relevant emotional dispositions exist and nothing gets in their way', and this will not be enough to guarantee that the values the theory defends are within the reach of most people, or even most members of a particular society. To put the point another way, advocates of the normative approach are often more interested in articulating political values than in considering what it would take to realize them, and this reduces their concern with the emotional dispositions that can promote or undermine the realization of the values they hold dear.[12]

For theorists who take the issue of realizability more seriously, these criticisms of the normative approach provide reasons for thinking that it will not be enough to build our political theories on a set of common sense assumptions about the emotions to which people are habitually prone. This stance yields only a weak interpretation of realizability. But if we aim for a stronger one, will the floodgates not open? It seems that we shall need to be alive to the great variety of emotional dispositions that shape our political lives, to the types of situations in which they arise, to the multifarious ways in which they change, and to the historical and cultural circumstances that can embed specific dispositions in the psychic lives of individual communities. But to yearn for this sort of sensitivity is to yearn for the very thing we cannot have—a systematic under-

[12] At least two other types of political philosophy are not concerned with realizability: conceptual enquiries which aim exclusively to articulate our political concepts; and descriptive enquiries which focus on the extension of these concepts. See Sally Haslanger, 'Gender and Race: (What) Are They? (What) Do We Want Them To Be?' in *Nous* vol. XXXIV.1 (2000), p. 33. The normative approach I discuss here does not fit into Haslanger's classification, as far as I can see, though the approach I go on to defend is what she calls an analytical form of enquiry.

standing of our emotional dispositions in all their richness and diversity, and a grasp of their relation to political life. We must, of course, put this unachievable ambition aside; but once we have done so, can we find a more manageable approach to the problem?

One way to attain a deeper appreciation of the emotional demands implicit in a theory is to try to make explicit the patterns of feeling that people would have to possess in order to live out the form of political life that it upholds. This way of exploring the relations between our emotional dispositions and our political aspirations provides, first of all, a means of clarifying the character of the theory in question which goes beyond the types of explication with which we are most familiar. As well as focusing on the theory's substantive claims (the principles of justice it defends or the criteria it proposes for judging equalities and inequalities) and on the reasons it offers in their defence, this approach urges us to look at the psychological capacities that it demands. If we apply it, for example, to Rawls's theory of justice, it encourages us to reflect on the fact that he envisages a just society in which a wide range of emotional dispositions are highly valued in citizens: a deep respect and admiration for just institutions and those who uphold them; indignation with officials who act unjustly; solidarity with the victims of injustice; an absence of resentment when one's property is redistributed in accordance with the difference principle; an adequate sense of self-esteem; an absence of contempt or hatred for other groups within the polity whose conceptions of the good are different from one's own; and shame at feelings of covetousness or partiality which conflict with the demands of justice. If this list is psychically ambitious, it is not because of the emotion-types to which it appeals; after all, admiration, indignation, self-esteem and so on are the ordinary stuff of our emotional lives. Instead, its ambition lies in the objects to which these feelings are directed, together with the implicit requirement that our feelings for these objects should be stronger and more enduring than others. Shame at covetousness, for example, must outweigh the pride that people take in their private wealth if they are fully to endorse Rawlsian principles.

This sort of exploration can help us to appreciate the ideal emotional profile embodied in Rawls's conception of a just society, but he does not expect or require it to be consistently realized. The realizability of his view depends on the existence of a majority of citizens who will initially vote for, and then continue to support, just institutions, and on the existence of officials willing and able to enforce just rules. (The fact that a minority abides by these rules merely out of fear of punishment, and in the face of their other feelings, is not enough to undermine the just institutions around which society is organized.) This less stringent demand nevertheless embodies its own emotional requirements. It assumes among other things that citizens possess the emotional dispositions needed to sustain democratic institutions. (When votes threaten to go against them they must be able to restrain their anxiety, resentment, or desire for domination, and when they are defeated at the polls they must be able to control their frustration and anger.) At the same time, it assumes that officials are sufficiently immune to feelings which fuel corruption—whether greed, envy, or delight in the exercise of illicit power—to refrain from undermining the just institutions they administer. So Rawlsian principles will only be realizable where these dispositions exist.

By examining the emotional dispositions that a theory requires of citizens or subsets of citizens, we can build up a picture of the psychic demands it contains, and acquire a richer understanding of what it would take to realize it. A proposal which initially appears to be realizable may turn out on closer inspection to depend on emotions or emotional capacities that are relatively unusual in the societies we are familiar with, so that we would need to reform our patterns of feeling in order to attain it. Equally, a defence of a policy which initially appears to be beyond our reach may turn out to appeal to familiar emotional dispositions and to be in this respect realizable. This kind of investigation resembles the normative approach I have criticized in that it relies principally on our everyday knowledge of emotions and their relation to action. (There is nothing to prevent it from appealing to more specialized psychological results as well, though it reckons to get by without any overarching, systematic theory of the passions.) But whereas the normative approach takes it for granted that specific emotional dispositions are widespread and dominant, the one I am proposing puts this very assumption in question. By encouraging us to look as closely as possible at the emotional dispositions presupposed by a theory, and to ask where, if anywhere, such dispositions are to be found, it holds out a conception of psychic realizability which is more than hypothetical, and is equipped to play a role in the critical evaluation of political philosophies.

Alongside this strength, the project of unearthing the emotional dispositions on which theories implicitly rely is fraught with complications. A first complexity lies in the fact that these emotional dispositions are not determinate, but range between those of the ideal citizen and those of the good-enough citizen who is sufficiently in sympathy with the normative principles around which a society is organized, and sufficiently cowed by the restraints it imposes, to go along with it.[13] The dispositions of the good-enough citizen and her companion the good-enough official set a lower limit which would enable a given polity to bump along, while those of the ideal citizen and official hold out a prospect of conditions in which it would flourish. In investigating the demands a theory imposes, we need to be sensitive to both upper and lower limits.

A second complication arises once we notice that coercive institutions can compensate for many forms of apathy, discontent and resistance, so that the ways in which a polity needs to worry about the emotional dispositions of its citizens will depend on its own constitution. An authoritarian regime may be untroubled if citizens feel anger or hatred for it and its officials, but concerned if it loses the knack of generating fear. A more open society, by contrast, may be anxious to cultivate the emotional dispositions required for democratic practices, and disturbed by a strong desire for conformity. These differences will be reflected in political theories, where principled accounts of the limits of legitimate coercion will partly determine the range of emotional dispositions that each theory relies on. Where this relationship is settled, it may be possible to see how emotions associated with coercion, such as fear, or pleasure in the exercise of power, are expected to intersect with other emotional dispositions, such as envy or a love of justice, to uphold a given set of values and institutions. But where it remains indeterminate, there will be no single answer to the question: what emotional dispositions does this theory presuppose?

A third complication stems from the sensitivity of our emotions to circumstance. Political theories focus on political values and institutions, but it is relatively rare for them to say much about the social and economic arrangements with which the state is intertwined. Yet our feelings about the apparatus of the state vary with our broader circumstances so that, for example, economic satisfactions can offset political alienation, and religious fervour can generate political discontent. I have suggested that we can recover some of the emotional dispositions that a political theory assumes; but when we do this in the abstract, without knowing anything about the circumstances in which such a theory might be put into practice, we are not in a position to say what else would be needed to keep these dispositions in place, or how resilient a political system might

[13] See Susan James, 'The Good Enough Citizen. Citizenship and Independence' in Gisela Bock and Susan James eds. *Beyond Equality and Difference. Citizenship, Feminist Politics and Female Subjectivity* (London, 1992), pp. 48–65.

prove to be if its supporting institutions were to alter or decline. Our emotional dispositions are only one of many types of condition that make a political theory realizable, and these different kinds of conditions interact in ways that are frequently difficult to map and impossible to predict.

As these complexities indicate, an exploration of the emotional dispositions that are required for a political theory to be realizable will be schematic and imprecise. But this need not prevent it from throwing light on the character of the theory, and helping us to appreciate the scope of its ambitions. Does the theory assume only emotional dispositions that are already widespread in our own societies, or does it envisage a community of individuals who have different patterns of feeling from our own? If the latter, what would it take to realize feelings like that? A significant advantage of this approach is that it focuses our attention on the central role played by our emotional dispositions in shaping our political lives. The loyalty, distaste, hatred or sympathy that we feel for the institutions and functionaries of the state, for the state itself, and for other groups within civil society, can not only make or break governments, but also mould much less earth-shattering political events. Our emotional dispositions both facilitate and limit the political arrangements under which we are capable of living, and arrangements that are perfectly acceptable to one community may be anathema to another. If political theories are to be realizable in more than a minimal sense, they need to take account of this diversity and the emotional commitments that sustain it, and the approach I have outlined offers a way to begin bridging the gap between theory and practice.

A further advantage of the approach I have sketched is that it points to a line of investigation which has fallen into disuse. Given that our emotions are not always submissive to our beliefs, it is not always enough to offer people good reasons for changing their beliefs, expecting their emotions to fall in line. Instead, we may have to recognize the force and rationale of existing emotional dispositions that are powerful and hard to shift, and may have to return to an old philosophical topic—that of the techniques and principles involved in the cultivation of the sentiments. Perhaps it will turn out that contemporary philosophy no longer has much to say about ways of bringing about this kind of change, but we should not rush to this conclusion. With luck, we might embark on a style of political philosophizing alive to the sources of political conflict, and sensitive to the difficulties of dealing with it.

XIV. Don't Worry, Feel Guilty*

J. DAVID VELLEMAN

Introduction: the Worry

One can feel guilty without thinking that one actually is guilty of moral wrongdoing. For example, one can feel guilty about eating an ice cream or skipping aerobics, even if one doesn't take a moralistic view of self-indulgence. And one can feel guilty about things that aren't one's doing at all, as in the case of survivor's guilt about being spared some catastrophe suffered by others. Guilt without perceived wrongdoing may of course be irrational, but I think it is sometimes rational, and I want to explore how it can be.

If guilt were essentially a feeling about having done something morally wrong, then feeling guilty about self-indulgence or survival would of course be irrational. The only reason why I can conceive of guilt's being rational in these cases is that I think the emotion need not involve any judgment or perception of immorality. But I also think that the emotion of guilt must involve a judgment or perception whose content is normative in a more general sense. In particular, I believe that guilt requires a sense of *normative vulnerability,* which I would define as follows.

At the bottom of normative vulnerability is the sense of being somehow unjustified, of having nothing to say for oneself. But feeling unjustified in some respect does not by itself amount to feeling guilty, since one doesn't feel guilty, for instance, about beliefs or assertions for which one is aware of having no justification. Guilt arises only when the sense of indefens*ibility* yields a sense of being defence*less* against negative responses of some kind, variously thought to include blame, resentment, retaliation, or punishment, though their precise nature remains to be specified by a philosophical account of the emotion. One feels defenceless against these responses in the sense of having no claim or entitlement to be spared from them, because they are warranted. One thus feels defenceless in a normative sense.

The concept of normative vulnerability helps to explain why guilt is a feeling of both anxiety and diminished self-worth. The

* Thanks to Justin D'Arms, P. J. Ivanhoe, and Nancy Sherman for comments on an earlier draft.

J. David Velleman

anxiety comes from feeling oneself exposed to something untoward. The sense of diminished self-worth comes from conceiving of that exposure as a matter of being stripped of a claim or entitlement. Any attempt to analyse guilt as lacking at least this much normative content is bound to fail, in my opinion. The most promising attempt of this kind, to my knowledge, is Freud's analysis of guilt, which focuses on the element of anxiety at the expense of the normative element. According to Freud, a guilty mind is anxious about the prospect of being punished by an internalized figure of authority, the super-ego. Freud notably avoids saying that this punishment is viewed in normative terms, as warranted. As I have argued elsewhere, however, this omission threatens to leave a gap in Freud's analysis of guilt, since anxiety that was merely about harsh treatment from a controlling figure might amount to nothing more than fear of a bully.[1] Unlike brute fear, guilt has a concessive or self-deprecatory quality, by virtue of which it disposes one neither to flee nor to fight but merely to hang one's head or to cringe. And the only way to read this aspect of guilt into Freud's analysis, I have argued, is to imagine that his description of being punished by an authority is, in fact, the description under which the guilty mind itself grasps the object of its anxiety—namely, as punishment administered with proper authorization. When thus reinterpreted, Freud's analysis ends up crediting the subject of guilt with a sense that his punishment is somehow warranted.

The resulting analysis raises a worry about the rationality of guilt even in cases of admitted wrongdoing, since it implies that such guilt is rational only if there really is some justification for punishing wrongdoers. If there is no justification for punishment, then it cannot be warranted, and so one would be irrational to feel vulnerable on that score. The worry is that punishment is difficult to justify. The most persuasive justifications apply to punishment carried out by a legitimate state for the violation of valid laws. But guilt is felt on the basis of wrongs that are not and could not reasonably be subject to legal punishment—the breaking of intimate promises, minor injuries to people's feelings, and so on. Feeling guilty about private wrongs could perhaps involve the mistake or the phantasy that they are crimes punishable by law, but then guilt would be ripe for debunking. If guilt about wrongdoing is to be vindicated as rational, then wrongdoing must genuinely warrant that to which guilt makes one feel normatively vulnerable; and I do not see how

[1] I argue for this claim at length in 'A Rational Super-Ego', *Philosophical Review* **108**, 529–58 (1999).

the private wrongs of adults can make one normatively vulnerable to punishment.

Freud thinks that the authority figure envisioned in guilt is an internalization of the parent who disciplined the subject when he was a child. But if an adult conceives of himself as having done something that would have warranted parental discipline when he was a child, then he will have no grounds for anxiety in the present; and if he conceives of himself as warranting parental discipline in the present, then he is simply confused. He may of course entertain the phantasy that he is back in childhood facing an angry parent, and this phantasy may even cause him real anxiety. But this anxiety would evaporate under reflection on the facts about who he really is and where he really stands. Unless he can rationally think of punishment as warranted, a sense of normative vulnerability to it will be irrational.

Freud is not worried about this possibility, because he is not interested in vindicating human emotions as rational. He is satisfied to show that they are intelligible in light of external circumstances as viewed through phantasies, misplaced memories, and other sources of distortion. But moral philosophers are inclined to worry about the rationality of an emotion such as guilt. And I have undertaken to consider the rationality of this emotion in cases involving no moral judgment, where feelings of normative vulnerability are even less likely to make sense.

I will approach these problematic cases by way of the less problematic case of guilt felt about perceived wrongdoing. I will propose an unfavourable response other than punishment to which perceived wrongdoing can make one *feel* normatively vulnerable by causing one to *be* vulnerable in that sense, so that the feeling is at least potentially rational. I will then turn to the cases in which guilt is felt about matters other than wrongdoing. One of these cases will lead me to consider yet a third response that may be the object of anxiety in guilt. The result will be a disjunctive analysis of the emotion, as a sense of normative vulnerability to any one of several unfavourable responses.

Guilt About Wrongdoing

Freud sometimes gives a slightly different analysis of guilt, saying that it is anxiety over having alienated the internalized parent's love.[2] Freud doesn't clearly distinguish between this analysis and

[2] *Civilization and its Discontents,* in *The Standard Edition of the Complete Psychological Works of Sigmund Freud,* James Strachey *et al.* (eds), (London: the Hogarth Press), vol. 21, 59–145, p. 124. See also *Outline of Psychoanalysis,* S. E. 23: 205.

J. David Velleman

the one based on punishment, since he suggests that the loss of parental love is anxiety-provoking because it will lead to harsh treatment of the sort that makes for punishment. But Freud's conception of love is hopelessly consequentialist, in my opinion, and should be discarded.[3] The result of discarding it will be, at least initially, to divide his conception of guilt into two independent conceptions, one tracing the constitutive anxiety to anticipated punishment and the other tracing it to the anticipated loss of love.

The latter analysis of guilt is plausible on phenomenological grounds. Typically, the only specific danger that alarms a guilty mind is the danger of discovery, which is alarming because it would lead to whatever contingency is the ultimate object of anxiety. Beyond discovery, however, the prospect looming before a guilty mind is extremely vague: no very specific contingency is clearly in view. Discovery must therefore be expected to yield something nebulously conceived, and this expectation must provoke a fairly unfocussed anxiety. The subject of guilt fears a generalized loss of security, as if discovery would leave him standing on shaky ground. Such insecurity is precisely what a child would fear at the prospect of losing his parents' love. Having done something that might alienate them, he would vividly fear their discovering it, but only because he would then expect banishment to a no-mans-land of which he has no more than vague apprehensions.

As before, however, we have to wonder whose love the guilty-minded adult is afraid of losing, and why he should be afraid of losing it. Surely, an adult doesn't think that his mother will stop loving him, after all these years, simply because he has cheated on his taxes. If, alternatively, his feeling of guilt is a revival of anxiety that he felt about his parents when he was a child, then it is simply misplaced. And he is unlikely to think that there is any love to be lost from the tax-collector—or, if there is, that there would be much harm in losing it.

Forfeiting trust

Something that the guilty-minded adult might realistically anticipate losing, however, is trust; and the loss of trust results in the kind of nebulous vulnerability that might arouse the anxiety constitutive of guilt. Losing trust is indeed a kind of banishment to a vaguely imagined no-mans-land—a status that would strike the subject as inherently dangerous without posing particular, specifiable dangers. Losing trust, like losing love, would leave him out in the cold.

[3] See my 'Love as a Moral Emotion,' *Ethics* **109**, 338–74 (1999).

Consider the familiar strategy for dealing with iterated prisoners' dilemmas.[4] The strategy is to co-operate with others until they fail to co-operate, and then to withhold co-operation from them until they have resumed co-operating. This strategy requires a player to classify his fellow players as co-operators or non-co-operators, on the basis of their most recent behaviour, and then to co-operate or not with them, accordingly. If most of the players adopt this strategy, then any player who makes an uncooperative move can expect to lose his reputation as a co-operator—which would be, in effect, to lose the trust of his fellow players, who would then stop co-operating with him. His anxiety about having warranted this response might then constitute a feeling of guilt for his own failure to co-operate.

This kind of anxiety might account for guilt about wrongdoing if the moral choices in life were one long series of prisoners' dilemmas, to which morality was the co-operative solution. In that case, being a co-operator would consists in treating others morally, and a reputation for being a co-operator would elicit moral treatment from others in return. Conversely, wrongdoing would jeopardize one's reputation for co-operating and justify others in retaliating with similar wrongs. Anxiety about thus having forfeited their trust would correspond to the feeling of guilt for wrongdoing.

This account of guilt has its points, but it needs some adjustment. It characterizes guilt as a feeling of normative vulnerability to retaliatory wrongdoing, and so it vindicates this feeling as rational only if such vulnerability is real, because retaliatory wrongdoing is

[4] The prisoners' dilemma gets its name from the following philosophical fiction. Two prisoners are questioned separately, under suspicion of having committed a crime together. Each is offered the following plea bargain: if he gives testimony against the other, his sentence (whatever it otherwise would have been) will be reduced by one year; if he is convicted on the other's testimony, his sentence will be increased by two years. Each person will benefit from giving testimony against the other, no matter what the other does; but if both avail themselves of this benefit, each will be harmed by other's testimony, and the harm will be greater than the benefit of testifying.

The discussion in the text refers to 'iterated' prisoners' dilemmas—that is, a series of decision problems of the same form, as would confront a pair of hapless recidivists who were repeatedly caught and offered the same bargain. This series of decision problems is often described as a game, in which the prisoners are "players" who make successive "moves." In the context of this discussion, 'co-operating' is defined in relation to the other prisoner, rather than the authorities—that is, as withholding one's testimony.

J. David Velleman

indeed warranted. But retaliatory wrongdoing isn't warranted: morality is not a co-operative scheme from which wrongdoers can justly be excluded. So if guilt is anxiety about having forfeited trust, the trust at stake cannot be represented by inclusion in the moral scheme.

Forms of trust

The trust that is forfeited by wrongdoing is expressed, not in moral treatment, which is owed to the trustworthy and untrustworthy alike, but in morally optional transactions that depend on mutual assumptions of good will. One is obligated not to lie even to a liar; what one doesn't owe to a liar is credence.

Attitudinal trust. In verbal communication, one person utters a sentence with the intention of thereby giving others reason to believe it, via their recognition of that very intention. This communicative intention necessarily depends on being recognized as a good intention. Its being recognized by the hearers as the intention to give them reason to believe wouldn't actually give them reason to believe unless they assumed that it was based on the speaker's own awareness of such a reason. If communication wasn't assumed by the hearers to be well-intended in this sense, it wouldn't succeed; and so if the speaker didn't assume that it would meet with that assumption, he wouldn't be in a position to intend it, in the first place. These mutual assumptions of communicative good will are the rational infrastructure of conversation.

Now consider why someone's telling a lie warrants others in refusing to trust him on future occasions. One possibility would be that the lie betrays his lack of some truth-telling disposition without which others have no grounds for trusting his word. In that case, his consciousness of having told a lie would make him feel that he had warranted others in withdrawing their trust specifically from his word, and the resulting anxiety would have a specific content that might earn it the name of liar's guilt. But guilt about wrongdoing is not divisible into specific modes for specific wrongs— liar's guilt, thief's guilt, and so on. If it were, then there would be modes of guilt only for common, repeatable wrongs that betrayed the lack of dispositions essential to warranting trust for various common purposes.

In reality, however, moral guilt is a unitary emotion, whose quality and content remain constant across many different occasions. Whatever serves as the object of anxiety in moral guilt should therefore be the same across different occasions for the emotion. If the object of anxiety is a loss of trust, then the trust at stake must be

240

such as any guilty-minded subject can think of himself as having forfeited, by means of any wrongdoing. So what's at stake for the morally guilty mind must be the prospect of being regarded as well- or ill-intentioned *tout court*—of being simply included or simply excluded from the company of those who are recognized as persons of good will. Wrongdoing must be regarded as warranting a loss of trust, not because of any specific disposition that it might betray, but because it simply betrays a failure to consider the wrongness of the act or to be deterred by that consideration. And what such a failure warrants from others is a refusal to engage in any dealings that require a reliance on the wrongdoer's moral sensibility or motivation. The vague insecurity with which the guilty mind feels threatened must then be a general exclusion from optional dealings that depend on an assumption of good will.

This conception of guilt would explain why guilt tends to motivate acts of contrition and apology. Such acts are explicit expressions of the emotion, whose tendency to motivate them is therefore a tendency to motivate its own expression. The explanation of this tendency is that guilt seeks expression as a means of restoring generic trust. If the wrongdoer wants to regain acceptance as a person of good will, he must somehow demonstrate that the moral quality of his acts is indeed a motivationally effective consideration for him. Expressing a sense of guilt demonstrates that he is even now considering the moral quality of an act as justifying a loss of trust, and that he is hereby motivated by that consideration—too late on this occasion, of course, but in time to repair his ways for the future.

To accept the wrongdoer's apology, according to this conception, is to restore him to his previous position of trust, in effect readmitting him to the company of the well-intentioned. To forgive is not literally to forget, but it is to forget for practical purposes, to erase the practical consequences of the act's being remembered.

Practical trust The practical consequences of losing trust can sometimes be described, in themselves, as a loss of trust, because they amount to the loss of what might be called practical trust. What I mean by 'practical trust' can best be explained if trust is defined as reliance on someone's good will. Merely to assume that someone is well-intentioned is already to rely on his good will in an attitudinal sense; but one can also rely on his good will in a practical sense, by doing something that puts one at risk if his will is bad. What one does may be mental rather than physical, since it may consist in no more than believing another's communication, on the assumption that it is well-intentioned. The point is that assuming a communication to be well-intentioned is one step short of believing

J. David Velleman

it, and the intervening step represents the difference between attitudinal and practical trust.

Practical trust often involves *en*trusting someone with something — one's credence, a task, a piece of property, a secret—on the assumption that it will be treated with good will. (That with which the trustee is entrusted can then be called a trust in yet a third sense of the term.) But that with which someone is entrusted, in receiving practical trust, may be quite intangible and hence difficult to identify.

Consider again the trust involved in communication, as expressed by the various senses of the verbs 'to listen' and 'to hear'. To listen is always to attend in a way that makes one susceptible to hearing. But there are many kinds of hearing: hearing that consists in merely detecting sounds; hearing that consists in understanding sounds as words uttered with communicative intent; hearing that consists in weighing a communication as a possible reason for belief; hearing that consists in believing on the basis of that reason; hearing that consists in taking the belief to heart, as a basis for action; and perhaps further, or intervening, levels of hearing. At each level one can listen without actually hearing, and one can hear at one level without listening at the next. (That's why it can make sense to say either 'He listened but he didn't hear' or 'He heard but he didn't listen.') Beginning at the third level, listening becomes a form of practical trust. Attending to a communication in a way that makes one susceptible to regarding it as reason to believe; attending to it as a reason in a way that makes one susceptible to believing; attending to the resulting belief in a way that makes one susceptible to taking it as reason for acting—all of these ways of listening entail practical reliance on the speaker's good will.

With what does one entrust a speaker by listening to him in one of these ways? What one entrusts him with, obviously, is one's susceptibility to hearing in the corresponding senses. (That's why listening is aptly called 'lending an ear.') And since one's susceptibility to hearing, in all of these senses, includes one's susceptibility to his words regarded as reasons for belief and action, listening to him can entail entrusting him with nothing less than one's mind, or indeed with oneself. One entrusts a speaker with oneself by placing one's beliefs and actions under the influence of his words in a way that puts one at risk if his will is bad.

Another example of entrusting oneself to others is the formation of shared intentions.[5] A shared intention is formed by the

---

[5] See my 'How to Share an Intention,' in *The Possibility of Practical Reason* (Oxford: Oxford University Press, 2000), 200–220. My conception of shared intention is based on the theory of Margaret Gilbert (see Gilbert's *On Social Facts* [Princeton: Princeton University Press, 1992]).

pooling of individual intentions each of which is conditional on the others. Each agent has an individual intention of the form 'I'm willing if you are,' and the agents 'pool' these intentions by expressing them so that, as all can see, the stated conditions on the intentions have been satisfied and the agents are now jointly committed to acting. Contributing to the pool of intentions doesn't necessarily require saying 'I'm willing if you are' in so many words, since the requisite intention can be expressed tacitly—for example, by holding out a hand in readiness to shake. But even a tacit contribution entails entrusting oneself to others, first, because their decision whether to reciprocate will determine whether one's intention becomes a positive commitment to act; and second, because that commitment will then be a commitment to do something whose point depends on whether they abide by their reciprocal commitment.

Even without joining a shared intention, one can do things whose point depends on the actions of others, and these shared activities may barely differ from actions based on shared intentions. Whether an extended hand is a signal of a willingness to shake if the other is willing, or the beginning of an actual handshake whose consummation is left up to the other, depends on subtle differences of expectation, resolution, timing, eye contact, momentum, and so on; and in the end, its status may be indeterminate. Whether or not one expresses an antecedent intention, however, doing one's part in a shared activity puts one at the other's disposal, by leaving the success of one's activity up to him.

Losing practical trust: a form of punishment

Withdrawing practical trust from someone thus entails refusing to do anything with him, in the sense of 'with' that applies to shared rather than parallel activities. It also entails not listening to him and hence not conversing with him, either. In short, withdrawing practical trust from someone entails excluding him from social interaction.

To exclude someone from social interaction is to shun him, at least to some extent, and shunning is a form of punishment. As I have explained, Freud thinks that anxiety about being punished will develop out of a child's anxiety about losing his parents' love, because the child will expect unloving parents to deal out harsh treatment of the sort in which punishment is generally thought to consist. But anxiety about losing trust, rather than love, may already amount to anxiety about being punished, if the trust at stake is practical trust, the loss of which amounts to being shunned.

J. David Velleman

Shunning sounds like an archaic and perhaps barbaric form of punishment, but in fact it is practised by liberal-minded parents of the post-Spockian era, in the form of the 'time-out.' When parents require a child to take a time-out, they exclude him from the conversation and shared activities of the family, precisely on the grounds that he cannot be trusted to participate. The rationale of the time-out is not that the child deserves the suffering that accompanies this punishment; it's that the child's misbehaviour warrants the withdrawal of trust in which the punishment consists. Enlightened parents will convey to the child that his exclusion from the family circle is not intended to make him suffer but only to put the family out of the reach of untrustworthy hands. Of course, they will also convey that he will be readmitted to the family circle as soon as he shows himself ready to be governed by a good will. And, finally, they will convey their confidence in the child's ability to be governed by a good will—a confidence that underlies their respect for the child and perhaps even their love.

For an adult, the loss of practical trust often entails no more than being met with fixed smiles and deaf ears, treatment that is outwardly nothing like being sent to one's room or made to sit in the corner. But a guilty-minded adult can still recognize that, in forfeiting trust, he has warranted treatment that would have been formalized as a punishment when he was a child, and this recognition is a rational counterpart to the phantasy attributed to him by Freud, that he is even now a child facing punishment from an internalized parent. Thus, the present analysis of guilt, as anxiety about having forfeited trust, can serve as a rationalist revision of Freud's analysis. According to this revision, guilt is anxiety about having warranted a kind of treatment that is sometimes formalized as punishment.

Guilt Without Wrongdoing

I now turn to a consideration of guilt that is not about perceived wrongdoing. My first example is the guilt that we sometimes feel about being self-indulgent, by breaking a diet or shirking exercise. I'll call it self-disciplinary guilt. My second example will be so-called survivor guilt, which will lead me to consider a different analysis of the emotion.

Self-disciplinary guilt

I think that Kant has the right account of self-disciplinary guilt. For Kant, actions fail to be well-intentioned when they are

244

performed for reasons that cannot be universalized; and reasons resist universalization because they must be regarded as applying either just to ourselves or, as Kant puts it, 'just for this once.'[6] I suspect that reasons regarded as applying just for this once are the basis for failures of self-discipline, which involve making one-time exceptions to some regimen to which we are otherwise committed. These actions violate the Categorical Imperative and therefore count, in Kantian terms, as violations of duty—specifically, of duties to ourselves. When we fail to be self-disciplined, we cheat ourselves in some way.

But why do we feel guilty about cheating ourselves, if guilt is anxiety about having forfeited trust? Whose trust do we forfeit by eating a second dessert?

The answer, to begin with, is that we forfeit our own trust, by undermining our grounds for relying on the commitments we make to ourselves. If we cannot count on ourselves to stick with a diet, then we cannot accept the commitment we make to ourselves in starting one, and then we cannot honestly claim to be on a diet, in the first place. Indeed, every future-directed plan that we make entails a commitment on which we ourselves must be able to rely in deliberating about related matters.[7] A loss of self-trust can therefore undermine our ability to organize and co-ordinate our activities over time—a consequence that is certainly a proper object of anxiety.

What's more, the violation of commitments warrants a loss of trust from people other than those to whom the commitments were made. If we break our word to one person, we provide grounds for distrust not only to him but to others who might consider relying on our good will. And grounds for distrust are similarly generalizable even from instances of breaking our word to ourselves. Insofar as we are un-self-disciplined, we are unreliable, and insofar as we are unreliable, we are untrustworthy. Self-disciplinary guilt can therefore be a genuine and rational form of the emotion.

Of course, this account of self-disciplinary guilt, if followed to its Kantian conclusion, implies that failures of self-discipline are moral wrongs, because they are violations of the Categorical Imperative. Strictly speaking, then, the account does not show the rationality of guilt in the absence of perceived wrongdoing. Yet the moral status of Kantian duties to oneself, and of the corresponding wrongs, is

[6] *Groundwork of the Metaphysic of Morals,* trans. H. J. Paton (New York: Harper, 1964), 91 (p. 424 in the Royal Prussian Academy edition).
[7] See Michael Bratman's *Intention, Plans, and Practical Reason* (Cambridge, MA: Harvard University Press, 1987).

J. David Velleman

not taken seriously by many present-day readers of Kant. The region carved out by the Categorical Imperative is not what is currently regarded as the moral realm. What I have argued is that it is nevertheless a region in which guilt can be rational.

Survivor guilt

Let me turn, then, to survivor guilt, which is felt by those who have survived catastrophes that others have not. There may be an argument for the rationality of survivor guilt, but it would require a different analysis of guilt altogether. I will therefore make a brief digression, to explore this alternative analysis.

Of course, survivors may feel guilty because they accuse themselves of wrongdoing—of having exerted too little effort to save others, or too much effort to save themselves. They may also accuse themselves of indulging in immoral thoughts and feelings—for example, relief that others died in their place. These instances of guilt on the part of survivors can be accounted for by the foregoing analysis of guilt. But I am using the term 'survivor guilt' to denote guilt experienced about the mere fact of having survived, which cannot be regarded as wrong or as warranting the loss of trust.

Survivor guilt would be rational, however, if guilt were anxiety about having warranted resentment rather than the withdrawal of trust. Just as the victim of wrongdoing feels resentment against the wrongdoer, so the victim of misfortune often feels resentment against those who are more fortunate. Hence a survivor, like a wrongdoer, can be anxious about the prospect of being resented. And if resentment were warranted against both, then both could rationally be anxious about having warranted resentment, and survivor guilt would be just as rational as guilt about wrongdoing.

A possible objection to this analysis would be that resentment about another's good fortune is a modification of envy, whereas the resentment about wrongdoing is a modification of anger. But I see no reason why survivor guilt and moral guilt could not be two distinct species of the same emotion, precisely by virtue of consisting in anxiety about having warranted two distinct species of resentment. Indeed, anger and envy rise to the level of resentment under similar conditions—namely, when tinged with the bitterness that accompanies a sense of injustice. One can be envied even if one's good fortune is acknowledged to be deserved; only if it is regarded as undeserved, however, will envy turn into resentment. One can incur anger by causing harms accidentally or through the vicissitudes of fair-play; anger will turn into resentment only if the harms

246

one causes are thought to be unjust. Thus, envious resentment and angry resentment form a natural pair, of emotions embittered by a sense of injustice.

Another objection to the proposed analysis would be that envy is never warranted at all, especially not when it rises to the level of resentment. But why shouldn't envy be warranted? I can imagine saying that envy is pointless, counter-productive, and even potentially vicious. But I cannot imagine claiming that the victims of misfortune have no grounds for envying those who are more fortunate, or for resenting those whose good fortune is undeserved; and so I have to admit that a beneficiary of good fortune may rationally feel anxiety about providing others with grounds for resentment.

Yet a third objection would be that if someone is literally a survivor, then the victims of the corresponding misfortune are dead and hence in no position to resent him. But third parties can feel resentment on behalf of the deceased, a resentment that can only be sharpened by the thought that its proper subjects are no longer alive to feel it. And a survivor can rationally feel anxiety about providing grounds for such vicarious or sympathetic resentment.

Conclusion: Don't Worry

So is guilt about distrust or is it about resentment? I don't know what would count as the right answer to this question. Surely, we feel anxiety about having warranted both of these reactions, and both are warranted by wrongdoing as well as by related matters, which include failures of self-discipline, in the case of distrust, and undeserved disparities of fortune, in the case of resentment. The term 'guilt' is applied to anxiety about all of these reactions, and there seem to be no grounds for ruling any of these applications incorrect.

I therefore conclude that guilt is a family of emotions, including anxiety about having warranted not only distrust but also angry or envious resentment and perhaps other, related reactions as well. This conclusion helps to explain the confusion we often feel about whether guilt is appropriate. We often criticize ourselves for feeling guilty when, as we say, we have nothing to feel guilty about. But we shouldn't criticize ourselves for having no grounds for distrust-anxiety or angry-resentment-anxiety, if what we're feeling is envious-resentment-anxiety instead. The fact that we haven't wronged anyone doesn't necessarily show that we have no grounds for feeling guilty; it may show only that we need to interpret our feelings more

J. David Velleman

carefully, as anxiety about warranting envious resentment rather than anger or distrust.

Correctly interpreting our emotions can thus alleviate our worries about feeling guilty. What a relief.

Index

Antony, L. 182, 183, 188, 198, 199
Aristotle. 115, 117, 124, 128, 199, 203, 218
Arnold, M. B. 73, 85, 116
Arpaly, N. 181, 186, 188, 195, 199
Averill, J. 3

Baier, A. 6
Bal, M. 202, 203
Barnes, A. 169, 170, 177
Baron, J. 165
Bartels, A. 83, 85
Benjamin, J. 221
Bennett, J. 186, 199
Ben-Ze'ev, Aaron. 147, 148, 149, 152, 155, 157, 162
Bergson, H. 156
Blackburn, S. 211
Blake, W. 5
Bourdieu, P. 15
Bower, G. 171, 174, 175, 177
Boyd, R. 183, 231
Bratman, M. 245
Brewer, T. 145
Budd, M. 122
Burge, T. 190, 199
Burnyeat, M. 102
Buss, D. 47
Byrne, A. 111

Calhoun, C. 3, 9, 186, 199
Campbell, J. 102
Carroll, N. 208, 218
Carruthers, P. 111
Cassam, Q. 102
Charland, L. 44, 48
Chevalier-Skolnikoff. 42
Chomsky, N. 114
Clore, G. 3, 76, 85, 174, 179
Collingwood, R. 211, 218
Collins, A. 3

Cosmides, L. 48, 63, 138, 139
Critchley, H. D. 71
Currie, G. 202, 206, 209, 214, 216, 218

D'Arms, J. 120, 128, 132, 211, 218, 235
Dalgleish, T. 64, 65, 66, 169, 171, 177
Damasio, A. 2, 5, 70, 71, 85, 113, 114, 116, 122
Danto, A. 17
Darwin, C. 40, 41, 42, 63, 102, 114
Davidson, D. 6, 92, 103
Davidson, R. 138
Davis, W. 170, 177
Deigh, J. 43, 63, 131, 144
Derryberry, D. 171
Descartes, R. 3, 5, 11, 13, 63, 83, 85, 113, 114, 116, 199
Dewey, J. 8
Dowell, J. 145
Downing, G. 14
Dretske, F. 46, 63, 78, 79, 85
Dreyfus, H. 15

Eibl-Eibesfeldt. 42
Ekman, P. 13, 14, 41, 42, 44, 48, 49, 50, 51, 53, 54, 55, 63, 64, 65, 67, 83, 93, 102, 132
Evans, C. 55, 56
Evans, G. 92, 103
Evans, R. 216

Faulkner, W. 159
Fernández-Dols, J. M. 50
Fish, S. 215
Fodor, J. 3, 78, 114
Foot, P. 127, 128, 135, 136
Forgas, J. 170, 171, 171, 174, 175
Frege, G. 6

Index

Freud, S. 10, 35, 36, 70, 85, 207, 235, 236, 237, 238, 243, 244
Fridlund, A. 49, 50, 51, 52, 53
Friedrich, J. 165, 166, 168
Frijda, N. 13, 39, 40, 54, 64, 116, 152

Gasper, P. 183, 231
Gaulin, S. 47, 48
Genette, G. 202
Gervey, B. 179
Geuss, R. 221
Gibbard, A. 211
Gigerenzer, G. 166, 178, 183
Gilbert, M. 242
Goldie, P. 7, 12, 211, 213, 218
Goldman, A. 182, 204
Gordon, R. 3, 8, 137, 204
Greenspan, P. 3, 8, 41, 64, 115, 129, 130, 134, 186, 199
Griffiths, P. 1, 4, 11, 16, 39, 41, 43, 44, 46, 48, 49, 61, 66, 82, 116, 120, 121, 123, 131, 133, 139, 144
Gur, R. 163, 178

Ha, Y. 165, 178
Harlow, Harry. 57
Harré, R. 82, 85
Haslanger, S. 230
Heal, J. 204
Heidegger, M. 15
Helm, B. 145
Henley, W. 18
Hinde, R. 52, 53, 58, 59
Hjort, M. 202
Hobbes, T. 11
Honneth, A. 221
Hug, K. 166
Hume, D. 6, 70, 85, 127, 128, 132, 135, 205, 207, 222, 223, 224, 226, 227
Husserl, E. 9

Ivanhoe, P. J. 235
Izard, C. 41, 44

Jacobson, D. 120, 128, 132, 211, 218
Jaggar, A. 186, 199
James, S. 233
James, W. 8, 12, 13, 15, 16, 18, 20, 48, 70, 71, 79, 94, 103, 117
Johnson-Laird, P. 84, 86, 138
Johnston, M. 170
Johnston, V. 47
Jones, K. 119, 145

Kafka, F. 201
Kant, I. 152, 153, 244
Kenny, A. 3, 72, 85
Kieran, M. 218
Kierkegaard, S. 201
Kilter, D. 173
King, N. 207
Kirby, L. D. 162
Kirkpatrick, L. 169, 171, 172
Klayman, J. 165, 178
Korsgaard, C. 190, 192, 199
Kunda, Z. 165, 178

Lamarque, P. 202, 213, 215, 216
Lane, R. 2
Lange, C. 48, 70, 71, 85
Laver, S. 202
Lazar, A. 169, 178
Lazarus, R. 3, 41, 44, 65, 73, 74, 75, 76, 77, 85, 86, 138
LeDoux, J. 2, 45, 47, 65, 80, 85, 121, 139, 139, 185
Livingston, P. 209
Liwag, M. 55
Lorenz, K. 42, 56, 58

Margalit, A. 221
Marler, P. 55, 56
Martin, M. G. F. 95, 102, 103
Matthen, M. 121
McBurney, D. 47, 48
McDowell, J. 91, 103, 211, 219
Mele, A. 63, 163, 164, 165, 166
Merleau-Ponty, M. 15
Millikan, R. G. 46
Moran, R. 214

Morton, A. 218
Musil, R. 202

Nash, C. 215
Nesse, R. 141
Neu, J. 3, 5, 8, 10
Nietzsche, F. 4, 7, 117, 201, 218
Nisbett, R. 75, 86, 165, 178
Nudds, M. 102
Nussbaum, M. 41, 66, 72, 73, 86, 156, 224

Oatley, K. 84, 86, 138
Öhman, A. 44, 45
Olsen, S. 202, 211, 215, 216
Opton, E. 3
Ortony, A. 3, 4, 12
Owen, D. 181

Panksepp. 2
Papineau, D. 218
Parkinson, B. 49
Pascal, B. 161
Peacocke, C. 92, 103
Pears, D. 96, 103, 163, 169, 178
Pinker, S. 114
Pitcher, G. 72, 86
Prinz, J. 48, 66, 69, 74, 79, 82, 86, 111
Pugmire, D. 123

Quattrone, G. 163, 178

Rawls, J. 16, 231, 232
Raz, J. 190, 192, 200
Redding, P. 152
Regan, D. 205
Ricoeur, P. 202, 219
Roberts, R. 3, 122, 131, 133
Rock, I. 162
Rorty, A. 11
Rorty, R. 215, 219
Roseman, I. J. 73, 86
Ross, L. 74, 86, 114, 165, 178
Rousseau, J-J. 222
Rozin, P. 44

Ruiz-Belda, M-A. 50
Ryle, G. 15, 22, 23

Sackeim, H. 163, 178
Sartre, J-P. 59, 60, 66, 117
Scanlon, T. 190, 192, 200
Schellekens, E. 218
Scheman, N. 186, 200
Scherer, K. 40, 41, 66, 67, 73, 86
Schroeter, F. 181, 190, 200
Schwarz, N. 174
Searle, J. 27
Seligman, M. 141
Selman, L. 221
Sharpsteen, D. 169, 171, 172
Sherman, N. 235
Shklar, J. 221
Skinner, Q. 221
Smith, Adam. 223
Smith, C. 74
Smith, C. A. 162
Solomon, R. 1, 3, 9, 43, 46, 66, 72, 73, 86, 118, 129, 130, 199, 200
Soteriou, M. 102
Sousa, R. de 4, 8, 9, 10, 118, 120, 124, 171, 178, 199
Spelman, E. 221
Spinoza 3, 10, 11, 155, 162, 223
Stern, R. 221
Stocker, M. 3, 10, 12, 186, 200
Storms, M. 205
Strack, F. 75, 86
Strawson, P. 90, 92, 103
Svarvarsdottir, S. 145, 181

Taylor, C. 96, 103
Taylor, G. 134
Teasdale, J. 41, 45
Tesser, A. 170, 179
Tooby, J. 48, 138, 139
Totten, J. 205
Trivers, R. 163, 179
Trope, Y. 165, 166, 179
Trout, J. 183, 199
Tversky, A. 163, 178
Tye, M. 111

Index

Velleman, D. 102

Wallace, J. 192, 200
Walton, K. 3, 202, 211, 214, 215
Watson, G. 190, 200
White, H. 215
Wiggins, D. 127, 211

Williams, B. 183
Wilson, T. 75
Wollheim, R. 39, 41, 206

Zajonc, R. 44, 67, 73, 74, 75, 76, 77, 86
Zeki, S. 83, 85